Mobile
Commerce

Don Gressv

Breakthroughs in Application Development Series

Series Editor:

David Orchard
Solutions Architect, IBM
Burnaby, British Colombia

The Breakthroughs in Application Development series is dedicated to providing hard knowledge in the form of detailed practical guides to leading-edge technologies and business models in modern application development. This series will identify, define, and stimulate emerging trends in the industry, covering such rapidly evolving areas as electronic commerce, e-business, inter/intranet development, Web architectures, application integration solutions, and the intersection of business and technology. Each title will focus on a new innovation in the field, presenting new ways of thinking and demonstrating how to put breakthrough technologies into business practice.

1. The Business of Ecommerce: From Corporate Strategy to Technology • *Paul May*

2. e-Enterprise: Business Models, Architecture, and Components • *Faisal Hoque*

3. Mobile Commerce: Applications and Technologies of Personal Electronic Business • *Paul May*

4. Practical WAP: Developing Applications for the Wireless Web • *Chris Bennett*

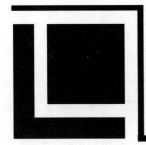

Mobile Commerce

Opportunities, Applications, and Technologies of Wireless Business

PAUL MAY

CAMBRIDGE
UNIVERSITY PRESS

PUBLISHED BY THE PRESS SYNDICATE OF THE UNIVERSITY OF CAMBRIDGE
The Pitt Building, Trumpington Street, Cambridge, United Kingdom

CAMBRIDGE UNIVERSITY PRESS
The Edinburgh Building, Cambridge CB2 2RU, UK
40 West 20th Street, New York, NY 10011-4211, USA
10 Stamford Road, Oakleigh, VIC 3166, Australia
Ruiz de Alarcón 13, 28014 Madrid, Spain
Dock House, The Waterfront, Cape Town 8001, South Africa

http://www.cambridge.org

© 2001 Cambridge University Press

Any product mentioned in this book may be a trademark of its company.

First published 2001

Printed in the United States of America

Typeface Garamond 3 12/14 pt.   *System* QuarkXPress® [GH]

A catalog record for this book is available from the British Library.

Library of Congress Cataloging in Publication Data
May, Paul, 1963–
    Mobile commerce : opportunities, applications, and technologies of
wireless business / Paul May.
        p.   cm. – (Breakthroughs in application development series ; 3)
    Includes index.
    ISBN 0-521-79756-X (pbk.)
    1. Cellular telephone equipment industry.   2. Mobile communication
systems.   3. Wireless communication systems.   I. Title.   II. Series.
    HD9697.T452   M39   2001
    384.5 – dc21   00-069764

ISBN 0 521 79756 X paperback

To my wife, Helen

ABOUT THE AUTHOR

Paul May, B.A. Oxford, M.Sc. City University (London), is author of *The Business of Ecommerce: From Corporate Strategy to Technology* (Cambridge University Press, 2000). A former software developer, he has been an independent business technology author, consultant, systems architect, and business development executive in the business systems architectures and e-commerce field since 1991.

He formed the independent e-commerce consulting practice Verista (www.verista.com) in October 1998, undertaking strategy and implementation projects with well-known global companies such as BP Amoco and De Beers, and with B2B and B2C e-commerce start-ups around the world. Prior to starting Verista, Paul launched and led the e-commerce practice at ECsoft (Nasdaq: ECSGY; London: ECS), a leading European consultancy and systems integration organization. He and his team were active in a range of business sectors, including finance, retail, and transportation and offered services from business and technology strategy through architecture, design, implementation, and deployment. He regularly presents on object technology and electronic commerce at international conferences.

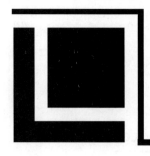

Contents

2 Types of Mobile Commerce Services   69

3 Technologies   161

Foreword

At the dawn of the new millennium, some 5 billion people inhabited the earth. In the year 2002, the estimated number of cell phones in use around the world will be 500 million. That is to say, roughly one-tenth of the total world population will soon be using cell phones. Of these devices, perhaps 20 percent (rapidly increasing) are fully equipped for all facets of mobile commerce, including purchase, sale, and trading actions. This gives mobile commerce a significant market.

Once a useful gadget for notorious chatterboxes, the cell phone has significantly reshaped some basic activities of our daily lives. Thanks to an increasingly "always-on" lifestyle, shopping, banking, and making reservations are now commonplace transactions "in your pocket." Expert observers take it as gospel truth that the majority of working adults will use a mobile device for their major commerce activities by the middle of the decade. For the business world the mobile commerce area beckons with a variety of opportunities to rejoin customers and partners in a decentralized, service-rich environment.

Hardware and software manufacturers are jumping on the bandwagon and heavily investing in the mobile commerce area. New technologies are designed to improve the bandwidth, speed, and performance of mobile devices, establishing them as serious competitors to fixed-line services once the desktop market is saturated. Because both the established leaders and aspiring new faces are keen to create new markets for their products, chances are that mobile commerce will successfully disrupt the current monotonous landscape of a few operating systems, leading to a greater diversity of market share.

Thanks to extensive media coverage of business-to-business offers and business-to-consumer launches, entrepreneurs are aware of the unlimited possibilities of mobile devices and the channel these devices represent. By disconnecting their equipment, people are becoming increasingly connected – a paradox business cannot afford to ignore.

Mobile Commerce: Opportunities, Applications, and Technologies of Wireless Business is one of the first books to map this emerging wave of electronic commerce. Although the Web and specialist journals abound with white papers, project reports, technical standards, and observer opinions, a coherent and authoritative guide to the subject has not yet surfaced. *Mobile Commerce* fills this void. This book is the perfect companion for both technical and nontechnical staff, from software developers to business decision-makers. Paul May, a technologist-turned-business-consultant, expertly explains both sides of the story in clear, intelligent language. Indeed, the author is a well-known authority in the area of electronic commerce, and *Mobile Commerce* is the logical sequel to his excellent first book, *The Business of Ecommerce: From Corporate Strategy to Technology.* I'm sure this book will serve you well.

Tom Jell
Senior Principal Consultant and Director of M-Commerce
Service Line System Integration
Siemens Business Services
Munich, Germany, and Princeton, New Jersey

# Acknowledgments

My thanks go to:

- Richard Taylor of Poqit, for debating many of these issues with me, guiding me along the WAP road and being an insightful technical editor.

- Lothlórien Homet of Cambridge University Press, for her belief in this book and her patience during its creation.

- Dave Ford of Webraska, for helping me understand and model the role of location in mobile commerce service development and for inspiring the generic model for mobile commerce services presented in this book.

- Michael Airey of Xtempus for providing the basis for the figure and discussion relating to cost components in Chapter 1.

- Stuart Evans of Vignette, for letting me use one of his slides as the basis of the figure relating to application emphases in Chapter 1.

- Everyone at WAPWednesday, particularly Grant Lemke, who founded the group and found room in it for me.

- Angela Green of Orange, for lending me my first WAP phone.

- Chris Pring of Bullitt and Thomas Golsong of RioBrand, for excusing my frequent physical (and occasional mental) absences during the writing of this book.

- My wife, Helen, for her unfailing support and encouragement.

Introduction

Rubber glvs, throwt, take tel off hook. . . . So began a list found stored in the personal organiser device of a bereaved London man, subsequently convicted in July 2000 of murdering his wife the previous December. The man's care in disguising the murder as a bungled robbery was destroyed by the small matter of the blood on his clothing, and the telltale list – which ended, "ring mobile just befor yo leave".[1]

Meanwhile, young vacationers partying on the island of Ibiza – the summer centre of the European dance craze – could get free entry to the most popular clubs by responding to text messages received on their cell phones. Almost one quarter of British citizens use text messaging services as a matter of course, and over one third of them have sent a declaration of love via the medium.[2] Lovers of music, books, and clothes purchase items from their cell phones or wireless organisers. Day traders on the beach execute trades with thumb presses, and night birds reserve theatre tickets by pecking at a hand-held screen.

The overorganised killer, the hedonist with an eye for a bargain, the tongue-tied lover: these are all players in a world in which mobile devices are common pieces of equipment, mediating our relationships and creating new ways for people to interact with their friends, employers, and co-workers and with a newly ubiquitous wireless business environment. The world is in everyone's pocket.

1. Angelique Chrisafis, "Killer left his plans in diary", *The Guardian*, 15 July 2000.
2. "I just text to say I love you", MORI / Lycos UK, 5 September 2000.

This book is about how people live their lives and fulfill their needs in a world of continuous, pervasive, personal, commerce-enabled systems connection. The book explores how businesses can respond effectively to this new world and create services that appeal to users, add value to their lives, and generate revenues. We also look at how the mobile channel changes the nature of business itself, transforming processes, capabilities, and expectations throughout tomorrow's successful enterprises. The book deals equally with business and technology concerns, reflecting the symbiotic nature of developments in both areas.

Mobile commerce is a building wave of change driven by consumer adaptation to wireless devices. GartnerGroup predict data-enabled wireless devices will outnumber Internet-connected PCs by 2003,[3] radically disrupting the e-commerce industries' hard-won models of customer behaviour, offer applicability, marketing strategy, and, above all, revenue generation in the fixed Internet setting. We are witnessing an evolutionary step as postindustrial humans climb out from their work stations and begin to populate an electronic savannah.

But readiness for the changes ahead is variable. Andersen Consulting's third annual survey of the e-commerce scene[4] found that most respondents had heard of mobile commerce (91 percent in the United States, 94 percent in Europe). Fifteen percent of European respondents reported they were already involved with mobile commerce, compared to 6 percent in the United States. Similar numbers of respondents in both regions were preparing for mobile commerce (27 percent in the United States, 28 percent in Europe). The most interesting disparity appeared when respondents were asked "Are you open to using [mobile commerce] but without definite plans?" Fifty-eight percent of European respondents agreed with the statement, as did 78 percent of U.S. respondents. On this evidence, European businesses seem to have more

---

3. S. Hayward, K. Dulaney, B. Egan, D. Plummer, N. Deighton, and M. Reynolds, *Beyond the Internet: The 'Supranet'*, GartnerGroup, 11 September 2000.
4. *eEurope 2000: Connecting the Dots?*, Andersen Consulting, 2000.

experience in mobile commerce practice, but less commitment to mobile commerce than their counterparts in the United States.

A series of new technology launches is set to improve bandwidth, speed, and performance of mobile devices over the next five years, putting pocket machines in a strongly competitive position versus fixed-line services. The consumer's pocket will no longer be the home of the wallet alone: it will also be a platform for personal, targeted, high-convenience, commercial services. And in the business world, tumbleweed will blow through cubicle prairies as people rejoin customers and partners in a decentralised, service-rich environment of enhanced relationships and accelerated action. This book is designed to equip readers for the changes in store.

WHO SHOULD READ THIS BOOK

The intended audiences for this book are:

- Business leaders and entrepreneurs seeking to understand the emerging mobile commerce arena and how they can take advantage of it.

- Software developers looking to understand the mobile commerce platform and its applications, so that they can develop new services or reposition their careers.

- Mobile technology professionals seeking to enhance their appreciation of the business applications of the technologies with which they work.

- E-commerce directors, e-commerce managers, and CIOs concerned to locate and embrace the leading edge of technology and business development in their field of expertise and to factor new channels, devices, and services into their strategy.

- IT managers looking to pre-empt the certain requirement to respond to mobile commerce challenges set by their colleagues in business development and corporate strategy.

■ Students of business and computing seeking an overview of mobile commerce concepts and technologies and their relationships to service definition and delivery within commercial organisations.

■ Everyone interested in how the development of mobile commerce technology will impact their lives.

How This Book Is Organised

This book has been organised in four main parts.

Chapter 1 focuses on the opportunities mobile commerce brings. We look at why the world is turning mobile and how an identifiable mobile lifestyle is emerging. We consider the economic and technology factors driving the emerging mobile commerce landscape and examine mobile commerce's impact on the newly established e-commerce industry. We look at ways of generating mobile commerce offers and propose a generic model for designing and evaluating mobile commerce business propositions. The chapter covers the topic of customer relationships and how they operate in the mobile commerce environment. Finally, the chapter looks at how mobile commerce affects systems developers and consumer expectations.

Chapter 2 surveys the leading types of mobile commerce services that currently exist or that are currently being developed to serve consumer and business user roles. We describe a basic functional platform over which mobile commerce services of all kinds can be laid. We then examine in turn the leading mobile commerce service types for consumers: travel, ticketing, banking, stock trading, news and sports, gambling, gaming, and shopping. Turning to services aimed at the business world, we look at mobile commerce services serving independent, collaborative, and management functions.

Chapter 3 collects, organises, and explains the enabling technologies of mobile commerce, from the various types of network technology available through evolving types of mobile devices and service development technology to the emerging standards relevant to the field.

Chapter 4 describes a number of live issues affecting the successful development of mobile commerce. These include distinctions between what is technically possible and consumers' desires and motivations; issues around security, trust and privacy; and concerns relating to health. We also consider the impact of unequal access to the benefits of mobile commerce, the implications of the blurring of the dividing line between work and private life, the re-emergence of geography as a key factor in electronic commerce, and the problems associated with obsolescence in networks, devices, and systems. Lastly, we look at the cost burdens on would-be dominant players in an often high-stakes game.

Appendix A contains a directory of existing mobile commerce services which readers can investigate further. Further sources of information and a glossary of terms complete the book.

A Note on the Text

Most companies referred to in the text can be found on the Web using the formula http://www.company-name.com. Where this is not the case, the URL for the company appears as an endnote.

Many names used in the text are trademarks and are recognised as such.

"He" and "she" are used randomly throughout the book.

I claim any mistakes in the book for my own.

Contacting the Author

Paul May can be reached at paul@verista.com. The book's Web pages can be found at http://www.verista.com/mobile/.

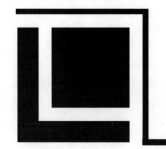

Mobile
Commerce

Mobile Commerce Opportunities

The Internet's arrived. The Net has changed everything, and nothing. Business has migrated to the Net, time has speeded up, expectations have been reset. And now there's a fresh rumble sounding down the technology road. The noise is all about mobile commerce. Is it just the massed empty stomachs of the technology crowd, eager for a new feast? Or is it the next vehicle to a brighter business future?

This chapter treats mobile commerce as a vehicle aboard which businesses of all kinds need to jump. We look at why the world is turning mobile – how the change to the mobile era is already well advanced and picking up speed. We consider how businesses can design opportunities in this emerging space by recognising the distinctive features of the mobile channel and respecting its differences from traditional channels. We present a new generic business model for mobile commerce that uses concepts of location, time, and mission as its touchstones. Customer relationships, and how they are created and owned in the mobile channel, are examined. We finish our survey of the space with a look at mobile commerce's headline effects on existing enterprise system costs and on individual users' interaction styles.

WHY THE WORLD IS TURNING MOBILE

We start our exploration of the business opportunities offered by mobile commerce with a portrait of the emerging mobile lifestyle, introducing some scenarios of wireless life that have already taken hold in markets around the world. We look at how businesses are beginning to respond to these changes, how explosive growth is triggered in mobile networks, and the key market drivers that are motivating the leaders in the mobile commerce space. Last, we question the classic model of electronic commerce and measure its effectiveness for decision makers in the face of the forces unleashed in today's mobile channel.

Mobile and Personal: The Emerging Mobile Lifestyle

Ted's time arrives in niches these days. Waiting for a traffic light to turn, riding in a lift, switching his attention from one work project to another – this former dead time is full of business. Ted has a real-time graph of his investment portfolio repainting itself in the palm of his hand. If he wants to alter his exposure he can buy and sell stocks just by changing the shape of the graph with a stylus. He also chooses to receive alerts about consumer products he might want to buy, based on his purchasing preferences and his current physical location. At the moment, some invisible software agent program is on the lookout for that model classic car he's chasing. Ted is also bidding in an auction for some used construction equipment, so he can use a spare moment to check the current bid on the lot and consider his next move.

When Ted takes an action, such as changing his investment portfolio, a bundle of transactions ripples its series of changes to a disparate collection of remote systems. At the same time, one cent of his current fortune shatters into slivers, the fragmentary payments flowing to the intermediaries who make this all possible: network operators, banks, brokers, retailers, portal owners. Ted makes thousands of such transactions every day, and interacts with tens of thousands of systems. He is continuously connected to an enveloping intelligent environment. Information, entertainment, and commerce flood the spaces in his life, wherever he is, whatever he's doing. He can switch it all off; but he can't make it go away.

Ted has a strange kind of liberty. He is free, yet tracked; mobile, yet contained. He lives in a world that is built of a myriad decision points and whose dimensions are time, location, and mission. He inhabits mobile commerce.

This scenario is already a daily occurrence in Japan, where major cellular phone operator NTT DoCoMo's i-mode wireless Internet service launched in February 1999. Growth of subscribers to i-mode has been phenomenal. The first million subscribers were acquired during six months of operation; thereafter the population curve climbed sharply, with the four million mark achieved around the first anniversary, and the five million mark a bare month after that. Subscriber numbers continue to climb at the rate of around one million per month. Users of i-mode have access to services such as banking, securities trading, airline reservations, and consumer purchases, as well as information and entertainment services ranging from yellow pages to horoscopes. By October 2000, 12.78 million users were generating revenues of $3.3 billion – around $300 each.[1] Looking beyond the consumer market, we find that i-mode is being used to connect field staff with corporate systems, so that logistics company DAT Japan, for example, has armed all its delivery staff with Web and e-mail access. DAT Japan claims a 90 percent cost reduction in call center costs from a $90,000 investment.[2]

Elsewhere in Asia, subscribers to Hong Kong's mobile service Sunday can receive offers from shops as they pass them in the mall.[3] In North America, Bank of Montreal customers can not only conduct their personal banking affairs by cell phone, they can also go shopping via the bank's partner Indigo. Meanwhile stockbrokers in the United States are rolling out wireless broker services that allow PDA (Personal Digital Assistant) users to make trades wherever they are, whenever they want. In Europe, teenagers send millions of text messages to each other using their cell phones' SMS (Short Message Service) function, conducting one-to-one and group conversations that fly beneath

---

1. Ian Murphy, "i-Mode's youth market could wipe out Wap", *Computer Weekly*, 30 November 2000.
2. Presentation by David Macdonald of NTT DoCoMo, Mobile Commerce (organised by IBC UK Conferences Ltd), London, 15–17 May 2000.
3. Falk Müller-Veerse, Durlacher, *Mobile Commerce Report* (no date; 1Q00).

the radars of their teachers and parents, and habituating themselves for a lifetime of mobile service usage.

Moving to Mobile

Though different geographical areas are at different stages of development, organisations from all sectors and nations are now responding to the growing market for mobile commerce services. For those that have already made the transition to offering services over the fixed Internet, adding some kind of basic service for the wireless channel is a small but significant step.

The consumer appetite for mobile services dictates that the leading banks in northern Europe, for example, cannot afford to ignore the new generation of WAP (Wireless Application Protocol) phones. While a bank's announcement that it would introduce a WAP banking service might lift its stock price in the first quarter of 2000, by mid-year, the *absence* of a WAP strategy was more likely to depress bank valuations. WAP also began to play a market enlargement role for European banks: *The Banker* reported in April 2000, that "MeritaNordbanken [. . .] is heavily investing in its WAP strategy because it has saturated the customer base that uses PC Internet banking in its domestic market".[4] Clearly, for banks at least, "wait and see" is not a viable option when it comes to mobile commerce. However we will suggest in this chapter that simply being first into the mobile commerce market will not guarantee success. Mobile commerce is a technology-enabled phenomenon, but sustained success in mobile commerce is a business issue.

We examine a wide range of mobile commerce applications in this book, but it is worth pausing here to ask why banking should be one of the leaders of mobile commerce. Personal banking transactions, after all, are rarely urgent, and being able to pay bills from a mobile device rather than hunt for a checkbook makes it no less likely that a customer will conduct her affairs more efficiently. Why should a mobile banking service be a "must-have" for the consumer market?

---

4. Kung Young, "WAP fever: Have you got it?" *The Banker*, April 2000.

From the bank's point of view, the wireless channel can be seen as a natural extension of existing phone and Internet channels. Customers increasingly choose the mobile mode as their preferred means of connection with all types of information, so the customer's bank must represent its relationship in that channel. This may be a positive impulse, but it may also be a rationalisation of a deeper pull from the customer. In the main, customers use banking technology to check the status of their accounts. Aside from their primary service as a convenient, automated wallet, ATMs allow customers to refer to their balances without keeping their own records. Consequently, balance checking outranks all services apart from cash dispensing in ATM networks.

The availability of balance information via a portable device makes the customer's balance an item that can be checked at any time, almost on an instinctive basis. In fact, balance checking can rapidly become as habitual as glancing at the time on a watch. We wear personal watches because we each own our own time, and we need constant connection with it. Similarly, we own our own money, and we need to keep seeing it. This intimate, emotional relationship is an example of the personal forces at play in the mobile commerce arena.

The theme of *personal connection* runs throughout this book. A soft issue that may not immediately fire the minds of a pure technologist, the individual user's willingness to interact with a mobile service is the major factor in composing and executing effective mobile commerce strategies. We break this willingness down into a number of component factors. The personal circumstances of the user, the physical means with which she interacts with a device and a service, and the complex of goals that make up her momentary mission, all interact to flex the mobile commerce project in ways that do not affect fixed Web-based initiatives. The personal factor is the twist that stops mobile commerce being a simple transition of "traditional" Web-based e-commerce to a wireless channel.

Network Effects

The emergence of this mobile, personal world is often charted in terms of the growth of mobile devices. These numbers are worth rehearsing, not only because they give some measure of the ubiquity of mobile connectivity, but also because they lay the foundation for the core commercial dynamic of mobile commerce, which is what economists call the "network effect".

According to Datamonitor, mobile phone subscriptions in Europe totalled 133 million at the end of 1999, and were forecast to grow to 270 million by 2005.[5] Launching their WAP service in February 2000 in the United Kingdom, Amazon said it expected there to be 48 million suitable phones by 2002.[6] Nokia, the leading WAP phone manufacturer, estimate this number at one billion by 2005.[7] According to industry researchers GartnerGroup, the mobile channel may account for worldwide e-commerce transactions worth up to $1.8 trillion by 2005.[8]

Why has mobile phone penetration grown so steeply in regions where common technology standards are available, such as the European GSM zone? And does the growth curve for device penetration tell us anything about the potential for mobile commerce? Economists explain the growth patterns of organisations such as phone networks by referring to "network effects".[9] In fact, network effects apply to many kinds of participatory systems: "network" is being used as a structural term rather than a strictly technological one. As Figure 1-1 shows, in a network in which all nodes can communicate bilaterally with each other, the addition of a single new node has a high impact on the overall value of the network. The number of potential interactions for a network with n nodes is $n(n-1)$. Increasing the value of n by 1 increases the potential interactions by 2n.

---

5. Datamonitor, *"The race for Mcommerce: Shifting paradigms in the world of mobile commerce strategy"*, March 2000.
6. "Amazon.co.uk launches 'Amazon.co.uk Anywhere'", Amazon press release, 23 February 2000.
7. Noted throughout Nokia's public information; see, for example, http://www.nokia.com/networks/mobile/get_more.html.
8. "Gartner unveils the shape of the wireless economy", Gartner press release, 11 September 2000.
9. See Nicholas Economides's site at http://edgar.stern.nyu.edu/networks/site.html for more information about network effects. The summary given here is based on his paper "The economics of networks", *International Journal of Industrial Organization*, vol. 14, no. 2, March 1996.

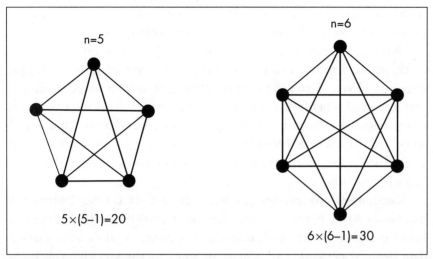

FIGURE 1-1. Network effects.

In other words, systems such as a phone network become more powerful for all users as subscribers sign up. If you are the only person in the world with a phone then the system has no value. If you have a phone that only will work in certain geographical areas, or with constrained subscriber groups, then the system's value is circumscribed by its candidate members. But if it is simple and compelling for other people to join the same phone service, regardless of where they live or which device they choose to own, then the service quickly becomes a major arena of exchange.

The Internet is our closest model of the network effect in action. Commercial online information systems and electronic mail systems existed before the Internet migrated to the public domain. These pre-Internet services could not achieve true mass market status because they formed a fragmented space. The Internet, and particularly the Web, took off because it uses common standards that allow anyone to become a user and a producer of content or services.

However, as economist Nicholas Economides points out, technical compatibility is not the sole driver of network effects. Equally important is users' *expectations* of the network's growth. By buying, for example, a WAP phone, a user is betting that he is making a mainstream decision. No one wants to be toting Betamax in a VHS world, because they won't be able to share content with others.

We can see expectations, and the management of expectations, at work in the leading Internet players' wars over instant messaging standards. Even clearer is the abrupt take-off of SMS usage in Europe that occurred when the network operators began to deliver messages across network boundaries in early 1999. As soon as the "home network" constraint was lifted, a true – and huge – "network" rapidly established itself. European users now send some 2 billion SMS messages per month.

Consumers buy phones primarily to talk, of course. Some commentators wryly point out that the "killer app" for mobile commerce is voice communications. But as mobile phones mutate into wireless data devices, network effects start to apply at the service level. If the mobile device that you buy is technically commerce-enabled, the basic determinant of your mobile commerce behaviour will be the availability of parties with whom to transact. If, for example, you want to do comparison shopping via a mobile device, you require that retailers be represented in the mobile commerce universe. You might even prefer a comparison shopping service to be available in the same channel; but again, you are more likely to use such a service if more than one exists.

The upshot of applying network effects to the mobile commerce arena is that, in general, mobile commerce initiatives experience a lonely period of unnerving quiet before encountering sudden explosive growth. In the European WAP market of 2000, services experienced slow growth due to the poor availability of WAP phones and consumer fears of buying into technology that would soon become obsolete in the wake of successor technologies. Yet the device manufacturers promise to prime the market by ensuring that every cell phone sold by the 2001 timeframe is WAP-enabled. Mobile commerce capability will therefore begin to arrive in mainstream consumers' hands whether or not they explicitly ask for it. As commerce becomes a default feature of the mobile device, network effects pull businesses into the game. Despite localised uncertainties about timing and technology, few businesses can afford to ignore the potential of the mobile channel and the market drivers that are accelerating its emergence.

Market Drivers

Mobile commerce is being driven by a number of distinct yet interrelated forces on the consumer demand side. As we have noted, the growth in ownership of connected devices provides potential critical mass. Three additional factors contribute to the take-off of mobile commerce: changes in the consumer funding model of mobile services, the establishment of fixed electronic commerce as a business phenomenon, and the accelerated service development environment ushered in by the Internet.

Before considering these factors, we need to note one market difference that favours the development of mobile services in Europe in contrast to the U.S. market. In Europe, a user calling a cell phone pays the call charges, whereas in the United States the cell phone user pays incoming call charges. As a result, European cell phone users are more likely than U.S. users to keep their phones switched on all day and to make sure that their friends and business associates have their number. Cell phone numbers in Europe have distinctive prefixes, rather than area codes, so a user always knows when he is calling a cell phone rather than a fixed phone. European mobile commerce service providers are advantaged over their American counterparts in addressing a market already committed to extensive daily cell phone usage.

The breakthrough growth factor in many mobile service markets has been prepaid voucher (PPV) contracts. PPV delivers a certain volume of calls with the phone when it is purchased. Postpaid billing contracts require upfront customer agreements, bank account details and credit checks, whereas PPV phones can be bought for instant use. This makes them particularly suitable for the youth market. Parents can buy PPV phones for children safe in the knowledge that they cannot run up unreasonable bills. Top-up vouchers extend the usable life of the phone in a manageable manner and also help to maintain a branded real-world relationship with the user. Prepay has commoditised mobile services, making mobile phones affordable items of personal equipment, and creating an electronic personal channel to a huge market of consumers. Many of these users will not be fixed Web users.

The second market driver is the success of fixed e-commerce itself. Consumers from all walks of life have embraced Web-based e-commerce and now expect to conduct transactions via electronic means. Using the Web has become a habitual daily part of work and private life for millions of consumers for whom mobile commerce promises a closer integration of online activity with other tasks. The fixed Web at once addresses and further stimulates users' desires for services. Any new consumer product or service must now place the Net in the foreground of its plans, regardless of its basic proposition. For companies offering business services, failure to provide an online component is unthinkable. Business has migrated to the electronic channel; mobile extends the electronic channel.

E-commerce has also created a new class of commercial organisations whose only effective existence is online. Companies as diverse as Yahoo! and buy.com can exist only in the context of the e-enabled world. The expansion path for pure Internet companies naturally lies in the direction of leveraging new electronic channels. Each new channel that can be recruited to deliver services to the market wrings additional profitability from existing infrastructure, processes, and expertise. The mobile channel is the logical arena for pure Net plays to enhance the value of their brands.

The third market driver that we consider here is time to market. While the Internet has irrevocably changed consumer behaviour and expectations and created a new layer of Internet-dependent companies, it has also changed business fundamentals forever. The change is not so much at the surface, where established enterprises seek to reposition themselves for the Web, nor is it discernible in the transient bandwagon effects of companies striving to be seen playing in the Internet space. Neither is it yet noticeable as savings in the supply chain, since many of these have yet to be proven. Digging deeper, we find that the one factor that has changed for all players is *time*, and in particular, time to market. The Internet economy has accelerated the development and deployment of offers and brands, shrinking the standard period of innovation. Startups expect to introduce service innovations on a monthly basis. Even the most traditional and ponderous of organisations expect their e-projects to deliver well within an earth year. Internet technology and Internet attitudes have undercut a thirty-year history of "big computer project" practice in many established businesses.

Mobile commerce is an ostentatiously fast-moving world where "Internet time" looks downright sluggish. The immediacy of mobile phone connection and the disposability of mobile devices combine with an impulsive, lifestyle-oriented usage relationship to create a market that expects rapid turnover of concepts, services and brands. Players across the board are actively looking to turn every feature of the mobile landscape into a time-to-market advantage.

For example, the PPV model can turn technology obsolescence into a virtue for network operators at the same time as it cuts away the administrative cost of top-up payments. Prepaid phones represent the best means of propelling new models of phones into the market, since they are more like commodities than lifetime possessions. Low-end GSM phones are treated as basic items of urban equipment in most European cities, and users expect to personalise and replace their phones at regular intervals. By introducing dual-slot phones that accept smartcards during 2000, France Telecom Mobiles handed its customers a phone that could process its own top-up payments. This saves the company money on administering payments, but it also effectively floods the market with fully commerce-enabled, personal point-of-sale (POS) terminals. Since all credit cards in the French market are smartcards, this single initiative does much to change the commercial landscape. Before the launch, there were some 600,000 POS terminals in France. With the launch of the new dual-slot phone, a further one million terminals were added.

The France Telecom Mobiles initiative has echoes of the French government's Minitel project of the 1980s, in which the state created an e-commerce environment by replacing the phone book with an online terminal. However, Minitel stayed within French borders; the GSM standard has a much greater territorial footprint, and those of the credit card companies are even larger. Certainly the initiative helps to create a large and powerful network, but its chief characteristic is its effect on time. By combining credit cards with e-commerce and putting the result in its customers' hands, the company is aggressively shortening the time to market that we might otherwise expect for this kind of development.

NTT DoCoMo's i-mode service in Japan makes a similar point. While players outside Japan sought an industry standard for interactive wireless data systems in WAP, DoCoMo went ahead in its own home market with a dedicated packet switched network as delivery platform and a subset of HTML as the content format. By creating a market from scratch, i-mode created it earlier than any competitor. i-mode established the rules of the game for service providers, including the revenue-sharing model. In this case, the company's first-mover advantage translates into sustained ownership of an extensive commercial platform.

Beyond E-commerce

Mobile commerce follows hard on the emergence of e-commerce via the fixed Internet. Can we use a generic business model designed for traditional e-commerce with this new field?

The classic model of e-commerce makes a fundamental split between business-to-consumer (B2C) and business-to-business (B2B) opportunities, as shown in Table 1-1. As we suggest in *The Business of Ecommerce: from Corporate Strategy to Technology,*[10] some of the power of the basic B2C/ B2B model comes from the strategist's ability to generate B2B applications from existing B2C applications, and vice versa. The B2C/B2B concept was never the last word on e-commerce, though it is often used to make basic distinctions between types of e-commerce venture. Mobile commerce is set to challenge this model more fundamentally.

To recap, B2C applications make up the majority of propositions amongst the so-called dotcoms, who tend to focus on the sale of mainstream goods and services such as books, CDs, and flowers. For such companies, e-commerce represents an efficient channel to market that

---

10. Paul May, *The Business of Ecommerce: From Corporate Strategy to Technology.* New York: Cambridge University Press, 2000.

TABLE 1-1. The Classic Generic Sectoral Model of E-Commerce

	PHYSICAL	INFORMATIONAL
Business-to-consumer	Books, CDs Tools Sports equipment	Stocks and shares Premium news
Business-to-business	Hardware Operating resources	Software Travel reservations

can be added to an existing business model. Other B2C companies focus on providing less traditional services: lastminute.com, for example, sells late-availability travel and entertainment products. On the B2B side of the street, the greatest success stories to date have been in online marketplaces, where users from one industry gain access to efficiently priced goods and services. Such services leverage the power of the Internet to deliver savings in time and money, and demonstrate the net's ability to remove the friction associated with traditional economic systems.

The B2B/B2C orthodoxy is bound up with *intention*. A Web-based online shopping site relies on the user deciding to go shopping, deciding to sit at a terminal device (and boot it up if necessary), and deciding to visit the target online store. A B2B exchange relies on a disparate set of employees located in different companies but with equivalent goals pursuing a set task at roughly the same time. In the roughest terms, we decide to be employees during the working day and consumers at other times; and though we might do a little light shopping at work and take a little work home, we are used to dividing our lives in this way.

Mobile connectivity puts pressure on this simple duality. Shopping at work and working at home are fairly simple and clearly bounded substitutions. But what about the executive who has a laptop and mobile phone but no desk? Is she at work or at leisure? She may switch between modes at the behest of an incoming call or in response to some other event taking place in her immediate environment. How can she defend her own private time and signal that she is not available for work demands when her employer has made it simple and convenient for her to be always contactable? With real-time access to the resources of her corporate intranet, how can she ignore the pressure to monitor the business's performance in real time and to intervene when the situation demands, wherever she is and whatever time it may be? Mobile connectivity creates a potential 24-hour dependency relationship between businesses and their employees, allowing business activity to permeate our lives. While we bathe in a sea of commerce, entertainment and media services, the currents of our business obligations will continue to operate, claiming our attention and our identities.

The static B2C/B2B model necessarily simplifies the role of the user, making him a somewhat passive recipient of applications that have been designed to structure his behaviour in some theoretically optimal way. Mobile commerce lets people scatter in time, space, and goal orientation. We lose our commitment to static work sessions at branded Web sites and become users of relevant, timely, atomised services that mesh with our daily lives. In so doing, we allow our commerce behaviour to reassert some important features that have been suppressed by the fixed Web.

Consider, for example, how Web-based e-commerce fails to facilitate impulsive behaviour on the part of the consumer. Before e-commerce on the Web, shopping always entailed movement, surprise, and a peculiar mix of determination and randomness. The remarkable growth of non-Web advertising of Web sites shows that consumers still need to have their imaginations caught in real-world situations. We have to pull non-technologists onto the Web through advertising, and then seek to keep them in that world using sticky sites, entertainment, and discount offers.

Mobile commerce, on the other hand, seeks to integrate itself with the user's daily life: to be a natural, comfortable part of that life. On the Web, we build spaces and narratives that entrap users, structure their behaviour, and co-opt their goodwill: we invite them into a place and then read them the rules whereby they may reach some commercial outcome. With the mobile channel, the user invites the service provider to share some of her attention, and the user makes the rules. Not only do we have to deal with the possibility that the user might click to another site, we have to compete with incoming alerts, voice calls, *and* the event stream taking place in the user's physical and social environment. We have tried to persuade consumers that shopping is about research, comparison, and discounts because that fits the fixed technology we have had to date. When we have yearned for more, it has too often been for the bandwidth necessary to render three-dimensional store environments or animate convincing shopping assistant *avatars* – cartoonish onscreen helpers. But if we twist our point of view over towards the customer, we immediately see a new set of values associated with the activity of shopping. Shopping is as much about rewarding ourselves emotionally as satisfying rational needs. What we buy, who we buy it from, and what we are prepared to pay vary according to our mood states. We may be able to suspend some of the emotional element when we sit down to shop online at a desktop machine. We will be more vulnerable – or more empowered, depending on your viewpoint – as mobile commerce users. B2C applications will morph beyond recognition as mobile commerce insinuates itself deeper into our daily experience.

In challenging the boundaries of employee and consumer roles, mobile commerce reduces the significance of B2B applications as a major category within an overall model of mobile commerce opportunities. This is not to say that B2B disappears as an area of focus for companies developing business services or looking to realise efficiencies by using such services. The emphasis is rather on the enhanced potential of mobile commerce over fixed e-commerce to revolutionise business processes within businesses as well as amongst them. As with consumer services, business applications extend and evolve to perform in a broader, deeper usage environment.

B2C and B2B remain useful categories for describing certain capabilities that can exist profitably in many traditional and electronic channels. However, their usefulness shrinks in the context of the newly emerging model. We will explore this new model in more detail in the next section. For now, we must recognise that mobile commerce is not just an extension to the Web, with the cell phone handset or wireless PDA taking the place of the desktop PC. Mobile commerce has core characteristics that differ from those of the classic Internet, and these in turn demand a reappraisal of the B2B/B2C model. While the old model is useful for the static Web, applying it thoughtlessly to the mobile commerce world results in applications that merely replicate existing solutions on a new platform, without achieving additional benefits. Just as many first-generation Web sites were essentially 'brochureware', many first-generation mobile commerce ventures will merely be the Web without wires.

The shift to a mobile channel undermines the service provider's traditionally superior position with respect to the user. The provider of a traditional Web-based service can reasonably guess that the user is sitting down and focusing on the task of using her computer and that the user is either in the workplace or at home. But if a user can access your service at any time and from any place, then you can no longer predict the context in which he is consuming that service. We can no longer validly treat users as characters implicated in simple, stereotyped situations. Simple transitions from fixed Web to mobile commerce will necessarily replicate a single, fixed set of assumptions about service usage, and thereby fail to connect – on the lifestyle level – with the target market.

One term popularly associated with the emergence of mobile commerce is *convergence*. It normally refers to the coming together of the fixed Internet and mobile communications systems to create what is often called the mobile Internet. The existing Internet and existing mobile communications systems certainly now *intersect* to give us Web-style services on mobile devices, but the implications for mobile commerce going forward are more profound than a meeting-point of technologies. The convergence prompted by mobile commerce is that of consumer and business lifestyles.

At the same time, mobile commerce behaviour is born of mobile phone usage rather than fixed PC usage. The characteristics of phone usage influence usage of other mobile devices and dictate the major contours of the mobile commerce landscape. In particular, phone systems are neither inherently business-to-consumer or business-to-business. They are person-to-person.

CREATING MOBILE COMMERCE OPPORTUNITIES

We have looked at how mobile commerce has started to emerge in the business landscape, its growth patterns and drivers, and the limited applicability of existing generic e-commerce models. Mobile commerce is changing the landscape within which it is appearing, and we need updated guides if we are to find our way. In this section we explore methods of finding business opportunities in the world that mobile commerce is rendering around us. We consider the practice of mobile thinking – a habit of projecting ourselves into the usage patterns of users. We suggest a new generic model for planning mobile commerce services. We also consider the ongoing relationship between fixed and mobile channels and the role of experimentation in service development.

The Uses of Intuition

The scientific element in business opportunity development is vanishingly small. In the absence of any guaranteed mechanical means of generating ideas for business lines and applications, imitation and intuition naturally take over as the decision-maker's guides. This is the way it should be. After all, our ventures are tested in the fire of the market, not the laboratory kiln. But these are sharp tools – and they need to be used with care.

The dangers of imitation are obvious. As we have seen with Web-based ventures, a rash of me-too imitators follows any innovative idea, leading to saturated markets with poor differentiation. Despite the investments made by both startups and established enterprises in online brands, and in particular the expensive ingenuity dedicated to their promotion in traditional media, brands cannot of themselves guarantee market success. Where an imitator has a genuine twist on an established formula, maintaining distance from the pack is a major challenge. But at the fundamental level, many businesses simply choose to imitate the wrong model. The rush to "get online" has ignited some spectacular dollar bonfires as companies compete to borrow each other's clothing. Core competencies are dumped in an effort to gain the buoyancy needed to join the current crop of high-fliers.

This is not to say that businesses cannot learn lessons from the actions of others. This book draws from a wide range of pioneering mobile commerce applications precisely so that decision-makers can apply the industry's emerging wisdom. Imitation that is not slavish is necessarily influenced by the second of our nonscientific guides to idea generation, intuition. Intuition is, of course, a subjective quality, and one person's insight can easily be another's irrelevance. The mobile commerce industry, like any cultural movement, tends to share its intuitions so that a body of opinion emerges and evolves over time. Theories come and go within this milieu, but a mainstream is usually discernible. However, it is somewhat misleading to think of the mobile commerce industry as a distinct grouping in its own right. The boundaries of such an interest group are at best fuzzy. Mobile commerce has rapidly become the concern of all businesses, and it therefore touches on the experience, responsibilities, and ambitions of individuals across the board. As a consequence, some of the intuitions that carry the most vocal support are not necessarily the most valid. In particular, a range of false intuitions arises from experience with Web-based e-commerce.

The Internet has been the defining technological phenomenon of our time. Its mode of use, role in our world, and structural relationships have come to seem "natural", though each is in fact peculiar. For most of us, the Internet is synonymous with the Web, even if we officially acknowledge the distinction. The Web is not the only model of an interconnected, information-rich, economically efficient world, and to assume it is denies the most interesting – and revolutionary – characteristics of mobile commerce.

The leading false intuition concerning mobile channels is that content needs to be rich: designed with colours and images, and multiple navigation paths. Those who have absorbed the Web as the only model of interaction are usually disappointed with first-generation WAP phones, for example. How can a device with a monochrome screen, limited graphics, four or five lines of text to a page, and no pointing device ever compete with the Web experience? The conclusion is that compelling content, and particularly entertainment, cannot be delivered to mobile users, or at least such services must wait until the full Web experience is brought to the mobile user. As we shall see, the prospects for information and entertainment services are very strong in mobile commerce despite this apparent handicap, and they in fact promise to overshadow revenues from fixed Web-based competitors.

For those who cannot make the leap away from Web-based content models, there is the option to make a positive denial of them. If rich content will not drive mobile commerce, then we could disregard content altogether, and decide the key attribute of mobile commerce is the ability to make transactions. Exchange of information is often seen as an afterthought in the Web world, with Web sites conceived as glorified magazines with occasional functionality spots pasted in. A number of mobile commerce players find their motivation in the reversal of this model. They design their offerings around discrete, atomic transactions and sideline issues such as customer dialogue and brand image.

Valid intuitions often come from thinking that predates the Web model or that suspends the hypnotic influence of its surface characteristics in favour of its successful underlying dynamic. Asked to identify the attributes of the "killer app" for WAP, transport information company Kizoom recommend designing services that are "simpler for the buyer and cheaper for the seller".[11] The phrasing is economical but precise. Kizoom's message is that mobile commerce users value convenience, while mobile commerce providers need to pursue cost advantages. The intersecting point on these two trajectories is the sweet spot.

Right Here, Right Now: Thinking Mobile

This message points us to the most profitable way of designing successful mobile commerce services. We need to identify what is distinctive about the mobile channel in its own right, and then pursue the implications of those differences in the context of user needs and desires. Web-thinking stops some corporate decision-makers from acknowledging that mobile commerce is different because it's . . . mobile. Rather than focusing on the perceived limitations of the current generation of mobile devices, let's look at where the mobile platform clearly wins out over the fixed Internet.

---

11. Presentation to WAPWednesday, London, 25 April 2000.

First, mobile devices are carried into different locations. A mobile phone or wireless PDA maintains its unique address on the network to which it is connected, but it operates in different locations. Various technology options allow us to fix the geographical location of a device at any time. This then allows us to develop *location-based* services. An entire class of applications that has little relevance on the Web emerges as a result of the device's portability.

Of course, desktop and laptop machines can be moved too. The next distinctive feature of the mobile channel is that it uses *personal* devices that tend to be carried as essential pocket equipment. Cell phones, wireless PDAs, and pagers are left on all day and stay with the user. Cell phones, in particular, are regarded as personal accessories like pens or watches and not shared with other users. They become personalised with snap-on covers, ringing tones, and boot-up icons. PDAs usurp the traditional functions of the paper schedule, address book, and notebook, their users coming quickly to rely on them as the repository of all their most important personal information. Personalisation of services is an important theme in mobile commerce, both from the point of view of the user's ability to customise a service to her own preferences and from the point of view of the service provider's ability to recognise a user and deliver relevant content to her.

The third distinctive feature of mobile commerce is the significance of a user's situation. At the basic level, this is a generalised version of the location attribute, in that as well as recognising where a user is, we might also take into account his generic surroundings. Is the user in an office or at home? Driving a car, catching a train, or on foot? He may interact with services in different ways in different situations. He may have more or less attention to donate to a service, depending on the current situation's physical and social demands.

In the fixed Web world, we know that most Web users are sitting at desks. They have chosen to concentrate their attention on interacting with a screen, keyboard, and mouse. But with mobile commerce we engage customers in mid-step and in mid-sentence. Customers initiate mobile commerce transactions on impulse, and service providers push alerts to them based on occurrences of events. Essentially, mobile commerce is integrated with people's lifestyles, while fixed Web-based e-commerce is a distinct task *inside* people's lifestyles. A mobile commerce user can engage with a service provider as the need or desire arises rather than seeking out a designated physical space such as an office, an Internet café – or a lap.

As well as generic situations such as in-car or on-foot, mobile commerce is distinguished by a deeper level of situation, which we call *mission*. Wherever a user is, and whatever type of generic situation he is in, users have one or more missions that they are attempting to progress. So, a user may be driving (situation) in Atlanta (location) to make a business meeting (mission). He may have longer-term goals that might trigger other missions, and if the service provider knows about these goals, then this knowledge could inform its outbound messages to the customer (personalisation).

Mission is the least discussed dimension of the mobile commerce space. This is partly because people are reluctant to jettison the fairly clearly demarcated components of the "traditional" e-commerce model, which tethers users to broad role definitions of "business" and "consumer". The concept of mission undermines most traditional applications, which are discrete bundles of functionality sometimes corralled into "suites", more often scattered across the metaphorical desktops of our best-loved operating systems. We are so used to generating point-and-click applications that we have forgotten that point-and-click is simply the best implementation of what users really want: think-and-do. Mobile commerce offers the chance to renew our approach to serving user needs, so that we offer solutions to specific goals as they arise, rather than attempting to package them into metaphor-driven entities.

The other chief reason that mission is rarely discussed is that most decision-makers on the technology side of businesses don't themselves yet live the mobile lifestyle. System architects are normally amongst the least mobile members of a company's community, working from centralised head office facilities. In addition, mobile commerce behaviour tends to be led by youth markets, so unless such decision-makers are blessed with children of the right age they may never consciously note the way users of the mobile channel integrate mobile services with their daily lives. Technologists may be early adopters of new device types, but they are rarely typical of the mass market user in their tolerance of buggy performance or, more importantly, their conception of what's cool.

Time for Push: Triggers and Bullets

The features we have discussed so far lead naturally from the characteristics of the mobile device itself. The importance of location is immediately obvious. Personalisation can also be appreciated as an important attribute by most people who follow consumer market behaviour. Situation and mission arise as attributes when we start to imagine mobile commerce in action, and we begin to identify mobile commerce with lifestyle changes. The last feature we will consider here is external to the device itself, but it has a major impact on the other features. It is *time*.

Time has played a very small role in the development of Web-based services. Search engines, for example, focus on the breadth and depth of the resources they cover and the ability to cast the most relevant items to the top of a result set. They do not concentrate on the timeliness of information. Indeed, the growth of the Web and the rate of change in its content makes it hard to imagine how a search engine that would confidently present timely information in response to a query could be built. In the e-commerce mainstream, stock trading services can send alerts by e-mail, but this still relies on the user connecting to the Internet and picking up his mail.

However, our world unfolds in time. More precisely, we live in an event-driven world. Events take place in time and cause other events to take place. A user places an item for sale on eBay, another user makes a bid, other users respond, and so on. An analyst issues a comment on a publicly traded company and investors react. An Amazon customer clicks through the checkout and a stock-picker receives a pick-list.

The technology implementing event-driven systems is often called *push*. Push technology was hyped as the next big thing for the Web in 1997, but did not achieve the goals sketched for it by commentators. The reasoning behind the big hopes for push was not unsound. The Web was beginning to overwhelm users with its wealth of content, forcing users to spend much of their time searching for relevant material. At the same time, the "pull" nature of Web usage meant that users were potentially missing relevant information simply through the happenstance of when they initiated their searches. The rationale of services such as PointCast, and services powered by Marimba's push technology was that users would subscribe to channels of content that would send relevant and timely items to the browser or desktop.

Unfortunately, most push channels compared unfavourably with broadcast media for content and quality of experience and failed to distinguish themselves from traditional broadcast channels through a faster churn of content. But push is alive and well on the Web in one small but significant feature: the stock ticker. The constantly updating stock-price window is an isolated example of effective event-driven service. For the business user, such event streams abound. Sales are made in real time; products are completed in real time; deliveries occur in real time; problems arise in real time.

In 1997 business technology consultant Simon Bisson coined the phrase *corporate ambient push* to characterise an environment in which relevant, timely corporate data was automatically sent to qualifying users *by any available channel*. Technology is now catching up with his vision. The proliferation of mobile channels and their integration with existing business information systems technologies is finally connecting the event streams of business with operating teams.

Events trigger actions, and the causal connection is formed by the transmission of information. Note that the information involved is relatively small and compact: a price, a stock level, an outcome. The quantum is bullet-like: discrete, direct, targeted. Today's mobile devices and network technologies favour applications where the information transferred is in small slugs. The less processing that needs to be done by the device, the less power it requires and hence the lighter its battery can be. Small chunks of information require lower bandwidth and can be transmitted with greater confidence across networks than can the sessions required for, say, video-conferencing. Networks with higher bandwidth and greater robustness will not cancel the validity of this model. As the performance of mobile networks and devices improves, the data required to describe an event will not enlarge by necessity.

Time, through events, adds a dimension to mobile commerce that is commonly absent in fixed e-commerce. Time also impacts user behaviour at a fundamental level. Put simply, mobile devices enable all users to spread their business and leisure behaviour around the clock face, rather than allocating each to specific bands of time. The time at which a user initiates or receives a service impacts the type and content of many services.

In the first instance, the interaction may be influenced by *urgency*. That is, an opportunity to achieve or avoid some outcome presents itself to the user. This could be the offer to sell a stock at a preset threshold price or a request to find a cab in a sudden rainstorm.

The second role for time in the user's experience is *schedule*. Every user's purposive life is governed by a patterning of time according to obligations and habits. At the personalised end of the schedule scale, we can imagine a service that buys travel tickets at the most opportune time ahead of a business trip recorded in the user's calendar, optimising fare deals with available credit and travel slots. At the generic end of the scale, services can be built to offer different services at different times of the day, suggesting lunch options around midday and theater ticket availability in the early evening.

A Generic Model for Mobile Commerce Services

How then shall we define "mobile commerce"? Simple definitions of the term are emerging in the industry, but most tend to serve the commercial interests of those who coin them. Thus for some mobile commerce is purely concerned with shifting existing online shopping services onto cell phones, while others focus on the creation of entirely new forms of consumer services for mobile users, such as location-based information services.

We take a fairly strict view of "mobile" and a wide view of "commerce". "Wireless" is often inaccurately used as a synonym for "mobile". Wireless technology certainly provides the technical basis of mobile commerce, but wirelessness does not always make for mobility. Wireless connectivity is, for example, a viable option for replacing domestic phone lines with broadband capability, but such solutions are not designed for use on the move. When we say something is "mobile" in this book, we mean that its primary usage environment is a mobile one.

Our usage of "commerce" is generous. We use the word to encompass activities which generate payment transactions, but also to include activities that create or enhance efficiencies in commercial processes.

Any simple definition of such an important term is likely to be inadequate for anyone seeking to act in the business space which it demarcates. We have therefore designed a simple generic model for locating, relating and evaluating mobile commerce services. The model, shown in Figure 1-2,[12] describes a three-dimensional space with axes relating to location, time, and mission.

In the example shown in Figure 1-2, the *weather* service is shown scoring low on all axes. This means that weather information has relatively little connection with location, time, and mission. This may seem counterintuitive since weather certainly takes place in real locations and at real times, and it affects real missions, all the way from picnicking to invasion. But from the point of view of the mobile commerce user, weather is a fairly neutral service. The weather for the user's current place and time is evident to the user without him having to use a service. Any mission that may be impacted by weather conditions will exist in the future, and possibly in another place. In other words, although it may be interesting to get a weather report on a mobile device, it isn't a vital service. At the most, a user may be interested in learning the current weather conditions in some other

---

12. This model was inspired by Dave Ford of Webraska, and developed with help from him. Most models of mobile commerce focus on time and location but fail to incorporate a concept of mission. This is generally due to their proponents' interest in establishing a particular niche service rather than describing an overall model for the field.

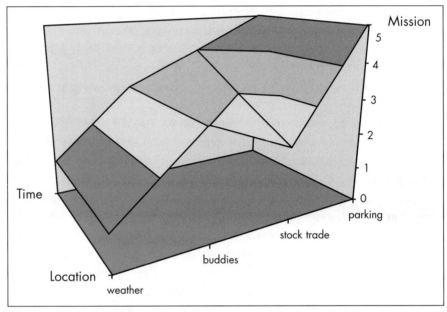

FIGURE 1-2. Generic model for mobile commerce services.

place, perhaps in the location of someone that she is about to call. Most weather services, however, focus on forecasts rather than current conditions.

The example shows the *parking* service scoring high on all axes. The service we envision here guides users to available parking spots in real cities in real time. The mission is pressing because the user is chasing a scarce resource, and failure to acquire a spot blocks her from embarking on the next mission. Time is of the essence, since parking availability and traffic conditions change by the second. Location is vital, since we need to present spots that are reachable from the user's current position. Parking is a service that cannot be put off to another time, done in another place, or abandoned as a means of terminating a journey. All drivers need to park, and relevant, timely information services in the mobile channel improve the parking experience and help to optimise the use of parking land.

Two other example services are shown in Figure 1-2. The *buddies* service scores in the middle of the range for location, time, and mission. We envision this service as a means whereby friends can check on each other's locations and intentions, so that they may jointly determine plans of action. As such, the service is an always-on awareness service. Users need to make constant reference to where they are, what time it is, and the goals that are available and desirable to the group.

The *stock-trade* service scores highly against time and mission, but slightly lower against location. We include this example to show that while mobility creates convenience for the user, the fact that a service is convenient to carry around does not make it location-sensitive. Stock trades are executed in real markets, which unfold in time. Stockholders have investment and liquidity aims, so their changing goals also impact on their trading behaviour. Their geographical location, on the other hand, is less significant. However, we have not scored the location dimension at zero. This is to demonstrate that the model may be used to prescribe a desired service as well as describe an existing service. In this case, we are imagining a stock-trading service that offers discounts on commission for users trading from vacation spots. Our imaginary stock-trading service has decided to corner the market in vacationing stockholders and has struck a deal with a hotel chain to include an ad for the service on the default page of the hotel's in-room TV service.

The parking service is based on one provided by Webraska and Schlumberger in the European WAP market. The buddies service is based on services provided by players such as Sessami and Room33. Weather forecasts proliferate on all electronic channels. The stock trade service is fictional.

We are careful to call the items plotted in the example space *services* rather than *applications*. The reason is that the term "application" smacks too much of the fixed Web space, where users access a defined, branded place and engage with a range of features. The services we describe here are lightweight and atomic. They target small, discrete opportunities. Each has the potential to establish a powerful brand associated with delivering solutions to actual customer problems or opportunities that unfold in time and space.

Fixed versus Mobile: Consideration and Action

In fixed e-commerce, users play *roles* with respect to *applications*. The available role types are limited to those of "consumer" and "business". Mobile commerce begins to challenge this rigid model, promoting mission as a more important determinant of service design than role, and introducing the dimensions of location and time. One way of picturing the resulting market is to use the hunter-gatherer society as a metaphor.

Hunter-gatherer communities make their living on the move; they gravitate towards resources rather than settling in an area and farming. We imagine them as living with higher levels of daily danger, though this is doubtless a romantic notion on our part, most of us being separated by several generations of industrial society and artistic idealisation from the harsh conditions of agricultural life. We also imagine them as moving in bands, or extended families, rather than settling in role-organised villages.

The mobile commerce lifestyle is increasingly seen in this romantic light: a return to an extended Eden, an electric savannah peopled by innocents who travel light and whose attention is easily captured by danger signals. The most popular mobile commerce scenarios play to this caricature, with bands of teenagers seen travelling through mall-shaped hunting grounds, tempted and warned by incoming alerts on their mobile devices.

The hunter-gatherer metaphor is useful to some extent. It helps us to lift some of the artificial constraints that we place on users of fixed e-commerce applications and is particularly useful in reinstating the role of impulse in shopping. However, the metaphor can be stretched too far. The types of behaviours associated with fixed e-commerce do not all evaporate because mobile commerce becomes available. Indeed, mobile commerce serves to clarify where the strengths of fixed e-commerce are located.

The different yet complementary natures of fixed and mobile commerce can be seen by comparing the utility of various applications

TABLE 1-2. Application Emphases in Fixed and Mobile Channels

APPLICATION	FIXED CHANNEL	MOBILE CHANNEL
News	Depth and context	Headlines
Shopping	Rich media catalogues, opinions	Hot deals
Stock trades	Research	Fast deals
Auctions	First bid	Last chance

in each channel. As Table 1-2[13] suggests, when applications migrate from fixed to mobile channels, the emphasis of each switches from *consideration* to *action*.

For example, the traditional Web-based application allows the stock trader to conduct deep and wide research into companies he is considering investing in. It allows him to compare performance of different stocks over different time periods and to read analyst reports and company statements. It will maintain details of his portfolio and value it for him. All of these functions are certainly doable in the mobile channel, but they are not best suited to the mobile channel. The analyst research function, for example, not only benefits from a large-screen format but also from dedicated, static reading time. Complex data comparisons usually require some iterative processing as the collection of stocks being analysed is varied. These are consideration functions.

The mobile channel, on the other hand, shines when it comes to stock execution. The deepest and widest research has value only when it can be applied in the live market, when it informs a decision to buy, sell, or hold. Securities markets are clearly time-based entities. Windows of opportunity open and close and are consumed by time. The ability to take action at the right time is crucial to optimum involvement in the active management of the investment portfolio. Mobile commerce provides this live link to the market without pinning the investor to a chair.

---

13. Adapted from a presentation by Vignette, Internet World, London, 25 May 2000.

Overemphasis on the hunter-gatherer metaphor can lead mobile commerce service designers to dismiss the importance of the consideration activity, relegating genuine desk work to an unfashionable, twentieth-century twilight zone. This is evident in some of the informal scenarios for youth-oriented mobile commerce that are discussed in WAP development communities. Hunter-gatherer enthusiasts extrapolate from European teenagers' mobile voice and SMS behaviour to posit a world in which groups of friends seek each other out to endlessly negotiate entertainment options using the mobile channel, sending revenues to information providers and ticket vendors as they do so. Yet this kind of behaviour cannot exist in a vacuum. The users involved have to take their lead from some set of shared data. For example, they have to be in broad agreement about what movies are worth seeing. Such a consensus cannot build up in any group of friends without two prior levels of information being in place. The first level is the list of movies currently on release. The second level is the media ranking of that list. Only when these levels have been provided can any group start to negotiate its own preferences.

There are two leading responses to this problem of complementarity between consideration and action. The first is to create a service that combines Web and mobile components to deliver a total experience. The second is to wrap consideration in the mobile service itself, by providing recommendations. The first strategy tends to be favoured by companies that already have established applications on the Web, whereas the latter often appeals to new entrants to the mobile commerce arena.

The first approach is illustrated by Brokat's stock-alert service. Here the user notifies the provider of her requirements at a Web site, and then SMS messages are sent to her cell phone in accordance with the profile.

One of the earliest illustrations of the alternative recommendations strategy is London-based Sessami. The company's first-release WAP service offers a list of *What's Groovy* in exhibitions and events, as well as form-based functions for finding *A Drink, A Bite, A Film,* or *A Taxi*. Searching for a bar, for example, is initially by neutral criteria such as area, but once a venue is chosen a short description characterises the type of experience on offer. The service will also link to a taxi firm that can take the user to the bar. At the inception of the service[14] this link gives only a phone number for a cab firm, but the potential to link straight through for a booking is clear. Minicab firms in London are allowed to offer their services only from fixed premises, unlike licensed black cabs, which patrol for custom. Since minicabs are cheaper than black cabs, the ability to book a minicab from any location to any other at a prearranged price is an attractive mobile commerce service. Sessami is playing a role somewhat like that of the official licensor. By recommending a cab firm, and ultimately by facilitating a transaction with that firm, it is implying a guarantee of some level of competence and value. The licence is a commercial one rather than one blessed by a regulatory authority. For companies like Sessami, success in making recommendations that ring true and choosing partners that deliver will determine their brand value.

Recognising Value

Mobile commerce is an immature market, and instinct naturally plays a large part in the formation of business propositions and the design of resultant services. The unfortunate flipside of instinct is prejudice. Just as it is easy to be trapped by a Web-formed view of commerce applications, so it is easy to make the error of projecting one's own preferences onto the market. This is a particular danger because mobile commerce represents a much broader consumer market than that of the fixed Web. Fixed, Web-based e-commerce has made great changes to the commercial landscape, but its achievements pale in comparison to the potential of mobile commerce. The mobile channel becomes a bonded, intimate part of people's lives, not the bounded, separate activity represented by interaction with fixed channels. We've learned a lot from Web-based e-commerce, but we still have little experience of mobile commerce. As the first lessons roll in, it's important to recognise where instant judgements may lead us astray.

---

14. May 2000.

Take, for example, the massive success of Bandai's cartoon character service for i-mode in Japan. Over one million i-mode users pay 100 yen per month to receive a new character image to display on their phones. Initial reactions to this undoubted success story in the west vary. One reaction is to dismiss the application as a peculiarity of Japanese culture and to deny that it would have such great value outside Japan. Another reaction is to cite the success of character-based phenomena such as Pokémon and Tamogatchi, measure the size of the youth market for mobiles, and conclude that character merchandising should be a massive business in western markets as well. Neither opinion is necessarily wrong, but each is perhaps over-cooked. The lesson to draw from Bandai's success is surely that successful mobile commerce services depend on the value perceptions of consumer groups, and that these will rarely look rational to observers from outside.

Part of the excitement in the emerging mobile commerce arena, and a source of stimulation for the enterprising, is the speed with which new applications confirm or confound prior expectations. Mobile commerce applications are being conceived, developed, and deployed with great speed, leading to a rapid stream of creative and corrective data. Amazon's WAP-based service, for example, turns out to sell many more CDs than books, even though the general expectation would be that the Amazon brand favours book buying. Why is this so? It is possible that buying music has always been more impulsive than book buying; consumers hear tracks playing in the car, and in stores and in clubs, and they associate certain songs or tunes with emotions and memories. Perhaps music is itself simply better integrated with lifestyle than reading – an action item rather than a consideration item? Or perhaps mobile users buy CDs when they are with other people, and it's simply cooler to be seen buying music than books in their current group.

Web-based e-commerce tends to take price as the key determinant of value in both the consumer and business markets. As we have suggested, for users with business missions, event-driven services have the potential to offer great value. For consumers, price is only one criterion in the decision-making process. In the action-oriented mode of mobile commerce use, price will sink in the user's list of priorities. The relevance of an offer to the user's current position with respect to our chief dimensions of location, time and mission will certainly take precedence over price alone. Social and emotional influences may also impact the rank position of price in a purchasing decision.

GR8 2 CU: Person to Person

As we have noted, the classic generic model for e-commerce revolves around businesses doing things "to" consumers and other businesses. The model requires users to adopt fixed roles and to engage with artificial application spaces that group together functions according to some metaphor. In the B2C part of the model, users push a metaphorical shopping cart through a shopping site and stop at the checkout. In the B2B part of the model, users represent players in a commodity exchange. The model is clearly derived from an IT systems world view, in which users' behaviour must be modified to suit the goals of an application.

We argue in *The Business of Ecommerce* that the future of B2B applications lies in system-to-system collaboration. Real efficiencies in the supply chain begin to arise when the knowledge states of cooperating parties can be combined on an automated basis. Most B2B applications today continue to recruit human users as actuators, but the most impressive implementations perform true cross-boundary collaboration with little human intervention.

Mobile commerce has a role to play in collaborative B2B systems. Unattended mobile systems fixed in trucks, trains, ships, and planes can communicate with logistics systems to determine routes, loads, and delivery times. The IT systems world view will be beneficial in achieving such applications.

However, when we switch to the B2C part of the model, our IT-derived viewpoint becomes a hindrance. We can no longer assume that "business-to-consumer" is the natural orientation of the commercial vector. The mobile channel is inhabited by active users who grasp atomic services at the time and place of need and who resist intrusion from businesses that seek to monopolise their choices or attention.

Above all, the climate of mobile commerce is created by users interacting with each other, conducting conversations with each other by voice and text, and playing online games with each other. The B2C agenda is being torn up by a massively enlarged, autonomous, and collaborative market of consumers.

As Figure 1-3 suggests, popular instant messaging services turn the control-oriented PC into a communications device. Phone-based messaging services and two-way paging services are much more convenient means of achieving the same results. Mobile messaging will haul many users away from the fixed Internet, making them less available for marketing messages provided by the fixed Web. As voice-recognition features are added to the growing number of buddy-oriented mobile portals, these services will rapidly siphon much of the zeitgeist out of the fixed chat rooms and online forums and relocate it in the mobile space.

Our conception of what is contemporary moved to the Net in the latter half of the 1990s, with e-mail viruses replacing hooliganism as a sign of social anarchy, day traders symbolising an accelerated, short-termist society, MP3 undercutting the entertainment industry, and movies like *The Blair Witch Project* promoted into mainstream success

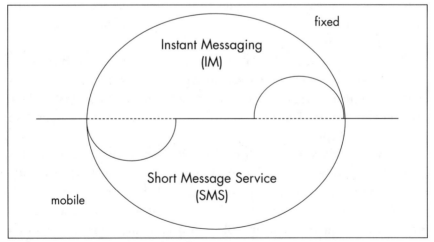

FIGURE 1-3. Convergent messaging systems.

by online marketing methods. The first decade of the new millennium will see contemporary culture migrating to the mobile channel and the younger generation creating the identity of the age outside of the immediate control of established businesses.

What does this mean, in practical terms, for business? First, businesses must accept that commerce activity is migrating to a domain that is primarily rooted in person-to-person communication, not in machine-determined processing. Technology is apparent in fixed e-commerce, transparent in mobile commerce. Businesses that would interact with customers need to invest in creating relationships with them – relationships that go beyond junk mail and satisfaction surveys. Businesses will need to employ ambassadors whose role is to mix with the mobile community, take part in online discussions, run with packs. They will need to understand better than ever before the factors that differentiate places and times from each other. Beneath the superficial genericity of a suburban shopping mall, for example, there is a real and changing local dynamic, influenced by incomes, employment, education, politics – and yes, even the weather. Behind the apparently uniform snarl-up that descends on every town at the sound of the school bell is a complex skein of missions concerning meals, sports, dates, and homework. The rich fabric of daily life yields an enormous opportunity space that makes the tidy B2C ventures of the 1990s appear unambitious.

E Is for Experiment

What goods and services will customers buy in the mobile channel? How will business users exploit the mobile channel to improve their processes? As we have seen, the mobile channel has different characteristics from those of the fixed Net, and these challenge our established application models. We are entering a period in which rapid experimentation cycles will predominate. Several such cycles completed during the writing of this book, and these are described with the relevant services included in Chapter 2.

Some general lessons have emerged early on. The first major lesson is that mobile commerce services find it hard to establish themselves in the market without portal relationships. Current mobile commerce devices and usage situations limit the amount of exploration the typical user will undertake. The mobile commerce user's online world needs to be highly organised, well signposted, and unambiguous. Sites that fail to gain prominence with a portal – or whose portal partner fails to command a significant user base – will need to seek other partnerships. For example, clothing brands may need to ally with retailers in branded lifestyle offers that include clothes, shoes, and accessories.

This does not mean that nonportalised sites are doomed to failure. Creative approaches to gaining customer mindshare are likely to include crossover brands, especially from industries that have a close affinity with mobile lifestyles. Music companies are ideally placed to crossover to the mobile channel: interactive commercial radio is arguably the next logical evolutionary step for the audio entertainment industry.

Travel nodes are also well positioned to become substantial mobile commerce players. The airport, for example, is an excellent domain for mobile business services. If a traveller can access flight information, buy tickets, check in, and penetrate the business lounge using his mobile device, then he is also likely to continue using the same service on the plane to order meals, shop for gifts, and sample the inflight entertainment. The same service could be pre-empting his arrival with offers related to his destination. The service knows the user's location, time, and mission states, so it is positioned to make highly relevant offers. Most importantly, it's "on". As long as the user isn't tempted to move elsewhere, the provider that initiated the customer interactions in the airport becomes the user's default travelling companion.

Many businesses have an inherent lifestyle hook that can be used to snag a mobile commerce service role outside the portalised space. Push services give companies the opportunity to sidestep the customer's portal relationships with compelling offers that lay the ground for longer term relationships. The cost of customer acquisition in fixed Web businesses is usually related to the marketing costs of the acquiring company. Each customer then has an average cost to the company, which can be set against the revenue projected to come from him. Mobile commerce allows us to use highly targeted direct e-mail, lowering the cost of customer acquisition and improving customer quality. Though users will resist junk alerts as strenuously as they resist junk mail and spam, the personalisation of devices and portals will allow users to set permission gateways for incoming offers. A mobile commerce player who cannot establish a permanent portal relationship – that is, take a slot on a prominent menu – may be able to negotiate a short-term, local area, outbound alert campaign with a portal. For example, a particular taxi company could become a sports portal's preferred outbound transport alert supplier on the dates of local sports fixtures. The user benefits from relevant offers, the taxi company gets a guaranteed shot at a predictable market, and the portal refrains from committing its brand to the taxi offer. This scenario is similar to that of targeted banner ads on the Web, though the alerts can be much more highly targeted, and they are as likely to take audio forms as well as text and graphic forms.

The second general lesson that has emerged from early experimentation in mobile commerce is that referrals, or "viral marketing", are key to service growth. The ability to forward content and links to other users is an essential aspect of the mobile device's role as a communicator. An experimental WAP site by myveryown.com shows how service providers can use atomic, lifestyle-oriented services to generate audiences and acquire user registrations. The company's WapGag:) service offers daily and random jokes.[15] The user also has the option to send a joke to a friend. This currently requires an e-mail address as the destination, and asks for an optional sender identification. The recipient receives the e-mail, together with a link to WapGag:). The ability to tag and forward items of interest, be they jokes, pictures, songs, or facts, will be a key feature of mobile commerce behaviour as users begin to participate in shared, online lifestyles. Companies that provide "send to a friend" functions can ensure that their copyright information and link-back is retained in the forwarded material.

---

15. WAP users can try WapGag:) at http://www.wapgag.co.uk/. Be warned that taste has not always survived the bandwidth restrictions of the service.

CUSTOMER RELATIONSHIPS

In this section we look at how customer relationships are formed and farmed in the mobile commerce world. We start by examining the vexed question of customer ownership. Users may not recognise the fact, but they are surrounded by a host of companies who would claim the right to enjoy exclusive relationships with them, and with their money. We look at where the concept of customer ownership derives from and how mobile channel realities are forcing would-be owners to share customers with each other. We also look at the bright prospects for personalisation in mobile commerce, whereby business/customer relationships reach a state of equal benefit to both parties.

Owning the Customer

E-commerce ventures take their lead from traditional service companies in valuing customer relationships as primary assets of the business. In the fixed e-commerce world, no player has a natural advantage when it comes to building customer relationships or keeping those relationships to itself. The fixed Web is a level playing field in this regard. However, the mobile commerce world immediately supplies a powerful instance of a relationship-centred player with whom all other players are obliged to treat. This is the mobile network operator. The network operator's ownership of the channel is a major difference to Web-based e-commerce, where no single company can restrict access to the Internet. The Internet is open by default; mobile channels are closed by default.

Cell phone networks, for example, naturally have to provide their customers with phones that work with their network. Service providers such as OmniSky supply wireless modems that attach to popular PDAs and enable access to their packet data network. In all cases, the tied relationship between the device and the network makes it equally natural for the operator to supply a default home page on a mobile commerce device. Since cell phones are aimed at the mass market rather than a specialist market, it is arguable that a supplied home page is a benefit to the user, since it removes the need to configure the device as an information appliance. The consumer simply uses the services contained within the operator's home page, accessing menu items for data services in the same way as she accesses the phone's own features, such as its address book or calendar.

This model is often called the *walled garden* model. The operator gathers a collection of key services and restricts – or at least discourages – the user from venturing beyond the garden's confines. Such models have arisen in the online world, but have struggled to withstand the open nature of the Web. AOL, for example, predates the Web and built its subscription base by offering proprietary content. Once AOL added access to the Web, its utility increased, but the majority of users still stay within the walled garden for much of their time online. The reason that AOL's proprietary areas continue to be successful is that they offer quality content. The greater competition added by Web access provides continuing motivation to maintain quality levels within the proprietary areas. Other pre-Web online service providers have not fared so well, and Internet portal brands such as Yahoo! have become the preferred guides to online content.

The full-service Web remains an unwieldy target for mobile access, and as we have seen in this chapter, does not exactly map to the requirements of mobile commerce. If mobile commerce were simply a case of connecting wireless devices to the existing Internet, then open access pressures would undoubtedly lead to the tearing down of operator-installed home pages and their associated walled gardens.

There is some evidence that this is happening in the WAP services world. Operators such as Orange in the United Kingdom provide a default home page that contains branded news, weather, and travel information. The operator also provides access to other WAP sites via a setting labelled 'othersites'. This setting connects the user to an alternate gateway that allows free access beyond the walled garden. The Nokia 7110 WAP phone has slots for five gateway settings, so an Orange Nokia user can also access the full WAP world by configuring a slot himself. This is not too difficult for a technically savvy user, though it would tax any user who has had problems configuring, say, a Web browser on a corporate network. The user needs to know the target gateway's connection type, security type, bearer type, dial-up number, IP address, authentication type, data call type, and data call speed, as well as a username and password. All of these settings have to be entered using the phone's keypad. Setting up a gateway is made simpler by portal services such as iobox. Here, the user registers a username and password with iobox, and the service updates the phone by sending it an SMS message.

At this point, our Orange Nokia user has potential access to every WAP site running on the Internet. But he is still limited to the WAP content that he can find, either within the chosen portal or via a directly inputted URL. (Note that not all phones allow this flexibility in the first place. The home page of the original Motorola Timeport WAP phone, for example, could not be altered by the user; nor could the user store any bookmarks on the phone.) How rapidly can an alternate WAP portal establish itself as the default starting point for a significant mobile user population? The leading Web sites built their initial communities through "word of mouse" – e-mail recommendations from friends and colleagues and postings to newsgroups. WAP services have a less fertile environment for growth. SMS remains a painful method of communicating text, especially URLs with their non-alphabetic characters. Voice may be a more natural way for users to spread the word about good sites, but the very time when it is impossible to make a voice call is while you are using the phone for WAP access. Iobox is building awareness of its brand through consumer advertising and its Web site.

The mobile network operator has a natural advantage in claiming ownership of the customer through the definite convenience it can offer in a well-designed default home page and portal. The operator's relationship with the customer runs deeper than that, however. By owning the billing relationship with the customer, the operator has an ongoing, unmatched financial route to the customer's wallet. Each traditional mobile customer contract establishes debit and credit facilities, while PPV schemes ensure cash is advanced to the operator ahead of the user's actual usage of the service. Each network has invested in sophisticated billing systems that combine complex tariff structures with call duration, location, internetwork connection, and discount schemes. The operator has a detailed, longitudinal view of a customer's behaviour over time, and can model her travel patterns if it so wishes. Most importantly, it can add noncall payments to the billing process with relative ease, giving it a currently unassailable lead as a potential collector of mobile commerce revenues. No other player enjoys this deep relationship with the customer. The high prices paid for 3G (Third Generation) network licences by European mobile network operators give some indication of the value operators place on customer relationships.

If we approach mobile commerce with the Internet as our only model of a network community, then the strength of the network operator's position looks anomalous. How can one party claim such dominance, and in particular why should it seek to restrict the user's experience through a default portal? This behaviour makes much more sense if we swap the Internet model for the phone network model. Phone companies – and mobile phone companies in particular – have been built up around customer service. Phones have always been designed to be as user friendly as possible, and in most markets around the world they remained the property of the phone company rather than the user, who merely "subscribed" to phone service. The earliest phone users asked operators to connect calls for them, while long distance and international dialling remained operator services for many years. Phone companies expect to run information services, particularly directory lookups. Mobile operators add a raft of customer service tasks to this traditional base, including bill queries, coverage queries, and number changes. The result is that as phone customers we are rather well looked after. Mobile operators are adding mobile commerce offerings to existing voice services, so they are selling incremental features to an existing customer base, who expect high levels of human assistance. Help is never cheap, so the more transparent the service can be, the better. Mobile operators are less than thrilled at the thought of handling queries that should be directed to third-party site owners or fielding complaints about poorly performing sites or offensive content outside their control.

Internet users, on the other hand, know better than to e-mail the owners of the Internet when their mail goes down or they find themselves 404'd. They have a high tolerance for confusion and failure. They accept that at certain points they have to get their hands dirty in order to make something work – or find someone who can help them out. There is still a frontier feel to the Net.

If Internet users were to transfer their forgiveness to the mobile channel, and if new mobile commerce users would acquire the stoicism of seasoned Net users, then the network operators' attitude could indeed be labelled patronising and even disingenuous. However, there are very many more phone users than computer users in the world, so the profile of mobile commerce users will inevitably skew towards the phone friendly, and Net intolerant. At the same time, we should remember that the same people behave differently when using different devices. A person may be relatively calm, savvy, and forgiving when using the Web for research, but frustrated and enraged by delays encountered using a mobile commerce device. Roughly speaking, the more a device looks like a phone, the higher our expectation that it will connect immediately and correctly to the destination we have chosen. The more it looks like a computer, the higher our expectation that we will have to clear a set of initial obstacles before reaching our desired destination.

Contenders for customer ownership include a range of players, of which the emerging mobile portals make up one segment. The other three leading contenders are device manufacturers, financial institutions, and retailers.

Device manufacturers theoretically stand to benefit from their physical representation in the user's hand. Brands such as Palm and Nokia are very strong in themselves. Can't such brands be used to take some stake in the user's mobile commerce transactions? The signs are that device manufacturers have decided, at least for the moment, not to pursue this direction, contenting themselves with revenues from the sale of their own products. However it is possible that as mobile commerce grows in significance, consumer appliance manufacturers and design-led personal device manufacturers such as Sony or Swatch will have different attitudes. At present, the device market is split between phones and PDAs, but as the range and types of personal communications devices grow, the existing incumbents may find themselves challenged by device-plus-service offers from other players. The mobile games market will be a key indicator in this area.

Financial institutions are traditionally the supreme customer "owners". Banks are licensed to ask all manner of intrusive questions in their quest to lend funds prudently. They are obliged to cross-relate the products a customer owns and operates in order to trap fraud and money laundering. Records of checking accounts and credit card accounts allow accurate profiling of customer spending patterns. Banks can not only assign each of us to an economic bracket, they can judge how well we match the stereotypical behaviours of the bracket. As commerce transactions migrate to the mobile channel, banks stand to lose visibility of their customers to the billing agents – the network operators.

Have phone network operators replaced banks as the leaders in customer transactions? It is as though funds transfer – the competence of banks – has been commoditised by the network operators, and the real-world transactions to which the transfers relate have been withheld from the banking system. A customer phone bill may contain many hundreds or thousands of data-related charges, nonvoice service transactions that the bank never sees.

It is hardly surprising that some commentators have begun to see the inevitability of banks buying network operators or network operators buying banks. However, we should not forget amidst such speculation that the profitable element of banking is not billing but lending and that the primary driver of profitability in the network operation business is network usage, not the carriage of personal debt. The area of retail banking that shows the most synergy with network operation is in fact the credit card business. The major credit card consortia are targeting mobile commerce as a growth area. We look at technology solutions for combining credit cards with mobile devices in Chapter 3.

Back in the offline world, the growth of loyalty schemes and the continued concentration of the groceries and household goods businesses in the hands of a small number of players already give the big retailers enviable customer profiling ability. Those that deliver goods to consumers' houses, whether they are traditional stores or pure Net plays like Webvan, have begun the process of becoming lifestyle partners rather than shopping destinations. Retailers can migrate their existing loyalty points schemes to the mobile channel with ease. They can also consider converting accumulated points for other forms of reward currency, such as Beenz, though, of course, this will send the customer's spending outside the immediate family, removing its visibility.

Retailers, like banks, have built detailed pictures of their customers' behaviour and will be loath to see it dissipate in the mobile channel. Some retailers have become so confident in their customer relationships that they offer retail banking services, usually rebranded from an existing bank. Retailers have responded to the Internet explosion by creating free ISPs. Free wireless devices, optimised for shopping the retailer's range, cannot be far behind.

Sharing the Customer: Meet the Mortals

Is exclusive customer ownership actually the ideal position for any player? The most likely scenario is that mobile commerce players will share ownership of the customer, relinquishing outright control over discrete subscriber bases in favour of smaller stakes in larger populations. The means of sharing customers is through a type of portal reinvented for the mobile era: the *mortal*.

Portal has become an overused term on the fixed Web, where it is often used to describe any site that isn't a coherent destination in its own right, such as a media brand or an online retailer. We define a portal as a site that guides users to resources and services that it recommends or that it partners with. The classic portal is therefore quite lightweight in its own right, and its value to the user increases with its comprehensiveness, relevance, and efficiency. Portal sites designed for specific industries (or "vortals", from the marriage of "vertical" and "portal") tend to be faithful to the original portal concept, providing online marketplaces as well as directories of goods and services.

Consumer portals naturally have to contend with a certain inherent ambiguity. They aim to attract users with the range and quality of resource references they gather together, adding original content where it cannot be sourced from partners or where context needs to be added. At the same time, they benefit from users staying at the portal site, rather than following any of the collected links. Where revenue sharing in partners' e-commerce transactions is part of the portal's business model, the portal is in an even more complex situation. To maximise its revenue opportunities from each customer, it must encourage them to take up offers with partner e-commerce sites and then return to the portal.

Portals offer convenience for users of the fixed Web, but for the mobile commerce user a good portal is a necessity. In the first place, whatever kind of personal device a customer uses to access mobile commerce services, it will be smaller in size than a desktop machine and have a more limited user interface. Today's cell phones have small screens and limited graphics capabilities, so terse and unambiguous menus are vital. Users of larger format devices, such as the current generation of PDAs, have a little more space to play with, but they too require well-organised, authoritative information choices. Customers buy PDAs in order to organise their lives better, they appreciate efficient applications design, and their time is precious. All types of customers appreciate some level of packaging of the potential wealth of mobile commerce services. Consumers arriving in the mobile commerce world from the cell phone user population will expect portals that are transparent, reliable, and credible. They will not be particularly concerned about the portal concept itself and will have low tolerance for branding and advertising messages that require repeated clicks. Such users will increasingly seek portals that express group affiliation by content and design rather than generic portal brands. Portals for sports fans, for example, have their herald in the United Kingdom's highly successful WAP site for the world-famous Manchester United soccer team. Customers who are approaching mobile commerce from the vantage point of the PDA user will expect to be able to configure the portals they use, personalising them to their own interests and tastes.

The portal paradox lies in the simultaneous need to retain and redirect users. The success of a portal, therefore, ultimately relies upon the user's propensity to return to the portal site after she has been redirected, either during the same usage session or on another occasion. The portal's brand carries the burden of inspiring this loyalty. The brand must have a strong life of its own, so that it functions as a memory-anchor for the mobile commerce user. This factor is stronger in the mobile commerce world than in the fixed e-commerce world. In mobile commerce, the portal brand is competing not just with other portals or destination sites, as on the fixed Web: it is also competing with all the alternative sources of information, advice, and distraction that make up the mobile user's environment. Mobile commerce is integrated with lifestyle, not desk life, so mobile commerce brands, and especially would-be market-controlling brands such as portals, need to be world-beating, not just Web-winning.

One strategy for achieving this dominant mindshare is to create a multichannel portal brand, which we call a *mortal*. Instead of designing a niche portal for a particular user group, we build a portal service that functions across several channels, such as wireless, Internet, and voice telephone. One such example is Strategy.com, a venture of the data management company MicroStrategy. Strategy.com offers a series of information channels, including financial, weather, news, sports, and traffic information. Users sign up to the channels that interest them, and can receive them on the Web, on a wireless device, or over the phone. We can categorise Strategy.com as an all-channel push initiative. The company demonstrates how the static portals of the fixed Web are mutating into active, lifestyle-integrated, push-y mobile commerce portals. Users become mobile, and portals follow suit, chasing their users across the growing range of electronic channels. We can expect to see mobile portals adding interactive TV and in-car delivery options as the market matures. Serious contenders for leadership in the mobile portal business will need to invest in multichannel, multiplatform services in order to compete for customer loyalty in a highly connected environment.

An alternative example of a multichannel portal or mortal brand is Breathe. Breathe aimed to become a constant companion to users by combining typical consumer Internet services and extending them to mobile channels. The company provided toll-free ISP service in the United Kingdom and Web-based e-mail, as do many other providers. Services for mobile users began with SMS text messaging from the

Breathe Web site to any phone in the United Kingdom. This feature, pioneered by BT Cellnet's Genie portal, is many users' first experience of a practical connection between the fixed Internet and the mobile channel. Corporate users in particular may find it more convenient to send text messages to field staff by this means than by entering the message into a phone keypad. This is also a lower-cost option for outbound SMS messaging than using a phone to compose and send a message. Breathe also offered to manage users' schedules on their behalf, as well as offering links to a select number of online retailers. The company's plans included full integration of different messaging technologies, so that, for example, e-mail messages could be automatically read to a user over his cell phone. Breathe collapsed under the weight of its debts in December 2000, underlining the huge expense associated with creating a multichannel player from scratch.

As we can see, the term "portal" is rapidly becoming inadequate as a descriptor for services such as Breathe, which will take increasingly influential roles in the user's life. There are signs in the WAP market that other types of player will gravitate towards playing this role as well. For example, the Wapmap search engine, launched during 1999 to provide links to WML pages, evolved quickly into Mopilot.com. The company's proposition now involves personal data management as well as information retrieval, aiming "to be your first choice for the latest issues and up-to-date mobile content – anywhere, anytime". Early leaders in the WAP market have also tended subsequently to de-emphasise the importance of WAP technology in their offers, so that their customer proposition can come to the fore. Even sites aimed at technologists are alive to the importance of befriending the user rather than just servicing his needs. For example, the developer-oriented resource Waptastic rebranded itself as AnywhereYouGo.com and introduced the tag line "the global wireless development community".

As mobile commerce players of all types continue to converge on customer intimacy as the key determinant of success, what happens to the brands of those businesses that *aren't* portals of any kind – the destination commerce and media sites? There is a conundrum here. If the portal is the senior partner in any commercial relationship in the mobile commerce world, then the portal should expect to take the major share of any customer-generated revenues deriving from commerce transactions. However, the portal needs credible partner brands in order to remain compelling for a user. Without partners of recognised quality for its commerce options, the portal is a gateway to nothing. This is most obvious in mobile channel operators' scramble to sign up branded news suppliers. CNN is a must-have partner for U.S. users, whereas in the English-speaking world in general the CNN and BBC brands compete to represent accuracy, completeness, and timeliness in unbiased world news reporting. Portal players need to take a media programming approach to their partnering strategies, populating their channel as carefully as a cable TV supplier and monitoring the performance of the partner sites.

Retail destination sites have a greater challenge in asserting their brand values in the mobile channel and acquiring portal slots than media brands. Traditional media brands may be broadcast in nature rather than personally targeted, but their content is renewed on a regular basis. This makes them closer in spirit to mobile services than stores. Users don't feel that a TV version of a news source such as the *Wall Street Journal*, or an e-mail addition to a print magazine that already has a Web version, stretches the brand unacceptably. The mobile channel seems like a natural extension. Retail stores, on the other hand, have already been challenged in their transition to the Web. Initial attempts to construct online spaces that would replicate or virtualise the physical retail experience have largely withered, partly due to bandwidth problems but also because of customer indifference. Retailers who have migrated existing mail order businesses to the Web, or imitated the mail order business model, have generally fared better. The Web's paradigm of surf, research, and transact is functionally close to the manual process of browsing a catalogue, studying a product, and completing an order. This approach transitions well to the mobile channel, with the exception of the research phase. As we have already seen, the process of searching, learning, and comparing is better suited to the consideration mode of fixed e-commerce than the action mode of mobile commerce.

Retailers can exploit the complementary nature of the fixed and mobile channels and at the same time augment the strength of their brands, enabling them to fight the all-important battle for the mobile user's attention and loyalty. The example of Kitbag makes this clear. Kitbag sells sports clothing in the European market. Its Web site offers a full e-commerce service in the now-familiar style. For the Euro 2000 soccer event held in the Summer of 2000, Kitbag offered replica team shirts for sale on its Web site. Users of the Breathe WAP portal could also navigate quickly to Kitbag, choose a team, a shirt size, and a quantity and place an order. The order could be completed only if the user was already registered at Kitbag. This means that the Web site is being used to establish a commercial relationship with the customer and the mobile channel is being used to sell one specific line of goods.

For users who are already signed up with Kitbag, buying a shirt on the mobile channel may be attractive as a group activity. Buying something on a mobile device can be made into a social event, and can even be used as a reward gesture for a member of the group or family. Assuming that stock levels can be managed successfully, the mobile channel also allows fans to buy shirts in line with the unfolding success of their teams in the competition.

Users who are unfamiliar with Kitbag who find it via a portal service may also be motivated to visit the Kitbag Web site and register as users. Any portal must limit the number of commerce partners it showcases, so in this case Kitbag enjoys a spotlit position as a sports clothing supplier. There is a technical disconnect between the appearance of the Kitbag option on the mobile device and the user's ability to access its Web site on a fixed device and also probably a time disconnect as well. However, the motivation to seek out the Web site is likely to be stronger than that provided by a passive advertisement, for example. The user knows that his phone includes the capability to buy Kitbag shirts and that visiting the Web site will effectively unlock that feature. The opportunity to shop for this particular item at this particular time in history becomes a current attribute of the device and therefore easier to action than the millions of other potential purchases that will be present in the customer's universe at this time. Clearly, if the Web site registration step could be removed from the process, the sale would be even more likely to succeed.

Retailers profit from portals, and portals profit from retailers. The key to happy unions between portal operators and retailers is a shared mental model of users' behaviour patterns and motivations. The portal addresses itself to users who want to feel involved, informed, and empowered; Kitbag seeks to understand and serve sports fans; in choosing to offer replica shirts during a major sports event, the two partners demonstrate an acute awareness of location, time, and mission.

How many portals can the mobile commerce world support? The experience of the fixed Web is that only a relatively small number of brands can survive as mass market consumer portals. Establishing such a brand is an expensive business. The world's leading mobile portal is iobox, born in early 1999 in Helsinki, Finland, and claiming around half a million customers one year later. Those customers were spread around Finland, Sweden, Germany, and the United Kingdom. A $13 million funding round in December 1999 enabled the company to open new headquarters in London and to spread its message through large-scale consumer advertising. Iobox has racked up a number of firsts, including the first retailer partnership in mobile commerce (Boxman, an online retailer of CDs[16]). The portal offers personal management services such as address books and calendars and is particularly well regarded for its fun services, which include ringing tones and icons. Each user acquires a mailbox at iobox, which can be configured to check other e-mail accounts. The extra benefit of the iobox address is that the first 160 characters of incoming e-mail are forwarded to the user's cell phone, together with an alert beep. The e-mail address also helps to further strengthen the user's relationship with the portal provider, since it may become his preferred address for all his e-mail activity.

Users who register with iobox receive thirty credits they can use to buy services. Further top-up credits can be bought when the initial set is used up. Whether or not users will buy sufficient credits to generate a significant revenue stream remains to be seen. In the mean-

---

16. Boxman ceased trading in October 2000; iobox continues to add retail partners to its offering.

time, the portal's partnerships with retailers such as Boxman and content aggregators such as Yahoo! give it customer credibility as well as a share of transaction revenue and syndication fees.

Some realignment in the mobile portal business is inevitable as players reconsider their options and as the currently fragmented mobile channel landscape begins to cohere. Iobox's arrangement with Yahoo! in Europe may not translate to the U.S. market, where Yahoo! already acts as a lifestyle brand through its merchandising, print magazine products, and credit card. AOL Europe began working with Nokia and Ericsson in February 2000 in order to ensure that AOL's mobile portals would be compatible with the manufacturers' WAP handsets. This suggests that the company is using Europe as a test ground for its general mobile portal strategy. As we have seen, the mobile network operators have their own interests in being portal players and are less likely to yield the portal business to other players in the same way that the ISP business eluded the fixed phone companies. The latter situation arose out of legislation, with U.S. telcos barred from offering ISP service. Access to mobile commerce channels is not similarly regulated.

While European players lead in the creation of mobile portals, they are acutely aware that their lead is rapidly shortening. Vodafone and Vivendi launched their multichannel Vizzavi portal six weeks ahead of schedule and declared that the portal had twelve to eighteen months to succeed in its aims of becoming Europe's favourite portal.[17] The mortality rate for mortals is likely to be high as national brands are consolidated by regional initiatives of this kind.

Customers ultimately make commitments to specific feature sets, rather than types of player. In other words, they rarely define themselves as "Sprint PCS people" or "Vodafone Airtouch people" or even "Nokia people" or "Motorola people". These brands are important, but mobile commerce enhances the utility of the mobile network and the mobile device beyond the level they are used to represent. Can a mobile network's name, or a device manufacturer's name, add any

---

17. "Vizzavi challenge to US rivals", *The Guardian*, 18 May 2000.

weight to an online retail offer? For example, does it make any difference to a customer's attitude to Boxman if she is using an Ericsson phone on the Orange GSM network? As the lifetime of phones continues to shorten, and as multiband phones and network-roaming agreements become more common, such factors withdraw further into the background. A portal such as iobox can command loyalty across every platform: it is lifestyle-portable; it is mortal.

The mobile network operators have been keen to stake their claims in the mobile portal area, and this is partly because customer retention is a core concern in their business. Network operators measure one variable above all others, and seek to influence it: churn. Churn is the rate at which customers abandon a service provider. Cell phone customers are notoriously flighty, easily lured by competing packages and no-strings relationships. A mobile portal may be one feature that can improve a customer's propensity to stay with a network operator.

Can the famed "stickiness" of successful Web sites be sprayed on to their equivalents in the mobile channel? Stickiness refers to the length of time visitors remain with a site, and for mobile network operators this translates directly into airtime revenues, or, with packet networks, into data usage. Stickiness has a long-term effect too, in that the stickiest sites usually have high levels of repeat visits.

A default portal will help to establish default behaviour, but will not in itself build loyalty. If the user does not put something substantial of herself into the portal, then it will be easy enough to quit when she buys a new mobile device and finds it set to some other launch site. Portals therefore need to solicit information from customers; they need to take on some of the burden of the customer's life, so that they become indispensable. The hardest part of moving from any type of supplier to one of its competitors is the need to retrieve information from the existing supplier and repeat it to the new supplier. This is why mobile portals are keen to offer address book and calendar services, and why they are happy to forward e-mail.

The network operator's close billing relationship with the customer now becomes a hindrance. Customers are unlikely to entrust their personal information with the party that is already proving with supreme efficiency its ability to track their conversations, movements, and purchases. As an analogue, consider a bank's role in storing a customer's nonbanking personal information. If a bank could encourage its customers to deposit their personal data with it, then it might create further discouragement to customers tempted to move their accounts elsewhere. But traditionally banks' personal data services are limited to safe deposit boxes, which are treated as sealed property. It may therefore behove network operators to offer personal data management services on a "sealed" basis. In other words, a customer can manage his life through the portal, but he is not hindered in any way from removing that information in a coherent mass and lodging it with another service. If the customer is not coerced to keep his information with one portal, then the likelihood of his joining the portal – and staying – will be higher.

Restricted portals in the European WAP market have enjoyed very short lifetimes. Nokia's attempt to create a "Nokia Services" default WAP site involving content providers such as CNN was discontinued after a demonstration phase. In March 2000, as WAP phones started to filter into the U.K. market, all the network operators enabled access to all WML content. Some commentators had feared that several years would elapse before this step was taken.

Technical openness helps to create a viable competitive portal climate, though network operators can still influence user behaviour according to the emphases they place. Orange's Nokia 7110 WAP phone comes with the Club Nokia site preinstalled as a bookmark, for example. Virgin Mobile, which resells capacity from the One2One network, provides links to Virgin brand goods and services on its handsets – and users enjoy preferential discounts. In the United States, OmniSky "provides one-touch access" to a set of partner sites including E*Trade and Travelocity. Quality rather than coercion will govern the success of all would-be portal players.

As mobile commerce develops, players will share customers across multiple sets of access points, and they will turn away from coercing customer lock-in. Attention will then turn to share of the customer's commitment, with different players aiming to control different fractions across different customer sets. Figure 1-4 shows how individual customers will be striated by collaborating service providers.

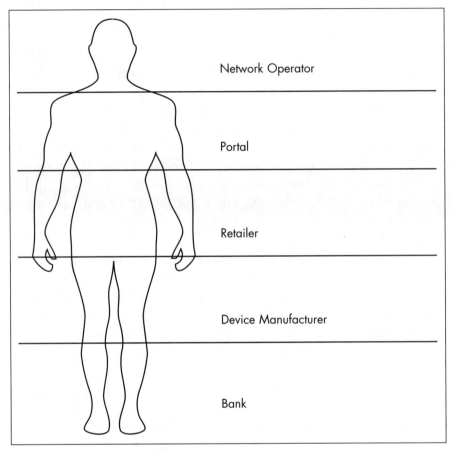

FIGURE 1-4. Customer share.

121 4 Real: Truly Personal Marketing

The competition for portal power amongst mobile commerce players is focused in the short term on establishing market share and capturing transaction revenues. The long game is concerned with the lifetime value of customers. A successful portal has the potential to serve in every area of a customer's concerns, from the relatively simple business of managing her schedule to the complex activities associated with managing her career.

For the network operators, a share in transaction revenues is an additional benefit to the revenues they earn as carriers. In circuit-switched networks, such as the pre-GPRS GSM networks in Europe, the network operator earns airtime revenue for all the customer's interactions, regardless of the type or value of the service that the customer is using. For packet-based networks such as those of OmniSky and i-mode, the network operator can charge for actual data usage. In practice, customers cannot be expected to place a value on undifferentiated data. A mobile customer is unlikely to agree to pay by the byte, and content providers will be hard-pressed to price their wares in this way. We are more likely to find that all packet-based networks will offer "all you can eat" deals, whereby the customer can access as much data as she wishes during the monthly billing period. Correct pricing for these offers will necessarily follow experience in the market. At the time of writing, data usage rates for mobile commerce are hard to predict.

One exception to the "all you can eat" model may be messaging. European SMS users have been conditioned to pay a fee for each message they send, with the fee loosely pegged to candy-sized amounts. Operators may be loath to see this tolled revenue disappear into a data usage bundle. Messaging is closest in kind to traditional voice communications, so the operators may find it easier to continue charging explicitly for it by use than for access to retail or media sites, which are associated with the free access Web model.

Other portal players need to fix on secondary revenues, particularly commission on sales made by the mobile channel. Where the mobile channel differs most strongly from its analog on the fixed Internet is its proactivity in stimulating the user to buy. Portals are wary of sending e-mail messages to users, though companies such as Amazon and Xoom are successful with this approach. Whether or not mobile users will appreciate sales messages pushed at them remains to be seen. But a proactive portal need not be intrusive. By applying insight into the target population's situation, a portal can stimulate purchases in ways that fit the customer's current position with respect to location, time, and mission.

Take the example of Virgin Radio in the United Kingdom. As we have noted, the Virgin brand is applied to around 130 consumer brands from airlines to vodka. Using a WAP phone, a Virgin Radio listener can find out what song is playing on the station at that moment – and buy it online. This service is a natural extension to the radio station: a form of subtitling, with clickthrough to purchase. The concept also supports the role of the single, which has traditionally been something ephemeral – the collective mood of a moment. The singles charts survive and thrive as part of our popular culture because the rankings tell us how we all feel this week. As the weeks go by, singles file themselves in the nostalgia departments of our memories. The ability to buy the song that's playing – right here, right now – is the perfect expression of mobile commerce's fundamental advantage over fixed e-commerce. Mobile commerce is part of our lives, not an add-on.

Virgin is arguably the world's first pure portal brand. Virgin companies are distinct entities with operational autonomy. They share the group's brand value and its collective expertise. They generally outsource the manufacturing or service delivery function to another party, just as an online portal sources its content and commerce services from outside the company. Services such as Virgin Mobile and Virgin Bank are rebadged services operated by other companies. The Virgin name already acts as a guarantor of value – and of a unique attitude to life – across a wide spectrum of consumer goods and services. A mobile portal may not choose to follow a multichannel strategy and establish itself on the Web and interactive TV, but it must aim to become a part of the customer's emotional landscape.

This kind of natural intimacy between businesses and the consumers they serve has long been the aim of one-to-one marketers. The idea of one-to-one marketing is that businesses can create personal profiles of individual customers' preferences and behaviours, and thereby tailor offers specifically for them. One logical extension to the idea is just-in-time manufacturing, where products are specified personally by the customer and then manufactured. A less radical use of the idea is to fine-tune the market segmentation that the company uses to target its products or services, aiming for a model with a larger number of member categories. For example, a bank might use data about a customer's account-usage patterns to assign him to the category of Young-Urban and then target credit offers connected with group travel products. Although one-to-one marketers would be appalled at such a diluted version of their approach, this kind of segmentation is often the practical outcome of many well-intentioned one-to-one efforts, given the paucity of customer behaviour data held by the campaigners.

Mobile commerce provides an important engine for committed one-to-one marketers. First, it is an entirely automated channel, with all transactions routed through a common technology gateway. In the case of a marketing offer being made to a prospect, there is no need to integrate e-mail interactions with Web form interactions, for example – let alone process inbound reply-paid cards. Second, the mobile channel delivers transactions that have time and location data built into them. Time is available to marketers in the fixed e-commerce channel, but it becomes vastly more meaningful when combined with location. Third, the portalisation of mobile commerce provides the marketer with some indication of the user's mission. The offer of a restaurant meal discount, for example, may fare better when placed alongside a theatre listing service than when included in a list of restaurants. In the first instance, the offer adds convenience to the theatre-finding mission, whereas in the second the offer distracts from the restaurant-comparison mission.

One-to-one marketers will use portals to triangulate sales opportunities and target offers. If portals fail to control the majority of mobile commerce behaviour, marketers will need to look at real-time analytical tools in order to form theories about users' missions. For example, by grouping transactions or queries according to time and location, the marketer may be able to find a correlation with an event, such as a sporting fixture. These analyses will necessarily have to be performed in real time in order for the marketer to capitalise on the revealed mission. Services that provide event scheduling and monitoring will therefore become valuable assets. Marketing professionals may find themselves actioning campaigns suggested by software agents – and doing so, of course, from their mobile devices.

The debate over customer ownership is therefore concerned with much more than staking a claim to a level of revenue share that might be acceptable to a fixed e-commerce player. The power of one-to-one marketing in the mobile channel has the potential to generate a larger proportion of consumer transactions online than marketers can achieve on the fixed Internet. Mobile commerce will make the e-commerce pie bigger by embedding itself in the moment-by-moment lives of its users, responding to customer desires and suggesting relevant, attractive actions.

DISRUPTION AND RECONFIGURATION: LIVING WITH MOBILE

In this section we look at how mobile commerce disrupts conventional processes within commercial enterprises, leading to changed technology priorities within the organisation. We also consider some parallel technology effects in the personal domain, whereby evolving consumer attitudes to mobile commerce lead to changes in device and system design.

Enterprise Systems Impact

So far we have discussed mobile commerce purely as a matter of opportunity for businesses. The implications of migrating to mobile commerce that we have considered have been concerned with business strategy, primarily with designing services and making them available in the mobile channel. Moving to mobile also entails a series of accommodating measures at the back end.

There are many ways of illustrating cost components in enterprise IT systems. The diagram in Figure 1-5 focuses on three major elements of concern in e-commerce systems.[18]

The first element, labelled *transaction*, refers to the system processes that must be in place to conduct commerce transactions with the customers. These processes include ordering, confirmation, and in the case of digital products and services, delivery.

---

18. Derived from work initiated by Michael Airey at Cognizant Solutions, February 2000.

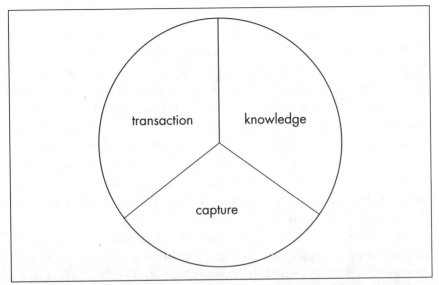

FIGURE 1-5. Major cost components in e-commerce and mobile commerce systems.

The second element in this cost model is *knowledge*. This element refers to the systems that we build to retain information about customers, their behaviours, and their preferences. This element also includes effort expended to provide tailored, personalised experiences to customers.

The third element is termed *capture*. This element expresses the costs associated with the actual processes of acquiring knowledge about customers and entering their transactions, as opposed to storing and analysing customer knowledge or processing customer transactions.

Mobile commerce has the effect of inflating each of the three components. The components maintain their respective proportions, but the pie as a whole grows.

First, the *transaction* area of the model grows. Mobile commerce entails a massive increase in transactions with backend systems. Why should this be? The reason is that convenience drives frequency. When it is easy to check a bank balance or package delivery status at any time and any place, then users will do so much more often. Such checking transactions may not in themselves provide revenue to the bank or the delivery company, but each will place an incremental processing load on their backend systems. Purchase transactions will also increase as consumers buy products in smaller quantities at greater frequencies. In other words, basket sizes will decrease while visit counts increase. Customers may maintain their effective purchasing level, but generate a larger number of transactions. As an example, consider the mobile music buyer. We may find customers buying sub-single recordings for download in large quantities, with an accompanying fall-off in sales of full-length CDs. Record companies may find it harder to repackage and represent classic repertoire in album-sized portions, but easier to recoup investments in new acts whose entire careers may never go the full 74 minutes.

Anecdotal evidence in the European WAP market and from i-mode sites in Japan suggests that e-commerce systems managers should be prepared for a 10X growth in transaction volumes in the first three months of operation for a mobile commerce version of the service. Designing systems for scalability has never been more crucial to enterprise success.

The *knowledge* area also grows because we can acquire, retain, and analyse a much larger body of knowledge about each customer. We also propel our services into a much larger potential market than that envisioned for fixed, Web-based e-commerce, simply because we are presenting services in a market that is primed for mass market consumer behaviours rather than the specialised, high-barrier platform of fixed e-commerce.

The increase in retained customer data suggests that data warehousing will continue to be a key area of focus for enterprises. Storage solutions continue to evolve in response to the growth in business data, not least in traditional fixed e-commerce systems. Data analysis tools will continue to become more sophisticated in response to the growing mass, and complexity, of customer data collected by mobile commerce systems. Mining this kind of data for patterns is already a core competence of telcos, which analyse calling and payment data to determine factors that might prevent – or inspire – a customer to quit the service.

We show the third element of the systems cost model, *capture*, also enlarging under the impact of mobile commerce. At first sight, this seems wrong. Surely mobile devices allow us to cut the cost of capturing customer data and triggering transactions? After all, we expect to deliver highly tailored, context-specific services that are sensitive to the dimensions of the mobile commerce space, location, time and mission. We are released from the expensive multimedia obligations of fixed, Web-based commerce. Content shrinks, design retreats, navigation goes unidirectional.

There are two reasons why this reaction is misleading. The first is that although current mobile commerce applications may favour stark graphic presentations and simplistic navigation, increased bandwidth and device capability will facilitate richer mobile commerce experiences. The costs associated with content production will return – with a vengeance. Site designers will no longer be creating experiences for fixed screens with known characteristics being used by committed customers. They will instead be using distilled information, reference-rich compact graphics, and integrated audio to capture and commit flighty users. Today's banner ad artists will lead the pack in designing compelling mobile sites as the mobile channel combines with shortening attention spans to favour the skills of the miniaturist.

The second reason capture costs do not decline is the main factor in their increase beyond those associated with fixed e-commerce. This is the diversity of mobile platforms in the field. The IT industry has seen technology standardisation efforts wax and wane, but reach relative perfection at the user interface level in the ubiquitous HTML format of the Web. Yes, different browsers interpret HTML differently, and proprietary scripting and plug-ins complicate the picture further; but it is still possible to design effective commerce Web sites that deliver consistent experiences to all users.

Mobile commerce has no such standard and is unlikely ever to achieve one. In the WAP market, for example, different micro-browsers interpret the WML standard differently. But even if a consistent, industry-wide applications layer were to emerge, it would still be compromised by the diversity of devices that exists in the mobile commerce world. This diversity will increase rather than decrease. To understand why, we need to go back to basics.

The fixed e-commerce world works forward from the desktop

machine: a more or less standard device running, in the overwhelming majority of cases, some variety of Microsoft Windows and fitted with one of the two leading Web browsers. Most important, there will be a screen, keyboard, and mouse. Even in its most unconventional forms, such as interactive TV sets or in-store kiosks, the e-commerce appliance is a mouse-driven, qwerty-assisted, tube-staring machine.

Mobile devices, on the other hand, are designed to fit into people's lives, not their rooms. The Palm user taps with a stylus and writes runes, while cell phone and games console users drive with their thumbs. Cell phone and pager users expect to hear beeps when something interesting is happening. Walkman users play, skip, and fast-forward through life. Drivers squeeze, flick, and pedal. These are all well established forms of user interfaces, and they won't easily be displaced by keypads and roller balls.

Furthermore, mobile devices will continue to evolve in format and functionality. The Handspring PDA converts, via the Springboard interface, into an endless race of devices, effortlessly morphing from notebook to camera to cell phone to global positioning device. Other device manufacturers will compete for the customer's hand by building multifunctional mobile devices that extend the character of a distinct ancestor. So, for example, there will be fully commerce-enabled devices that look mostly like MP3 players, others that look mostly like game consoles, and others that look like phones. At the same time, as we discuss in the next section, devices will fragment around the body of the user, extending the user interface potential still further.

Systems developers will therefore need to invest much more energy in the user interface layer than they do for fixed, Web-based e-commerce. Smart developers will layer their architectures to make the most of common interaction functionality. Device-specific features can be isolated in a specialised User Experience Layer and designed to deliver themselves to the correct devices on demand. We examine such strategies in more depth in Chapter 3. For the time being, we need to be aware that the capture element of our cost model will grow at a similar rate to its sibling elements, knowledge and transaction.

Consumer Embrace and Pushback

People love mobile devices. Cell phones are phenomenally popular, particularly in youth markets. Sony's Walkman has had us toting pocket machines since the start of the 1980s. Professionals in the United States feel undressed without their Palm devices. There's no doubt that access to communications, entertainment, and information is becoming a base assumption for today's consumers.

As the market for personal devices matures, we are seeing the device types mutate, merge, and fragment. The most obvious pattern is the convergence of different device types into single machines. We each have limited pocket or handbag space, so consumers will be loath to carry too many separate devices with them. MP3 players incorporate FM radios and phone number lists. Microsoft's PocketPC platform plays MP3 files as well as other media formats. Handspring's Visor series of Palm-compatible handheld devices is extensible via its Springboard interface, so that the machine can become a camera, note-taker, or global positioning device with the snap of a module.

While devices continue to converge, they are also fragmenting into separate pieces. When we consider the user functions that a mobile device may be asked to carry out, we quickly see that devices might usefully disperse to different parts of the user's immediate environment. The move to "wearable computers" is being glamorised by implementations that turn components of the mobile device into jewellery items. An earpiece, for example, can be attractive as well as functional. Voice microphones can be built as brooches or buttons. Small screens sit naturally on wristwatches.

The dispersal of the mobile device around the user's body relies on effective personal area networks (PANs) which are themselves based on radio communications. (We look at the leading contender for short-distance intercomponent communications, Bluetooth, in Chapter 3.) But with the user's body space wirelessly live, what is to stop us merging the user with their locale? The user's systems can communicate with systems in the room, or in the street, as readily as they can with each other.

Clearly, our current notion of the mobile commerce user as being dependent on a *handheld* device will rapidly lose currency. Consumers' embrace of mobile devices will become increasingly intimate and at the same time increasingly transparent. Mobile commerce will become a property of the physical space we inhabit. We will be closer to the classic conceptions of cyberspace than ever before.

What does this mean for businesses designing services for mobile commerce? First, we need to remember that mobile commerce is personal. *Personalisation* is usually taken to mean that services are tailored for a specific individual, and we have followed this usage earlier in the chapter. But ideally personalisation is driven by the user, not the service provider. Users decide to join portals and to configure them for their own needs. More importantly, mobile devices belong to individuals in a way that desktop machines will never achieve. Anything that we choose to carry about our person becomes a part of our personality. Just as we prefer not to lend others our fountain pens or glasses (or wallets), so we will guard our mobile devices jealously. Intruding in this highly personal space without an invitation is a serious commercial error. Businesses that send unpermitted alerts to consumers risk the demolition of their brands. While we have learned to tolerate junk mail in our physical and virtual mailboxes, we have never taken kindly to random intrusions such as flies and sirens. Messages that wait for us in demarcated spaces may be burdensome, but they are not threatening. Intrusions that we can't control are perceived as threats and trigger our defence mechanisms. Online marketers will need to consider adrenaline as well as attention. Worries about invasion of privacy are going to become more acute as clumsy e-commerce players violate basic courtesy in ignorance of mobile commerce's radically different usage context.

Second, we need to consider that mobile commerce makes demands on users' *patience*. Users of fixed e-commerce facilities are conditioned to being controlled by the sites they use, and frustrated by the complex wealth of material available to them on the Web. Mobile commerce users aren't prepared to wait. For a start, they are probably doing something else while they are engaging with the service. They expect clarity and relevance. If they wanted a hard time, they'd find somewhere quiet to sit. Mobile commerce services have to be supremely easy to use, rapid in their response times, and designed with short runs to beneficial outcomes. In other words, consumers need to be able to get on, get it, and get out – without fuss, fumble or fear.

Considerations of privacy and patience suggest that consumers are not easy pushovers for mobile commerce players. Indeed, as a truly mass market, mobile users are less tractable, and less forgiving, than technology sympathisers in the business and professional communities – those who have invested energy and ingenuity in learning their way around the Net. Mobile users overlay the general population more closely than do Internet users. As a result, gross consumer trends map quite closely to mobile commerce issues. Parts of Europe have experienced growing protest at the siting of wireless masts, for example. Rejection of masts is sometimes associated with suspicions about the health impact of radiation. In other instances, or amongst other groups, the chief objection is aesthetic. One U.K. mobile network has introduced masts disguised as trees. Both concerns map on to more mainstream environmental concerns, and reflect a questioning of technology benefits that is more prevalent in Europe than in the United States. But American players should not assume that the home market will roll over ahead of everything the mobile commerce movement would like to throw at them. Acknowledging that consumers are suspicious of the health effects of cell phone radiation, Sun Microsystems co-founder and chief scientist Bill Joy muses that "what you really want to do is break up the phone and put it into your shoes to get the electromagnetic radiation as far from your head as possible".[19]

Designing services for mobile commerce requires us to consider not only the lifestyle changes of our user base but also the variability of devices they carry, the permeability of the personal device horizon, and the sensitivity of that horizon. Prototyping a system for the desktop starts to look easy by comparison. For example, we make no concessions to anatomy when designing traditional user interfaces. Our users had better have reasonable hand-to-eye coordination or they're not

---

19. Lee Bruno, "Visions of Joy", *Red Herring*, May 2000.

going to be able to use our applications very effectively. Mobile commerce service providers, on the other hand, must design for visual output on a wide range of display sizes and distances from the eye. They must also place greater emphasis on audio output, particularly what we might call *iconic tones*: audio elements signalling events or options. Synthetic speech will also be an important output mechanism. On the input side of the problem, designers need to cater for input via button presses, pointing devices, speech instructions, and possibly even eye movements. Technologies developed to aid the physically challenged will stream into the general market place, as will technologies associated with stressful military control environments.

If all this sounds daunting, consider that while mobile commerce adds significant labour to the systems design project, the mobile channel also heralds new opportunities for product designers, and paves the way for a closer collaborative work style between content, software, and hardware producers. By combining their skills to deliver a customer service, each discipline can increase its value-add to the final experience.

The first mass-market example of a product category resulting from such a multi-disciplinary approach is the e-book. The Rocket eBook is the leading dedicated electronic book designed specifically for reading text. The entry-level model can store around ten typical novels.[20] Microsoft uses its own Microsoft Reader and ClearType font technology to improve the reading experience for electronic book users. The Printer R.R. Donnelley announced in November 1999 its commitment to electronic books. Stephen King's 16,000 word novella *Riding the Bullet* was released as an e-book in March 2000 and immediately broke bestseller records. Device manufacturers, software designers, content aggregators, and authors converge to create a mobile experience that is at once innovative and deeply familiar. King's ghost tale is a marker for a series of novel product-service-content combinations as yet unborn.

---

20. See http://www.rocket-ebook.com/ for more information about this product.

We'll let the last word go to a long-established company with its eye on the mobile commerce customer of the future, and a sure grasp of the new values of the emerging mobile commerce era: "Timex is interested in the real estate of the wrist. It's location, location, location. The wrist is the most exciting and accessible place on the body".[21]

---

21. Susie Watson of Timex, quoted by *Fast Company*, April 2000, from Peter H. Lewis, "State of the art: Look out! new wrist devices on the loose", *New York Times*, 20 January 2000.

Types of Mobile Commerce Services

This chapter surveys the leading types of mobile commerce services that currently exist or are currently being developed to serve consumer and business user roles. This is not an exhaustive survey. The services chosen for this chapter command the greatest attention amongst users and service providers alike. Each service includes a range of potential associated and follow-on services; indeed, each service could be regarded as an industry in its own right.

We purposely avoid labelling the services as *applications*. The term "application" implies a demarcated set of functionality designed for a known or ideal user group. Applications are traditionally installed on machines and packaged to fit into the prevailing desktop user interface model. The move towards application service providers (ASPs) in the business world is undermining this traditional concept. An ASP provides the functionality of a software application, such as a human resources application, on a remote usage basis. The customer no longer installs and runs an HR package, dealing with its upgrades and backups. He simply buys the ongoing servicing of his human resources administration needs over a network. An ASP takes on a role similar to that of a large corporation's computing department in the days of time-sharing computers and dumb terminals. The ASP aggregates a number of customers into a virtual organisation and supplies a centralised computing service targeted at common business needs. The ASP movement signals a shift in emphasis from software ownership towards contracted relationships encapsulating service benefits.

The computing service model is more appropriate to the mobile commerce world than the traditional software application model for two major reasons. The first reason is the majority of mobile commerce users will come to mobile commerce from a consumer, rather than a computing, background. Such users understandably resist the responsibilities of software product ownership. Even consumers equipped with home computers and used to using desktop machines in the workplace are not uniformly exposed to the nuts and bolts of application management. Many home computer users restrict their activities to use of Web browsers, word processors, and games, whereas most corporate users are discouraged from tinkering with their installed software platform. Users may have difficulty coping with e-mail attachments and locating and installing browser plug-ins. Few develop their own program code, and many are horrified by the command-line entry format of "real" operating systems. Computer users should not, of course, need to have any interest in software development, any more than a car driver need understand the principles of the internal combustion engine. But people inculcated in the mysteries of writing and installing software products develop a thick layer of skin that differentiates them from virgin consumers. Seasoned computer users are tolerant of systems' complexity, and systems' tendency to fail in unpredictable ways. Such users have some insight into the difficulties inherent in writing software, and their empathy with software developers can make them blind to an application's foibles and drawbacks. A consumer who takes on ownership of a computer elects to join a club where some of the normal rules of consumer life are suspended in favour of hobbyist indulgence. Products such as Apple's iMac and self-installing user-friendly software such as AOL's suite seek to remove some of this perversity and to put ordinary people back in charge of technology.

Phone users, on the other hand, have been educated in an entirely contradictory fashion. We have been conditioned to pick up a phone, acknowledge the friendly burr in our ear, and get going with our business. Dialling numbers and navigating voice-menu systems is as difficult as it gets. The phone network offers us benefits such as directory listings and weather forecasts, but these are not "applications": they are services located at numeric addresses. The speaking clock continues to talk even when no one drops in to listen. Phone services are aspects of the network environment, rather than discrete mechanisms that live in the handset.

Of course, few people are exclusively computer users or phone users. We all act in both roles at different times – and often at the same time. But our attitudes to and expectations of each device tend to abide by the strict demarcation between device types. Cell phones gain integral clocks, organisers, and games, yet they are still primarily communications devices. Computers gain DVD drives, headphones, and microphones but they still struggle to make it into the living room. Although today PDAs and phones compete as the focus of attention for mobile commerce players, the evolution of each device type is converging on a new class of mobile commerce device which owes its computing capabilities to the PDA but its overall usage mode to the telephone. In other words, however sophisticated mobile commerce devices become, most users will expect their functional benefits to be expressed as a characteristic of the overall product and service package, rather than as separately bounded applications.

If consumer expectations form the first major reason why we should approach mobile commerce from a service rather than an applications point of view, consumer *situations* form the second. Deskbound computer users find the desktop metaphor of computing congenial. In a context where people sit to concentrate on a set of tasks, turning their attention from one to another, filing and discarding as they go, the combined workspace and file cabinet metaphor underpinning traditional graphical interfaces is a manipulable, universal, and robust conceit. The mobile lifestyle is completely different. Mobile users are not fixed in place and fixated on a single visual display, but are moving in an environment with a much richer visual content. They are not contemplating a set of tasks that can be pulled out, worked on, and put away, but engaging with a set of goals developing in real time. Rather than being distributed amongst applications, their attention is fragmented by all the demands of life. The desktop metaphor attains utility only when a user chooses to halt the flow of life, extract herself from its manifold distractions, and address a set of tasks. At other times, other metaphors may have greater relevance.

Visually based metaphors may have little traction in the typical mobile usage context. At times the mobile commerce user may be better served through audible cues and soundscapes than by button bars and icons.

Even if visual methods retain a primary function in the user interface, visual resources are unlikely to be devoted to the business of manipulating icons on an abstract surface. The triumph of the Web interface has already diluted the full power of graphical user interfaces without sacrificing usability. In particular, drag-and-drop is not a feature of the traditional Web and its omission is not lamented by users. The Web encourages users to access information and service by in-context word labels and simple icons, directing users down pre-designed paths rather than making many options available on a simultaneous basis as traditional nonmodal GUI (Graphical User Interface) systems do. The Web browser has reduced the significance of the application icon by usurping much of the function of the GUI's desktop, while well-designed Web-based services have undermined the concept of discrete, identifiable applications in favour of fast routes to goal completion.

Thinking of mobile commerce in terms of services rather than applications has a liberating effect on the industry. Mobile commerce players can address the user in the round, as a freely acting individual with goals and desires who plays many roles in the space of a single day. Should we then not also abandon the distinction between consumer and business services established in the fixed e-commerce orthodoxy?

We believe maintaining a distinction between consumer and business services is valuable during the early development of the mobile commerce industry. One reason is consumer and business opportunities represent different routes to customer acquisition. A user may be sold a commerce-enabled phone for personal purposes but then use services provided by his employer to work away from the office. On the other hand, a user may acquire a mobile device as part of his work duties and then use it in his personal life. The rise of the Web demonstrated flows across the consumer/business divide in both directions. The Web reached public consciousness as a tool of the consumer domain, allowing individuals to access and publish information of interest to themselves. Corporate Web sites, intranets, and e-businesses followed as enthusiasm for the technology grew, with the Web ultimately displacing predecessor client-server environments. At the same time, e-commerce grew in popularity because people could access the Web at work and explore shopping and entertainment possibilities during work hours and without making personal financial commitments to home computers, modems, and phone lines. The feedback across the consumer/business line has resulted in business systems with greater usability and reduced needs for training and in consumer Web sites with database-driven, personalised, commerce-enabled features.

Another reason for maintaining the distinction between consumer and business services lies in the service developer's business model. Consumers and businesses take different attitudes to cost, value, risk, and loyalty. We may be able to sign up a user for a business service knowing that bills will be paid by an employer and knowing the user is one of a legion of users simultaneously joining the service from the one employer. The same user may be a credit risk for a consumer service such as a gambling service. Theories concerning the viability of business services are often easier to verify than those aimed at consumers. For example, an e-procurement service can credibly estimate how much the average company spends on administering the purchasing of supplies, taking into account the costs associated with maintaining a catalogue of approved products and processing users' orders, and thereby begin to craft a justification for an improved, automated service. An online consumer auction service, on the other hand, has much less to work with. How many consumers are interested in buying and selling any class of goods? What are their existing costs in buying and selling, and do they even account for these costs? These kinds of questions remain unanswered until the service is launched and promoted, and the public votes with its clicks. At root, successful business services fix known, measurable, recurrent problems experienced by parties with the financial means and motivation to seek solutions, and successful consumer services unearth largely unexpressed but commonly felt needs. Alternatively, we can say that while business services fix existing problems, consumer services detect desires and fashion them into necessities. Conceiving, developing and launching both types of services are equally hard in nature, while the processes differ radically in content.

BASE SERVICES PLATFORM

Before we look in detail at specific consumer and business mobile commerce services, we need to consider the basic functional platform over which mobile commerce services of all kinds are laid. The base services platform and its relationship with added-value services is shown schematically in Figure 2-1. Each of the base services described here has been identified at one time or another as the killer app for wireless devices. Collected together in one package, this base service set makes a convincing description of a mobile commerce-era multipurpose device: the Swiss Army knife of the wireless population. This piece of essential mobile commerce equipment is a device providing e-mail, Web access, voice control (and voice output), and location finding together with the means to store and play digital content such as books and music.

Service providers and manufacturers differ as to the specification of this base platform. Many players downplay this aspect of the mobile commerce movement, since any suggestion of a minimum credible platform for mobile commerce disadvantages players who cannot meet the minimum. Others argue that any specification of a base services platform is inadequate without high bandwidth network capability, and therefore considerations of device functionality or network service availability are at best misleading and at worst premature. Nevertheless, we describe a service set here that we believe represents the minimum viable service level for the enabling of mass market mobile commerce. Specialised devices and networks will doubtless target niche user populations as the market develops, but the broad future for mobile commerce lies in a commonly accepted repertoire of personal services available to the user, howsoever they may be formatted or delivered.

This section describes current incarnations of each base service and how each is used.

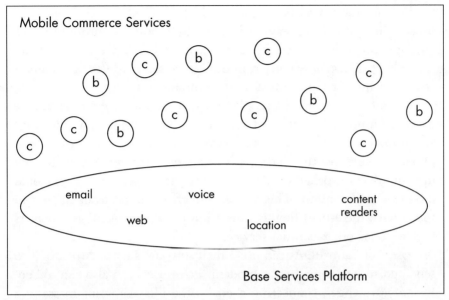

FIGURE 2-1. Mobile commerce services for consumer and business roles are enabled by a platform of base services.

E-mail and Messaging

E-mail is the prime suspect for mobile commerce's killer app. E-mail has insinuated itself into contemporary life as the leading flow of information (and noninformation) in the connected user's daily experience. In the business context, e-mail has taken over from the interoffice memo as the key weapon in the bureaucratic armoury. To be away from one's e-mail is to be – perhaps fatally – out of the loop. When road warriors hook up their laptops to the phone system, their first and often only purpose is to check on their e-mail.

Mobile users are also addicted to text. Paging continues to be popular in the United States, offering the best nationwide text communication services. SMS (Short Message Service) for GSM cell phones dominates the equivalent market in Europe. Mobile-to-mobile messaging has worked with the same consumer impulses to create two distinct cultures in the two continents. Visiting Europeans marvel at Americans' fondness for their BlackBerries and shake their heads at belt-loop pager users, while Americans staying in the Old World are surprised to see children pressing out messages on their mobiles. We have here an example of divergent evolution in devices caused by differing technical environments but expressing a single common user goal.

E-mail for cell phone users is now common for digital cell phone users in Europe. BT Cellnet's Genie service,[1] for example, will forward any e-mail sent to <username>@sms.genie.co.uk to the user's cell phone as a text message. The user's Genie mailbox can be used to pick up e-mail from other POP3 mail accounts, making it a personal mobile e-mail conduit. This simple and effective means of staying in touch with the e-mail flow is illustrated in Figure 2-2. Portal players such as iobox offer a similar service.

Users of Palm PDAs can use e-mail software such as MultiMail to send and receive e-mail via a modem. Palm users can also run Yahoo! Instant Messenger, connecting them to the global instant messaging community.

A cunning marriage of convenience between old modem technology and modern e-mail systems allows users without true wireless connectivity to stay in the e-mail loop. PocketScience's PocketMail service translates modem control characters and data into audio signals. Dedicated PocketMail devices, or Palm devices fitted with PocketMail's BackFlip accessory, act as acoustic-coupler modems. By holding the device against a normal telephone handset, the user can access her e-mail from anywhere. This strategy gives users the benefit of mobile access to e-mail without requiring a subscription to a wireless data service or the purchase of a wireless modem. Given the variability in coverage afforded by different wireless technologies and service providers, especially in the United States, PocketMail represents a cost-effective solution for mobile users.

Truly successful phone-based e-mail systems await three additional usability features. The first required feature is an improved means of authoring replies. The existing method of using the phone's

---

1. http://www.genie.co.uk/.

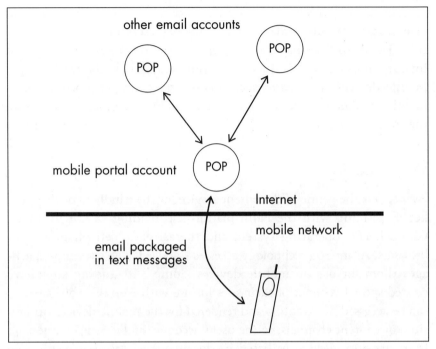

other email accounts

FIGURE 2-2. SMS-based solutions allow GSM cell phone users to read e-mail on the move.

numeric keys is cumbersome, even with predictive text entry systems which attempt to complete words for users as they type them. Alternative methods allowing users to click on letters in a scrolling alphabet are not much better. Efficient voice-recognition features that turn spoken words into reply text will greatly enhance the utility of mobile e-mail. The extension of character-recognition features from PDAs to phones will provide a further means of rapidly authoring e-mail text.

The second feature required for effective mobile e-mail services is some means of handling attachments. Images and documents appended to e-mails need to be viewable; otherwise mobile e-mail services will remain at the terse level of telegramese. PDA users have an advantage in being able to use reader software to open a number of file types. Adding intelligence to the cell phone platform will allow device manufacturers to preinstall readers for popular file types, especially image files.

The ability to forward content to another user completes our trio of necessary mobile e-mail enhancements. Users need to be able to refer friends to Web pages they have accessed on their devices, and to forward messages they have received to individuals and groups. Mobile devices are used as social tools, and the viral propagation of mobile content will be a key aspect of mobile commerce services in the consumer market.

Web Access

AvantGo is the prime Web content service for the handheld device market. Beginning with the Palm platform, extending to the Windows CE/PocketPC operating system and thereafter to cell phone micro-browsers, AvantGo's technology accesses standard Web sites and repackages them for use on mobile devices. Some 350 leading sites have created special versions of their sites for use with AvantGo, but any site can be accessed by AvantGo and rendered for the mobile device. Adding sites, or content channels, to the user's account can be done by selecting from the optimised sites listed in the menus at AvantGo's site. The optimised sites include branded news, stock prices, flight information, and entertainment listings. Alternatively, using a piece of script supplied by AvantGo as a button for the user's Web browser, the user can add any Web site to his account as if making a bookmark or favourite. AvantGo does not charge for its service.

AvantGo's basis in the PDA market means that the service is designed around synchronization. Having set up and configured his account, the user attaches his PDA to his desktop machine via its cradle, cable, or infrared connection. The synchronization software on the desktop machine then goes out to the Internet, dialling a connection if necessary, and checks the sites marked in the user's profile to see if their content has changed since the last synchronization event. Updated content is then fetched and fed to the PDA.

For the seasoned PDA user, the AvantGo service integrates seamlessly into his routine. By synchronizing his PDA with his desktop before he leaves his workplace, the user automatically packs the latest versions of his favourite Web sites along with his updated calendar, contact book, and working documents. The interactivity of form-based Web pages is also preserved to some extent by AvantGo. Any form submitted by the user is recorded and automatically sent on to its destination at the next synchronization event. This is adequate for simple forms such as service registrations, but does not cater to processes containing chained forms. Where a Web site presents a series of forms for the user's completion, the disconnected nature of AvantGo's solution becomes a frustration. However, if the user's PDA is equipped with a modem then AvantGo becomes a true mobile commerce service, as it does when used on a cell phone platform.

AvantGo's basic synchronization mode is particularly well suited to corporate users. Users habituated to accessing the company intranet for reference information can equip their mobile devices with the same data sets. AvantGo's corporate products also target non-Web information assets in the form of direct backend database access.

AvantGo's strategy recognises the Web's role as a complex publication environment. The Web contains masses of information users come to sort and prioritise according to their needs and the quality of what they find. Content partners who provide optimised content for AvantGo help to rationalise further the overwhelming quantity of information available on the Web by propelling their own offerings to the top of the pile. Users who regard the Web primarily as a repository of information rather than a channel for interaction quickly appreciate AvantGo's role in maintaining and refreshing their personal view of the Web. Such users have long since reduced the proportion of the time they dedicate to surfing or browsing, overlaying on the Web a simplified model of personal access. Personalisation services offered by leading portals such as Yahoo! and Excite already do much to serve such users' needs. AvantGo extends the principle to the user's offline – and off-desk – situation.

As AvantGo begins to stress wireless modes of operation for its service, its unique values start to diminish. This quickly became clear on Microsoft's PocketPC platform, which ships with AvantGo and Microsoft's own Pocket Internet Explorer browser. The PocketPC user can consult either the AvantGo version of a Web site, or access it natively through the browser. The AvantGo version reduces the number of colour components and minimises the graphic content of the page (including banner ads). The native version, on the other hand, retains colour and rescales graphics according to the device's screen dimensions. Pocket Internet Explorer also obeys frame sets. The first releases of the browser do not however accept plugins or execute Java applets. AvantGo suffers here from its origins in the synchronization strategy. AvantGo supplies rationalised, monochrome content to a wide range of devices, and has been doing so since 1997. With Pocket Internet Explorer, Microsoft is able to leverage its leadership in desktop Web browsers and target a truly mobile platform at the same time. Microsoft is an investor in AvantGo, and how the two approaches will coexist on the PocketPC platform is not clear at the time of writing. On the Palm side of the street, the Palm.Net service now enables all Palm devices in the product family to access Web-clipping services.

AvantGo creates content channels suitable for mobile devices by parsing and reformatting existing HTML resources. WAP (Wireless Application Protocol) uses an alternative strategy for composing Web-like content: WML, or Wireless Markup Language. WAP and WML are explored further in Chapter 3. For our present purposes, we need to note WAP's great success in creating general awareness for the mis-named "mobile Web" and in stimulating high awareness of the WAP brand itself. WAP has become a favoured term for all things mobile commerce. The term seems to have followed Linux and XML as a focus for media attention and investor activity. "WAP" has consequently come to represent rather more than its actual technical content. Mobile commerce services in the United States are frequently labelled as WAP services, even though many use HDML (Handheld Device Markup Language), a predecessor to WML that is inaccessible to users of pure WAP browsers. SMS is a not a component of WAP, yet many European users of text services believe they are using WAP. While early experience of WAP services on GSM networks has led to dismay from commentators and early adopters, the critical voices have not succeeded in stemming consumer enthusiasm for mobile commerce services. WAP via GSM may be slow and flaky, but "WAP" continues to be a powerful rallying cry in the market. The public's clamour for Web access on mobile devices is strong enough to endure suboptimal service standards.

The leading strategies for providing Web-style content to mobile devices are shown in Figure 2-3.

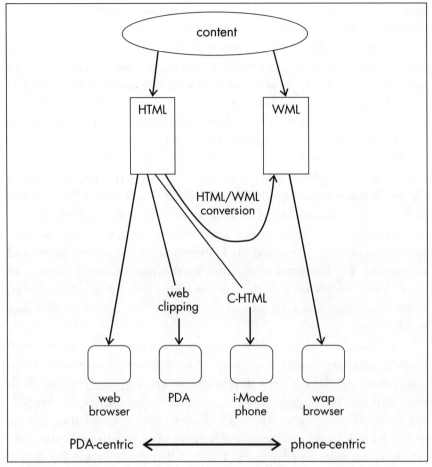

FIGURE 2-3. Main approaches to providing Web-style content to mobile devices.

Voice Dimension

Voice interfaces to computing devices have long been a goal of computer scientists. Science fiction shows us humans talking and listening to computers, while typing is a skill rarely noted in the genre's heroes. We act in a physical world and communicate via our voices; yet with fixed e-commerce we have constructed a commercial environment that favours simplified virtual spaces and constrained textual communication. The strength of the movement for mobile commerce lies in mobile commerce's alliance with naturalistic human behaviour. We want to move, act, talk, and listen. Mobile devices have the potential to integrate these functions in commercial space. The continuing explosion in cell phone ownership and surging interest in mobile commerce services bring voice control to centre stage.

With this convergence in mind AT&T, IBM, Lucent, and Motorola founded the VoiceXML forum, submitting the first version of the proposed standard to the W3C (World Wide Web Consortium)[2] in May 2000. VoiceXML is intended to bring voice control to Web sites, enabling voice-response sites similar to telephone booking services, replacing point-and-click menus with voice commands and supporting the integration of other speech-recognition functions in sites. VoiceXML's origins are in the development of phone-based interfaces to business systems and customer service centre applications in particular.

An agreed common standard for implementing voice control via a markup language brings two main benefits to service providers. First, a common standard allows developers to create voice-enabled Web sites without learning proprietary programming languages. Second, the responsibility for delivering the service to the end user can be shared by the mobile commerce service and the mobile network operator or some other intermediary. The mobile commerce service retains responsibility for designing and coding the service, and the technical functions associated with recognising and processing speech are supplied by the mobile network operator or an intermediary in the form of an ASP (Application Service Provider) or portal.

Voice enablement has one overriding attraction to mobile commerce service players. By making a service voice-enabled, the company can instantly address the mass consumer market. No special equipment or skills are needed for consumers to access such a ser-

---

2. http://www.w3c.org/.

vice. The mobile commerce service need no longer identify itself with the concept of networked computers, thus sidestepping the objections of consumers who are repelled, bored or frightened by the Internet. Consultants Kelsey Group estimate that 45 million cell phone users in North America will be using voice portals by 2005.[3]

Voice is also a natural medium for services consumed in hands-free environments, particularly the car. Text-to-voice translation software continues to improve and can be run efficiently on a backend server. A corporate user can therefore dial into a server and hear her e-mail read over a normal phone connection. Mobile commerce startup etrieve provides such a service on a monthly fee basis. Spoken driving instructions make a natural accompaniment to graphic maps in direction services and are already available to mobile commerce users from MapQuest.com.

As users become accustomed to interacting with services through vocal commands, voice recognition will become an unobtrusive element of user authentication. A user's voice print will serve to identify her to the backend system rather than a username and password. IBM's Voice Application Server[4] includes a function to register voice patterns, which can then be used by security routines.

The addition of the voice dimension to the mobile commerce model has considerable implications for service designers. Existing models for voice-controlled systems will rapidly prove inadequate to the task. Current automated customer service systems for the telephone improve productivity for the company that deploys them, but customers endure added complexity. The phrase "Press one for . . ." induces stress in us all. Listening to a recitation of menu options is by no means as user friendly as seeing them displayed. The customer is required to construct a mental image of the menu or to scribble the menu down. This test is repeated at each level in the hierarchy – until

3. Anne Chen, "Calling up e-com business", ZDNet, 10 July 2000: http://www.zdnet.com/ecommerce/stories/main/0,10475,2598327,00.html.

4. http://www-4.ibm.com/software/speech/.

the customer is favoured with an answer or a human conversation. This style of system will not propagate in the mobile commerce era. Users will expect to interact with services in ways that are more efficient for themselves, not the service provider.

This is not to say that they will expect to communicate with mobile commerce services in free, natural language. Consumers are more likely to coalesce on a relatively small number of common queries, much as they do in everyday shopping encounters. Mobile users will ask mobile commerce services questions such as "What's my current balance?" and "When does the movie start?". Rather than devising hierarchical menu structures, sticky features, and compelling banner ads, mobile commerce service designers will create pre-emptive query- and comment-recognition interfaces. Services will recognise common voice inputs and learn from those to which they cannot immediately respond. So, an e-book sales service may initially create a pre-emptive response structure for queries along the lines of, "How much is the new <Harry Potter>?", but subsequently learn that the service also needs to field questions like, "How do you spell <phenomenon>?"

Location Finding

The base services we have considered so far deal with user empowerment. E-mail, messaging, and Web access connect the user to the information world, whereas the voice dimension allows mobile commerce usage to become more naturalistic. These base services create a powerful customer-centric platform, but leave the user as an unlocated entity. While a wireless connection and a user log-on enable a service provider to identify a customer, we need some other means of pinpointing her physical location.

There are two main methods of determining the physical location of a mobile device. The first makes use of satellites orbiting the earth, whereas the second involves use of the wireless network infrastructure itself. Both methods rely on triangulation to calculate positions.

The Global Positioning System (GPS) uses 24 satellites and a set of ground receivers to determine the position of an object on the

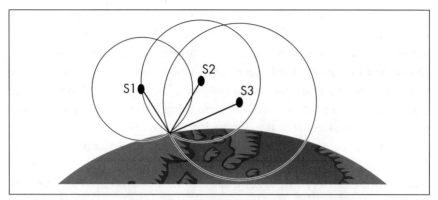

FIGURE 2-4. Triangulation from three satellites.

earth.[5] The object's position is found by calculating the intersection points of a number of theoretical spheres, where each sphere is centred on a satellite. Figure 2-4 shows how a point can lie on a number of different spheres centred on satellites. If we know the distance to one satellite, then we know that we are located somewhere on the sphere which has that distance as its radius and the satellite as its centre. If we also know the distance to another satellite, then we know we are located on two spheres. Our position must be somewhere on the circle of points created by the intersection of the two spheres. By measuring the distance to a third satellite, we can reduce the number of possible points of our location to two. With absolute accuracy in our measurements and knowledge of the satellite's position, we can generally regard one of these two points as obviously incorrect, because it will be too far from the earth's surface. In fact, GPS uses four satellites to determine position, with the fourth signal being used to provide a means of synchronising the measurements. GPS satellite signals incorporate psuedo-random code sequences which receiving devices can compare with their own code sequences to determine timing differences, and hence relative distance between satellite and receiver.

---

5. The simplified description of GPS given here is based on the excellent detailed GPS tutorial by Trimble Navigation Limited at http://www.trimble.com/gps/.

GPS is designed for use by relatively small devices and does not require large antennas. GPS devices are established in the marine sector and are becoming increasingly common as personal equipment. DeLorme's Earthmate GPS Receiver is a pocket-sized GPS device that can be connected to a Palm or Windows CE device. The GPS receiver works with Street Atlas USA software installed on the PDA to automatically locate the user on a detailed map.

GPS can be thought of as a device-based approach to location finding, since it relies on specialised electronics and processing in the user's mobile device. The chief disadvantages of GPS are that the system relies on line-of-sight communications, making it unworkable in many buildings, and the extra power requirements of dedicated GPS hardware. The alternative approaches to positioning are network based. Network-based solutions may offer less accuracy in positioning, but the technology and processing investments do not need to be made in the mobile device. The simplest means of providing a location for a mobile device within a network is known as Cell Of Origin (COO). Since a cellular network must monitor the cell location of every live device, the current value can be used to locate a user within a broad geographical area. The TOA (Time Of Arrival) technique involves the network's base stations monitoring the handover access traffic of devices, comparing the relative times of arrival of each signal, and triangulating a position. TOA requires modification of the network infrastructure, but can be used with existing cell phone populations. E-OTD (Enhanced Observed Time Differential) is a technique similar to GPS, using the cell base stations of the network in place of the satellite constellation but using the same principles of signal synchronisation and triangulation. E-OTD requires a software update to existing cell phones.

Mobile network operators have been motivated to provide location finding services as part of the base mobile platform by legislators in the United States and in Europe. U.S. cell phone operators are required to provide device positioning data to within 125 metres accuracy for emergency 911 purposes by the end of 2001. The European Union has targeted 2003 for a similar requirement covering the region's 112 emergency services. The incorporation of location-finding technology in mobile devices and networks for emergency purposes enables commercial services sensitive to location without requiring further investment by the network or the consumer.

Digital Content Products

Thanks to the high media profile of Amazon during the early years of e-commerce, books have an unlikely founder's role in the establishment of the Web as a mass commercial medium. A coincidence of history positions e-books as a key influencer in the development of mobile commerce. The e-book market is a pathfinder for the sale of all kinds of electronic goods to the mobile population, much as Amazon blazed the trail of general online sales with its book business.

Amazon initially focused on book sales because books make up the largest class of uniquely identified products. A traditional physical bookstore cannot hope to offer the world's entire catalogue of books in print, whereas a virtual player can. The online bookstore can offer rapid searching through this wealth of product, and price savings derived from its savings in brick-and-mortar retail premises. Books are assigned unique identifiers, making them ideal subjects for computerised catalogues.

The success of Amazon and the imitators it inspired established the concept of buying over the Web, allowing the principle to be extended to all other products and services. The e-book will perform the same market function in the mobile commerce market. The first reason for this is that books are naturally portable media. A reader rarely consumes a book in one physical location, unless he is consulting a rare work that cannot be transported or replicated. Books are used at desks, in armchairs, and in bed, as well as on trains and planes. An electronic book that can be stored on a portable device and read with ease fits naturally into the mobile lifestyle. Owners of mobile devices are clearly customers for e-books: they have already invested in the necessary technology, and they have adopted a mobile lifestyle that welcomes e-book usage. Voracious readers will also see e-books as a reason for committing to mobile technology. While books are portable, they also carry a cost of ownership. For titles that readers don't care to keep on their shelves, e-books propose an elegant solution. Instead of recycling books through charity shops or sending them to be pulped, readers can simply delete e-books from their devices. Furthermore, readers increasingly buy books from online stores, the main source of marketing messages supporting the uptake of e-books.

The second reason why e-books perform a pathfinding role in mobile commerce is their *unidirectional* nature. Books transmit information in a single direction, from author to reader. The book is the ultimate content package, and despite the efforts of some authors and publishers, books cannot be made interactive. Books may contain optional texts, but they do not contain multiple paths. When a book tries to incorporate a richer selection of consumption options, it becomes a multimedia experience. Our interactive age tends to look down on unidirectional information while simultaneously claiming that "content is king". Computer games form a unique aspect of our culture, yet the most successful game-type products are Hollywood action movies – consumed passively by audiences.

The category of unidirectional information embraces two gigantic businesses: music and movies. Like written text, audio and video content can be reduced to digital code and distributed with increasingly impressive fidelity and efficiency. Music is clearly a naturally mobile product. Consumers' interest in portable music drove the development of transistors and, ultimately, all contemporary consumer electronics products, while Sony's Walkman created the concept of a "personal" class of products, including the personal computer. The growing e-book business acts as a proving ground for the sale of digital music to mobile consumers. Since e-books contain mostly text, with the occasional graphic, file sizes can be small and reading software can be relatively simple. E-books are therefore ideal content objects for transmission in low-bandwidth networks and for storage on small form-factor devices. As sales of e-books grow, the consumer market becomes habituated to using unidirectional content that has shed its physical housing. This most traditional of physical products has dematerialised to reveal pure content, with publishers and readers alike weaned away from the problems of paper production, distribution, storage, and disposal. Where e-books go, e-music follows. Digital music requires larger file sizes than printed text, but music player software can be incorporated easily into mobile devices. Transmission time over low-bandwidth networks remains a barrier to the uptake of e-music in the mobile commerce environment, with music fans used to downloading MP3 tracks to desktop machines and then porting them to their mobile devices. As bandwidth improves, delivery of e-music to mobile devices will be liberated from the desktop, and sales promotion via digital radio will fuel a newly dynamic market.

E-books are often perceived as a ripple of disturbance confined to the publishing industry, but their influence on the development of mobile commerce is profound. The availability, pricing, and convenience of e-books will persuade many consumers to invest in PDA-type mobile devices, acting as a counterbalance to those joining the mobile commerce world via the cell phone. While this route to the general growth of the mobile commerce market will not be as large a factor as cell phone uptake, the e-book market will prove the viability of full-feature mobile devices that offer more than phone and text services. As e-book business models are joined by e-music offerings, cell phone producers will find themselves further challenged. We often assume that convergence between the cell phone and PDA markets will occur around screen services, with cell phone advocates pushing videophone services and PDA diehards envisioning TV services. E-music is likely to short-circuit these dreams, leading to triumphs for consumer electronic companies who focus on mobile music devices that also act as phones and computing platforms.

Several companies are looking to bring video content to mobile devices ahead of the emergence of high-bandwidth wireless networks. PacketVideo's technology transmits 5-frames-per-second content for use with its player technology. ActiveSky's player has been adopted by short-film publisher AtomFilms for its Atom To Go project. The ActiveSky player can be installed on a PocketPC or Palm device and play content from AtomFilms or other publishers, much in the same way e-books are displayed by reader software. Early content for

Atom To Go focuses on short animated features, and the immediate future for such strategies seems to lie in providing movie trailers. If mobile users can be persuaded to consume this kind of content, then AtomFilms (now merged with shockwave.com) and its competitors will have created a market similar to those in e-books and MP3 files. This scenario may be a far cry from full video programming or two-way video telephony, but it provides a stepping stone to commercial distribution of popular video content such as video post-cards (baby's first steps, feeding time at the zoo) and business applications such as video signoffs (receipt of a delivery, completion of a structure).

The main challenge to the e-book–led scenario for mobile commerce growth is the role of the physical artefact in consumers' value sets. Will book lovers jettison books in favour of content? Will music lovers buy music that is not accompanied by CD cases and artwork? Artefacts acts as symbols of affiliation in the unidirectional content class. Books do furnish a room, and speak volumes about a person's tastes, biography, and opinions. Disk cases make statements from the shelf and continue to relay messages about their owner while the content is silent. The urge to *own* a product, to see it in his environment, can be a powerful element of a customer's decision to purchase. Music companies may need to develop alternative methods of allowing consumers to own pieces of recording stars. E-music buyers may be able to order related merchandise to use as tokens of affiliation and ownership, such as clothing and figurines. E-book buyers may be able to buy author-signed certificates of readership to collect, frame, and trade. Serial readers of serial writers about serial killers may be eligible for lifetime award plaques.

MOBILE COMMERCE SERVICES FOR CONSUMERS

In this section we examine the leading mobile commerce services for consumers: travel, ticketing, banking, stock trading, news and sports, gambling, game playing, and shopping.

Travel: Direction and Connection

One of the most successful application categories in fixed e-commerce has been travel. Sites aimed at personal and business air travellers, for example, make excellent use of the web's strengths. Sites such as Travelocity allow users to specify departure and destination airports, preferred times of travel, and price brackets using Web forms. The user can then scan the options that match her criteria, make a booking, and pay in one streamlined process.

Travel has obvious synergies with mobile commerce. In fact, the concept of travel is so closely bound up with mobile commerce that thinking of travel as a discrete category of activity divorced from other activities, in the style of fixed e-commerce, is unhelpful. In the world of fixed e-commerce, a user plans a trip from her desktop. She then abandons the desktop for the trip itself. She may have downloaded a relevant city guide to her PDA before departing, but the Web has played its part in arranging the travel component of the trip. But if the PDA she sports has wireless connectivity, or her cell phone has data capabilities such as WAP, then mobile commerce can continue to play roles in the travel experience itself.

First, the established ability to book travel tickets electronically transfers elegantly to mobile devices. Travel information is naturally packaged into relatively small chunks, so the information is simple to translate to low-bandwidth channels. The information is composed of alphanumeric data (for example, names, dates, times, and prices), so a lack of colour graphics or multimedia capabilities at the client device does not present a barrier to implementation. More importantly, booking by mobile commerce allows users to develop and purchase their itineraries in flight – metaphorically and literally. The ability to make last-minute changes to routes and times and to choose alternate travel modes is greatly increased by mobile commerce. Users can search, compare, and buy tickets in their native language rather than struggling with a foreign tongue. They can rearrange their itineraries while sitting in a lounge, grabbing a snack, or browsing for gifts rather than joining a series of queues. They can arrange trips through their favourite suppliers, wherever they happen to be, without searching for a fixed Web appliance.

Best of all, extreme mission states allow users and service providers to optimise the deals they make with each other. A traveller who is pressed for time can choose to take a more expensive travel option in order to make a meeting, perhaps upgrading to business from coach class or opting for a taxi rather than the courtesy shuttle. On the other hand, a traveller who is looking to stretch his finances as far around the world as possible can choose to take last-minute surplus seats or even (depending on the type of travel) sell a ticket he already holds to someone whose need is more urgent.

Ticketing extends beyond travel, and we look at ticketing services in more detail later in this chapter. However, electronic tickets have an important role in seeding other travel-related mobile commerce opportunities. The first of these is the in-transit opportunity, which can be demarcated by the electronic actions of checking in and arrival. By beaming his electronic ticket at a receiving device, an air traveller formally checks in and registers his arrival within the terminal. The airline allocates his seat and confirms any dietary requirements of which he has notified them. The ticket continues to function during the customer's stay at the terminal, granting him discounts in stores. If his flight is delayed, the ticket may also be used to represent compensatory value, in the form of rights to purchase snacks. The electronic ticket may also serve as a gateway to sales opportunities during the flight itself.

The second seeding role of electronic tickets is their role in handing off the customer to partners after the travel experience is completed. A ticket may act as a discount to related travel, accommodation or entertainment offers, for example. The user beams his ticket at a participating business to receive his discount, or other benefit, automatically. The ticket's virtual stub acts like a click-through banner on a traditional Web site, with the added attraction that the mechanism is in the user's personal ownership rather than merely in his visual field.

Booking trips, paying for them, and using electronic tickets via the mobile channel adds up to an intuitive set of services. The mobile device is effectively replacing a mass of pre-electronic paraphernalia: timetables, route planners, calculators, cash, tickets, boarding passes, and receipts. Electronic passports, visas and customs declarations would streamline the travel process further. Mobile commerce is improving the travel process for both traveller and travel organisation, leveraging the personal wireless device to create greater convenience and coherence.

Mobile commerce has a second major part to play in the travel arena, beyond the booking-payment-ticket role. This is the opportunity to provide users with directions. As mobile commerce capabilities leak into the mass consumer market via the introduction of commerce-enabled cell phones, *direction* services will be as fundamental to users' lives as the *directory* services of established telcos. The primary problem in using communications systems lies in identifying the address of a target party – that is, knowing their number. Mobile commerce exploits underlying communications systems to create an intelligent, personal companion that goes everywhere with its owner. The mobile user still has the primary problem of identifying the addresses of target parties, which is why mobile portals are competing to offer organised links to commerce providers. But mobile users have a secondary problem, which relates to the mobile device's role as a travelling companion. As well as requiring addresses for the purposes of communicating, either with other users or commerce sites, the user also needs help in finding real-world places. She moves in real space as well as cyberspace.

Giving directions – the business of helping people move from A to B – entails calculating routes from map data, breaking routes into coherent and communicable segments, and feeding the segments to the user as the user requires them. A typical route segment will include a road number or name, a direction relative to the user's current position, and a distance. The clarity of directions can be improved through the inclusion of landmarks.

The direction service therefore creates an overview route, segments the route, formats each segment in a user-friendly fashion, and delivers the segments with reference to the user's progress through the route. The service encapsulates the behaviours of the perfect human navigator: a companion who knows where we are going, who can recognise the unfolding landscape and relate it to a plan, and who can give unambiguous and timely instructions to the driver. Direction services prove their sophistication when they can recalculate routes based on encountered obstructions or user deviation.

Not all mobile commerce travel services offer directions according to this scenario. They rely instead on the transmission of maps to mobile devices. In fact, map transmission services currently outnumber direction-giving services. Published maps are already stored in digital form, making them relatively easy to transfer from traditional publishing applications to the mobile channel. Ventures which already own comprehensively mapping data are naturally inclined to see map-reading as the single answer to mobile users' travel information needs.

However, the large number of players offering travel services comprised solely of maps may be unwittingly excluding half of their potential market. The reason lies in the different approaches men and women seem to use for finding their way. Researchers investigating cognitive differences between men and women have repeatedly experimented with route-learning exercises. Research suggests that women remember landmarks better than men and use these to orient themselves and construct mental routes. Men, on the other hand, seem to learn routes more quickly, though they tend not to remember landmarks as well. The current theory of the male strategy is that men use spatial data to create mental routes. Much newspaper ink has been spilt concerning the resulting academic respectability of the old routines about wives who can't read road maps for husbands who won't stop and ask where they are. A short sideways step takes us to explanations based on hunter-gatherer roles in early human societies, with the implication that women stayed at home and concentrated on where they had planted crops or hidden food, while men went out to hunt, oblivious to everything but the speed and direction of their prey and the distance it was taking them from home.

Whether or not such explanations convince, some people evidently prefer to construct routes using landmarks rather than vectors (combinations of distance and direction). A-to-B services using a mnemonic approach rather than a graphical map base may therefore find appreciative audiences. At the same time, map-based services that integrate points of interest with their maps extend their attraction to a larger audience. Combining mission-sensitive landmark information with directions produces services that cater to modern-day hunters and gatherers of all types.

For example, Maptuit and 724 Solutions have combined to provide target landmark services for the financial services industry. 724 is an established provider of wireless services to this market, and is particularly known for its work with Bank of Montreal. Maptuit provides maps, directions and points of interest to systems providers such as online retailers and logistics companies. Together, 724 and Maptuit can provide wireless place-finding services for integration with other service providers' offerings. Resources such as gas stations and restaurants can be located in relation to the user's current whereabouts, and a route created.

This kind of service is usually called a *location-based service*. In our *location-time-mission* model, we would place this service high on all dimensions. From an objective point of view, the service calculates a route between an origin (the user's location) and a selected landmark (the user's destination). But from the point of view of the user, the service collapses the conceptual distance between a goal and its satisfaction. Technically, the service is location-based. Emotionally, the service's sensitivity to the user's mission makes it compelling. In business terms, the service is an excellent mobile commerce opportunity area.

The best example of the power of combining directions with landmarks – and adding the urgency of time – is the parking service we noted in Chapter 1. Piloted in France in the summer of 2000, Webraska's WAP service uses Schlumberger's parking data to provide real-time information on parking space availability combined with traffic conditions, maps, and directions. Schlumberger is a leading smartcard company and also supplies parking meters. The parking meters can be upgraded to signal their current usage to a central server. Schlumberger aggregates all the status data from its parking terminals to produce an availability picture that can be matched with Webraska's map and route pictures. By calculating occupancy according to areas, and assessing whether availability is rising or falling in each area, the Schlumberger server produces a conceptual "heat map" from which the user can select a target parking area. The Webraska server then calculates a route and guides the user to the target.

At the finest level of granularity, the individual parking spot is a time-sensitive resource. The Webraska/Schlumberger parking service uses aggregated parking spots to select landmarks in accordance with users' declared missions. We can imagine other types of service that target the individual spot. Parking spots have value, identity, and fixed locations, so it should be possible for a customer to book a particular space. But somehow the vision of a would-be parker who has booked a space using his mobile device arguing with a driver who has happened upon it first is hard to accept. Parking spaces would not have any sanction against opportunist parkers, short of refusing their payment, which would seem to defeat the object of the game. Yet in all other respects, the parking problem is akin to any travel-related booking opportunity in mobile commerce: a resource related to time and location that a customer might pay to own. By distinguishing spaces that must be booked from first-come, first-served public places, parking providers could charge premium rates to more than cover the increased nonoccupancy time that such spaces might experience. In effect, contract parking schemes, whereby an employer provides spaces for the company's workers in a public facility, could be opened up to unaggregated customers. Some means of automated clamping could deter drivers who used spaces they had not booked: the space would not recognise their electronic ticket. Parking is already reserved for residents in busy metropolitan areas, a privilege for which they pay through local taxation. Mobile commerce will allow owners of valuable road space and parking lots to maximise their revenue.

As we shall see repeatedly in this chapter, mobile commerce does not simply extend the benefits of e-commerce to the mobile user, offering convenience and mission-related services. Mobile commerce also has the potential to change the way business is carried out. E-commerce has had a profound effect on brick-and-mortar retailers, with B2C online retailers challenging their traditional counterparts on price and range. Traditional stores have responded by enhancing their physical environments, making the shopping experience more rewarding – more real – than the online alternative. Mobile commerce reaches into many more areas of our lives and will consequently impact many more features of our world. Elitist parking is only one possible consequence of the addition of mobile commerce to our daily lives. Another is escalation in taxi competition as mobile commerce allows users to bargain for fares with local drivers. Once drivers and potential passengers are connected through the mobile channel, the combined population constitutes a market. Drivers may be able to negotiate premium fares in conditions of driver scarcity, and passengers negotiate discounts when the local area is flooded with empty cabs. Drivers will also be able to examine heat maps to determine where the best fishing is to be had.

Ticketing: The Stubs of a New Currency

From the perspective of a travel service provider, tickets are enablers. Tickets enable travelers to take up the travel facilities that they have booked, and tickets allow the service provider to maintain a mobile commerce relationship with the customer during and after their period of travel. Spin over to Tickets.com and you will find a different perspective. This Web-based ticketing centre lets customers focus on booking events in which they are interested – and then arranging travel to the events. The company helps customers organise entertainment events by creating packages of travel and entry tickets.

Travel and ticketing are close neighbours in our mental models. Ticketing is often regarded as an obvious mobile commerce service, and inserted baldly into lists of forthcoming attractions by WAP service providers. We elide mobility with travel, and travel with ticketing. But as we have seen, the mobile channel is concerned with more than the servicing of travelers. And tickets play roles in other industries than travel.

What *is* a ticket? A ticket is a documentary time-specific right to a human-sized space – usually a seat. The seat may be moving, as in a plane or train, or stationary, as in a movie theater or sports stadium. Travel and entertainment proprietors issue tickets so that customers can provide proof of purchase when they arrive to consume their purchase. The ticket acts as a pass for the customer, guaranteeing his option to enjoy the seat he has bought. From the point of view of the ticket's issuer, the ticket acts as an authenticating device, helping to ensure that nonpaying customers are rejected. Tickets are an efficient means of modelling distributed ownership of limited, time-based resources.

Contemporary ticketing services are among the leaders in migrating a traditional, paper-based activity to the mobile channel via proven fixed e-commerce mechanisms. The ultimate goal is to create systems that issue and receive electronic tickets. However, three precursor stages exist, as shown in Figure 2-5. These alternative strategies are worth examining because they reveal an ordering of benefits from improved ticketing processes.

The first approach to mobile commerce ticketing is simply to extend the ordering of paper tickets on a fixed e-commerce site to the mobile channel. In this case, tickets are acting like any other form of product that can be sold over an electronic channel. The provider minimises his technology costs in producing the system. He may use general e-commerce storefront software to create the system, specifying low graphic content and minimal text so that the system can be ported to the more constrained user interfaces of mobile devices. Tickets are low-weight, high-value, and time-sensitive products. They are therefore an ideal area of focus for metro area e-fulfilment players: that is, companies seeking to establish themselves as reliable and speedy deliverers of products bought via electronic channels.

Even if the service provider still delivers paper tickets to the customer, a mobile commerce ticketing solution can add benefit to the customer's buying experience. Motorola used ticketing to demonstrate the first use of a GPRS (General Packet Radio Services) network for mobile commerce in Barcelona in May 2000. (GPRS is a mobile packet network technology discussed further in Chapter 3.) The user entered a set of entertainment preferences in the service, and the back-end system negotiated with a range of suppliers to choose best-match tickets. The user could then receive notification of ticket selection and confirm booking via the cell phone. Credit card payments were actioned immediately with the completion of the booking.

Motorola's ticketing application makes a valuable point about the ticketing opportunity, as well as demonstrating an efficient commerce process. The ticketing service is not acting simply as a conduit for tickets, but as a value-adding mediator. The service runs a reverse auction

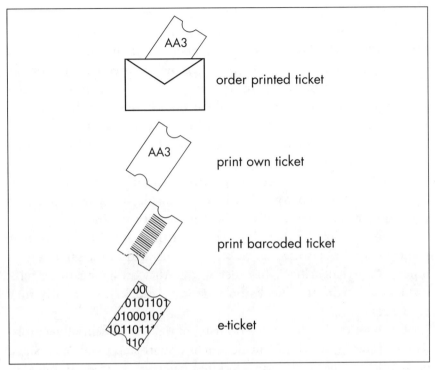

order printed ticket

print own ticket

print barcoded ticket

e-ticket

FIGURE 2-5. Precursors of full electronic tickets.

with event and venue operators to find attractive deals for its customers. In order to do so, it must learn about the customer's interests, schedule, and even the size of the groups she goes out in. The service must also have prearranged a payment facility with the customer, so that it can deal confidently with event and venue operators, knowing that the service's customers will honour any purchases they elect to make.

Our second stage of ticketing marks the start of a process of virtualisation of tickets. Several companies have developed services that allow customers to order tickets and then print them out at their own printers. Competition has been particularly strong in the movie theater business, with Cinemark, AOL MovieFone, and MovieTickets.com all introducing electronic ticketing services in 2000 and targeting the mobile commerce user.

The obvious benefit of enabling the customer to print her own ticket is that printing and dispatch costs are saved at the supplier end. Delivery to the customer is instantaneous, and the customer takes responsibility for creating the paper artefact. An equally important benefit of this approach is its low impact on the ticket-collection process. Home-printed tickets can look slightly different than theater-issued ones – in fact, they may well be of higher quality – but they can still be handled and checked by counter staff with no special treatment required.

Home printing of tickets raises the possibility of ticket counterfeiting. With customer-produced tickets displaying a wide range of print quality and paper types, the opportunity for fraud is greater. The main task of the ticketing service in this case is to ensure that identifying numbers used on tickets are generated in the same way as other security identifiers. In other words, they are going to be relatively long, contain checksum patterns, and belong to distinct sequences.

Once we realise that home printing of tickets is essentially a problem of printing security identifiers, it is a short step to our next stage of mobile commerce ticketing: printed barcodes. Barcode technology is a stable area of technology that has been proven in inventory systems around the world. Industry standards ensure that barcode printing and scanning are universally possible. The drawback to barcoded tickets lies in the ticket collection technology at the receiving end. Venues and transportation systems that already use barcoded tickets will be able to accept home-printed barcodes, but manual receipt points will not. Smaller venues may need to invest in barcode scanners in order to accept such tickets. The scanner is, of course, only the first component in an entire information systems strategy that needs to be in place to enable the venue for barcode tickets: there is no point in reading an identifier if it is not at least going to be verified against a table of legal values. The small venue operator therefore faces a considerable investment in technology if he is to welcome customers equipped with home-printed barcode tickets.

The barcode turns a paper ticket into a proxy e-ticket. The value of the barcode lies in the information it encodes. The barcode is chosen as a delivery mechanism for the ticket identifier because the technology to produce it is available in the customer's home, and the resulting artefact is highly portable. The barcode ticket's acceptance at the destination requires a level of technology commitment that favours larger operators, especially nonlocal transportation companies and theater chains. Perhaps surprisingly, full-fledged electronic tickets will remove these technology barriers in time, making e-tickets truly mobile and universal.

A true electronic ticket simply conveys the numeric information associated with a ticket as computer-readable data. The ticket may be displayed or printed out, but its effective existence lies in the electronic object, not any visual artefact derived from it. When customers of Austria's rail transport system OBB use their cell phones to check timetables and book tickets, confirmation is sent to the phone as a text message containing an authentication code. The traveller shows the code to the conductor aboard the train. The conductor then uses a handheld device of his own to check the code. The customer is charged for the ticket via his mobile phone bill.[6]

In this example, the train company incurs additional cost by equipping its guards with special devices for authenticating e-tickets. The organisation needs to be able to print receipts for customers on request, making the necessary equipment quite complex. However, with a cell phone solution of this kind, the authentication process can also be handled by a backend process. Swedish movie theater chain Sandrews Metronome trialled a mobile commerce ticketing solution in 2000 that proves the point. The customer buys his ticket via cell phone in much the same way as our Austrian rail traveler. At the theater, the customer can either show his authentication code to a staff member, or beam it directly to a staff member's mobile device by infrared connection.[7]

---

6. "Mobile Ticketing: The test-bed for mobile transactions", *Mobile Internet*, 1(1), 10 April 2000.
7. *Mobile Internet* [UK], 1(3), 8 May 2000.

This approach allows human checking to be removed from the ticket collection process. The receiving staff member's device can be preloaded with an application that matches incoming authentication codes against a list of valid codes. If the staff member's device is a PDA, then the valid codes for the day can be synched to the device from a desktop machine in the back office shortly before show time. If, on the other hand, staff use cell phones, then the phone can be programmed to send incoming authentication codes on to a back end server that checks them, issuing audible and visual cues for acceptances and rejections. The latter approach allows the process to be in real time, though it exposes the ticket-accepting company to network availability and performance risks – the standard trade-off between synchronising applications and true wireless applications.

As network coverage and reliability improve, and as packet-based mobile networks become the norm, the device-to-device solution for ticketing will grow in attractiveness to businesses of all sizes, but especially to smaller transport companies and independent venues. These smaller players will essentially be able to outsource their ticketing process to mobile commerce intermediaries while using standard consumer devices in the field. Mobile commerce ticketing services will handle the business of issuing, receipting and collecting payment for tickets across the full range of travel and entertainment opportunities. They will take a percentage of ticket sales to finance their operations and make a profit, choosing to boost value further by creating travel/entertainment ticket packages and undertaking preference-matching searches for customers. These added value services have the virtue of not interrupting the ticket purchase and consumption processes, as, say, ticket-embedded advertising would.

Ticketing services face classic intermediary challenges. First, they need to sign up participating organisations and convince them mobile commerce ticketing will deliver customers at an effective cost. The problem is analogous to that of B2B procurement suppliers in fixed e-commerce: an e-procurement service for corporate buyers is only as good as its collection of catalogues. Ticketing is not so much about nifty solutions for printing documents as building alliances to deliver content to users. Companies launching mobile commerce ticketing services can learn much from content aggregators on the fixed Web, in both the B2C and B2B sectors.

The next challenge to ticketing services is the breakneck speed of technology innovation at the device side. We blithely assume above, for example, that infrared is some kind of techno-lingua franca that all devices speak. The truth is that while most devices come equipped with an IR port these days, few will recognise ports outside their own product family. As we will see in Chapter 3, the Bluetooth movement is tackling this kind of connectivity headache. In the meantime, players have to recognise that diversity in the device population creates fragility in systems solutions. Territorial assessment of network availability and device type penetration is vital before launching a full ticketing service into a market.

The final major challenge to mobile commerce ticketing services as intermediaries is their ability to create a distinctive user experience for the customer. We are used to falling back on the mantra of "compelling content" when considering this challenge on the fixed Web. In the mobile channel, the solution lies more in the efficiency of the service and the implications of its brand values. To put this in human terms, we appreciate assistants who are both competent and likeable, not necessarily ones who are exhaustingly voluble or seemingly expert in every department of human knowledge.

Winning mobile commerce ticketing services will know their business and perform it with speed, accuracy, and grace. User interfaces need to be intuitive, exploiting the wealth of traditional experience in designing timetables and seating plans and rethinking those designs for mobile devices. Ticketing naturally allies itself with lifestyle services, so we can expect leading ticketing services to stake key positions in lifestyle-oriented portals. However, judging appropriate levels of obtrusiveness is a major issue for ticketing services in this context. While being prominent in the static lists of a portal is beneficial, being over-assertive in making direct offers to the customer must be treated with caution. Experience with fixed e-commerce suggests that customers appreciate relevant offers, but not if they are made repeatedly. Making your proposal once, in the right words and at the right time, will be crucial to proactive marketers.

Looking out to an environment where mobile commerce ticketing solutions are standard, what secondary opportunities can we see emerging? Ticketing will generate new types of related services related to customer empowerment.

Consider, for example, the effect of mobile commerce ticketing on a multiplex movie theater. Customers in the local area look at movie programs and reviews during the day, buying tickets as they go. They may be being influenced by recommendations from members of their buddy lists, notices in media channels, or personal preferences for film types or movie stars. Some may be influenced by the signage on the complex itself, as they drive past or use other facilities in the mall.

In effect, customer votes come in throughout the day, giving the theater management a real-time picture of demand. The theater may notice one movie reaching capacity on its designated screen. Management can then switch the movie to another screen, moving the booked tickets across, and at the same time reconfigure the exterior signage – electronic, of course – to put the favoured film in the most prominent position or to promote a movie that seems to be doing badly. The theatre can also develop offers for seats right up to show time by offering general discounts or discounted additional tickets to customers who have already booked.

In this scenario, customers determine the bill of fare at the movie house. We can extend this principle to imagine customer buying power creating actual events. Just as buying clubs on the fixed Web enable groups of customers to force product prices down, so groups of ticket buyers could force artists to perform additional shows. Promoters could make holding payments on venues and then sell refundable tickets for an event. At a certain trigger point, the show becomes viable and the early bookers are rewarded with a discount on confirmation. While music companies fret for their revenues in a world saturated with freely duplicated music files, artists will be able to continue earning from live performances, and, through the aggregated power of mobile commerce customers, entertain "by popular request".

Technically speaking, this could be done using the existing fixed Web. However, the effect is much more likely to occur in the mobile channel. In the first place, the mobile commerce customer population will be much larger than the fixed e-commerce population, simply because there will be more mobile phones and other personal devices in the world than desktop machines. Mobile devices will also be used a great deal more than desktop facilities. Mobile commerce has a truly popular base, and "viral" communications amongst users will drive currents of opinion at lightening speed. The ability to forward items of interest to friends will rapidly create pools of commercial opportunity for ticketable events. We must remember that entertainment events are group experiences and that customers buy the right to be part of a group as much as the opportunity to enjoy a particular sensory experience. Group propulsion of events via mobile commerce ticketing services ties promotion by word of mouth – or stylus or thumb – into automated resource optimisation and fulfilment.

Organisations that receive tickets are also empowered by mobile commerce ticketing services. While introducing e-ticket receiving terminals can be seen as an unwelcome expense, such terminals also represent the opportunity to play in many more mobile commerce opportunities. Once an organisation can accept and verify an authorisation code in an e-ticket, it can enable any other service that requires authentication. This could include release of goods held in temporary storage, for example. In this way a bus station could easily become a local distribution centre for e-commerce fulfilment companies, who deliver ordered goods to neighbourhood collection points for convenient customer collection.

One benefit of paper tickets that could be lost in the transition to personal e-tickets is their anonymity. Companies operating mobile commerce ticketing services need to ensure that while they take an interest in customers' buying patterns and expressed preferences, the customers can still transfer their tickets to others – within any prearranged or legal restrictions. After all, many tickets are bought in pairs or blocks. The ability to forward e-tickets allows customers to buy tickets on behalf of their partners, family, or group. This capability also enables an after-market in tickets, so that ticket speculators will still be able to operate. In effect, e-tickets can act as a form of currency and even a form of tradable equity.

Banking: The Suggestion Machine

We touched on mobile commerce banking services in Chapter 1, noting the leadership of European retail banks in the rollout of WAP-based services. We also looked at the strong fit between bank customers' desires to check balances frequently and the personal convenience of the mobile device. As cell phone-based banking services continue to proliferate, banking already seems a given of the mobile commerce landscape. As we shall see, the first generation of banking services is the forerunner to a more sophisticated banking presence in the mobile channel. But first we may ask, If mobile commerce banking is here and here to stay, what can it tell us about the design, launch and effects of other mobile commerce services?

Taking these attributes in order, we can immediately see that banking services for the mobile channel are designed for ease of use above all other considerations. WAP services running on nonpacket networks impose a functional discipline that contrasts with the bloated approach to applications design we have come to expect with desktop systems. The interesting data items at the heart of any consumer banking application are cold, hard numbers – usually depressingly small ones, or large ones with unwelcome debit signs attached. WAP phones of the 2000 vintage allow for no embroidery to soften the blow of the data. Control buttons are effectively limited to scrolling, clicking, and going back to the previous screen (or *card* in WAP terminology). Numeric data entry is, of course, a simple matter for a phone device; text entry is more tortuous, but less relevant to banking applications. The basic WAP user interface is ideally suited to displaying balances, accepting funds transfer instructions, and producing ministatements. At the same time, mobile commerce banking applications leverage the knowledge of systems developer and bank customer groups alike. ATMs prepare customers to operate their own accounts through a menu system, whereas ATMs and phone-based banking systems represent a layer of customer-facing functionality that can be readily converted to specifications for WAP systems.

The undecorated, terse accuracy of WAP banking services cements the conversion of a bank's image from that of a human institution to that of a simple machine. Banks invest heavily in correcting this imbalance, stressing the importance of person-to-person relationships in their advertising campaigns and their continued occupancy of physical retail space. However, there is no doubt that using the simple, widely available technology of the cell phone to maximise the convenience of their core competence exposes banks to erosion of their brand values. When a bank balance becomes a function of a pocket device, what happens to the authority status of the balance? Is the balance a trusted communication dispensed by a wiser, remote power or merely an item of the user's personal property that happens to be managed by an entity beyond the ether? Just as the power and water entering a consumer's home are hard to brand, giving competition in the domestic supply business an often desperate edge, so personal banking information becomes a bland commodity: an ever-present utility afforded low respect by its users. Mobile commerce banking services illustrate that the mobile channel strips the mystique from any commercial service centred on the provision of habitual data. Mobile commerce reduces all such businesses to machines.

Every business that depends on the supply of data for habitual checking or updating by consumers is in danger of being stripped in this way. One example is the entertainment channel listings business. As electronic program guides find their way into remote controls and then into personal devices, the brand value of listings publications begins to melt away. Listings are, after all, a form of software specification designed to be run by humans. We read through the listings, sort the information in our minds, and output signals to the TV or VCR. Mobile commerce can erase the more mechanical parts of this process by allowing users to click on show titles and thereby program their entertainment services. Listings publications have to fight back by adding less data-oriented content and encouraging community activity amongst users, otherwise the concept of listings as a discrete and valuable service will disappear into the all-embracing functional glow of the mobile device. Listings players will, in fact, need to emulate news organisations in their transition to the mobile channel.

Banking's major contribution to consumer mobile commerce may prove not to be in demonstrating how a mechanical business can be exposed as such without major loss of brand value, but in establishing a ready market for other services. Banks are keen to promote cell phone-based banking services, often giving away WAP devices to customers who sign up for the service. In so doing, they help to place mobile commerce devices in the consumer market while providing a mobile commerce service to educate and habituate users. Part of the banks' reasoning in priming the market is that if the banking sector is moving to mobile commerce, then each player must move fast to hold onto its existing customers and attract any strays from its competitors during the migration.

Another, more long-term, consideration is the banks' claim on subsequent mobile commerce revenues in a primed market. As mobile commerce transactions increase in volume and value, the incumbent bank in the consumer's palm stands to control at least a share in those revenues. While low-value transactions may be managed by network operators via their billing systems, bigger ticket items will require bank credit. Equally, transactions outside the direct mobile commerce space will also be impacted by the availability of mobile commerce services. For example, a consumer might buy a vehicle at a physical dealership, but secure finance for the purchase using his mobile device. When such an opportunity arises, the customer's bank is positioned to be the default lender. In this sense, being an unnoticed and undifferentiated part of the individual's mobile commerce environment is an advantage to the bank rather than a disadvantage. Why call attention to the fact that there are alternative supplies of credit just at the moment the customer is set to commit? If a bank can become a customer's "money button" for all financing opportunities, then the conversion of the bank from institution to machine is a benefit of the transition to the mobile channel rather than a drawback.

The fight for ownership of the money button will be especially keen given the mutability of the meaning of "money" in the mobile commerce era. Small transactions with remote suppliers will be effected via the network operator's billing procedure, while person-to-person transactions can use various forms of electronic currency. Banks will be able to pump electronic value to users' devices, making money more like a form of energy than a system of physical exchange. With the majority of payments becoming electronic payments actioned by individuals with mobile devices, the bank's role will increasingly be that of credit supplier. Banks will use mobile commerce to compete for ownership of consumers' borrowing behaviour. The business of banking has always been lending, with transacting and accounting being means to the end.

If we shift our viewpoint to that of an eager lender rather than a reluctant accountant, the mobile commerce landscape begins to look very attractive. In one sense, life is a series of opportunities to get into debt; those Victorian painters of morality parables knew to put the money-lending booths on the same path to hell as the dancehalls and booze joints. The emerging caricature mobile commerce lifestyle, associated with youthful, metropolitan consumers with high disposable income and few ties, is more closely allied to the concept of easy money than the technology of wireless transmission. With the money button acting as an ever-present temptation, consumers will at least be exposed to many more opportunities to consider borrowing money. Operators of mobile commerce banking services will benefit not just from increased rates of semiautomatic borrowing, but also from live insight into the market in which the individual consumer is acting. For example, a bank could provide a credit modelling function allowing the user to input any sum and select from a range of payment plans. Any use that the customer makes of this function adds to the bank's picture of her preferences and behaviours. If the bank is able to aggregate the data input to the credit modeller with the time and place of the interaction, then its picture grows in depth. If the modelling interaction is performed as a call-out from a Web page or text message owned or tracked by the bank, then the picture becomes very accurate. A bank, together with other commerce partners, will be able to make purchase offers to customers and observe not only whether they show interest, but also how much interest they are prepared to pay – in money. A loan calculator, provided as part of the basic mobile commerce banking service, becomes a passive intelligence-gathering device.

The bank can improve its knowledge of the customer further by providing modelling tools for savings as well as borrowings. A retirement-planning calculator, for example, could show the customer how unused balances in a personal account could be redirected into a pension fund, with any associated tax benefits and a forecast for the enhanced value of the pension vehicle at her retirement date.

The central role of money in consumers' lives gives banks the opportunity to generate personalised offers relevant to the business of the moment. By shifting our attention away from the utility business of performing transactions, we can see that mobile commerce allows banks to maximise the volume of opportunities for lending and saving. Each moment of each user's life becomes a niche in which a bank can propose an offer. Smart banks will do this unobtrusively, through the provision of modelling tools that propose and illustrate lending and saving proposals with accuracy, clarity and actionability. They will move rapidly away from the prevailing broad-brush marketing theories of life stages, whereby events such as graduation or marriage trigger offers to individuals. *Life moments* will flood the banker's marketing agenda, with the customer's every step converted into a potential financial turning point.

Stock Trading: Hand-Holdings

Mobile stock trading is perceived by most observers as the hottest space in mobile commerce. A high-visibility application in a broad, technology-friendly market, stock trading is highly geared to mobile, time-based decision-making. Fidelity Investments' ad copy for its Powerstreet service for the Palm VII says it all: "What if opportunity knocks and you're not home?"[8]

Stock trading has become a truly mass market phenomenon during the latter part of the 1990s. Much of the growth in interest in owning and trading equities derives from the growth of the Internet technology and e-commerce sectors. At the same time, the Net itself has made

---

8. Magazine campaign, June 2000.

the process of trading cheaper and more convenient for private investors. Online trading quickly grew to represent the largest source of trading volume for the leading brokers between 1997 and 1999 and propelled the dedicated Internet brokerage companies to the forefront of the industry. By the first quarter of 2000, trading via the Net accounted for 38 percent of all trades executed on the New York Stock Exchange and Nasdaq, 23 percent more than in previous quarter.[9]

Mobile stock trading has two main components. The first is the ability for investors to check the value of their portfolios and the second is the ability to execute trades.

In existing implementations, the valuation capability depends on the customer using the fixed e-commerce channel to register as a user and open an account. Valuation then becomes an add-on feature of online stock trading, whereby prices can be applied to stock symbols held within a portfolio and efficiently sent to a cell phone, PDA, or pager device. Alerts follow on naturally as a service, since it is straightforward to create a routine at the server side that will watch selected stocks and broadcast short messages to holders of the stocks. The data involved is compact, unambiguous, timely, and relevant.

The ability to execute trades is more challenging. This is not because it is a complex function: the data involved in a trade transaction are simple, and most of the data is provided by the broker rather than the user. The challenge lies in the security dimension, specifically the area of authentication. Does an incoming instruction emanate from the customer it claims to represent? Mechanisms to establish passwords via the fixed e-commerce channel alleviate this problem, though they need to be buttressed by an explicitly accepted agreement of liability between the two parties. We examine the issue of security in more depth in Chapter 3, along with forthcoming technology solutions.

Mobile stock trading has been available for some time. Fidelity Investments, for example, introduced the InstantBroker technology behind Powerstreet in January 1999. InstantBroker enables stock-

---

9. Mark A. Mowrey, "Battle of the Brokers", *TheStandard.com*, 15 May 2000.

trading capabilities on Palm's wireless VII model and also via Sprint PCS Wireless Web and the RIM 950 two-way pager. By June 2000, some 65,000 Fidelity customers had registered for the service, representing around 2 percent of the customer base. Competing broker Charles Schwab introduced a wireless portfolio-checking service for the Palm platform in October 1999, adding alert and trading capabilities in June 2000, with extensions to mobile phone and pager platforms following soon after.[10]

Does the small percentage of uptake experienced by Fidelity justify the industry's expansion of wireless services? Brokerage firms are relying on two effects to grow the market: the continued spread of mobile devices into the general population, and the mobile user's greater propensity to trade.

As we have seen, the plans of device manufacturers and mobile network operators guarantee that the consumer market will be flooded with mobile commerce enabled devices in the period up to 2003. Forecasts for the number of devices vary by analyst, and true rollout will be affected by regional variations and by manufacturing logistics. Inability to meet market demand for devices continues to frustrate timetables for mobile commerce service developers, with the slow emergence of WAP phones in early 2000 followed by launch delays for Bluetooth equipment. Although device supply continues to be a problem, stock trading customers are highly motivated to acquire the necessary technology. Many are already PDA users, making established platforms such as the Palm series an ideal route to mobile services. The wireless Palm VII and the OmniSky wireless service for the Palm V make many customers mobile commerce-ready, whereas the emergence of low-cost Palm clones such as the Handspring Visor makes the move to wireless trading an incremental cost for dedicated online users.

The second important source of potential growth for mobile stock trading services lies in the usage patterns of mobile commerce users. Experience at Fimatex, the first broker to offer trading on the Palm

---

10. Elisa Batista, "Taking stock of wireless trading", *Wired News*, 14 June 2000.

platform, suggests that mobile users tend to make more trades than users of other channels: an average of 13 per month.[11] Fidelity offered new customers of Powerstreet free trading for three months, up to a limit of ten trades. Will Fidelity customers match the appetite of their European counterparts? If so, customers will start to make charged trades during their second month of service. Stock-trading services may choose to offer a certain number of trades bundled in a monthly subscription fee in order to tempt new users and stimulate trading activity amongst all users. Fimatex's high level of mobile trades could reflect a customer base already skewed toward high-volume trading. Bundled trades would help to educate a broader base of users.

The market for related information services will grow as mobile commerce offers the customer more opportunities to trade stocks. News, research, and tips will be offered by a wide range of suppliers in the mobile channel. The initial model for stock-trading services has the customer create her profile on a fixed Web site and then check and trade that portfolio subsequently via the mobile channel. As transaction frequency grows, customers will want to take full control over all their investments from the mobile device. While the Web is a better medium for in-depth research than mobile devices, the real-time nature of securities markets forces mobile customers to rely on their devices for news and background. Financial information services that tailor content deftly for the mobile channel will become influential. Successful financial media companies such as CNBC have already integrated themselves into the lifestyles of private investors, and should transition well to mobile commerce. Audio channels dedicated to market coverage will be a major source of revitalisation in the talk radio industry.

Established financial media brands will find their biggest source of competition in the mobile stock-trading population itself. For customers arriving in the mobile stock-trading space from the cell phone route – the likely majority in a mature market – the person-to-person

---

11. Catherine Tillotson, "Wired for sound investments", *Internet World*, June 2000. Fimatex is a service of French bank Société Générale.

character of the mobile lifestyle will encourage herd behaviour amongst users. Many consumers will ignore branded financial news in favour of tips from people in their social groups. The "buddies" class of service that we identify today with younger age groups will evolve to incorporate a wider number of group concerns as its users age. "Buddies" services allow users to create consensus and anoint leaders: these capabilities transfer well to players in financial markets.

At the same time, services allowing consumers to bypass branded content channels will further empower individual investors. Take the example of Napster, the MP3 music-sharing software launched on the Net in 1999. Napster and its subsequent imitators allow users to see music files on each other's machines, and to upload and download those files to each other. Napster acts as a real-time exchange, whose mediation role is only realised in its database of user registrations.[12] Facilities like Napster threaten portal players, whose value to the user is their ability to corral links to relevant information. But Napster-like services let users rapidly zero in on particular types of resources and their value. In the case of music, the resource value of a track is its size and estimated download time. The Napster user can then action the ownership of a selected resource.

The Napster model can also be applied to mobile stock trading, as shown in Figure 2-6. Users could register for a service that would allow them to see each other's portfolios and examine their performance. They could then choose to imitate target portfolios or even shadow the trading activities of an individual trader. A user could set his trading service to alert him of the actions of a favoured portfolio holder whose track record he admires. Secondary services identifying virtual trader teams would create a new kind of tracker fund – one based on the performance of community stars rather than the validation of branded media channels. By connecting players in a community of actors, mobile commerce will enhance the financial markets, widening not just access to research and trading functions but also to leadership.

---

12. Other peer-to-peer technologies such as Gnutella do not use central servers for any purpose, thus further erasing the mediator role.

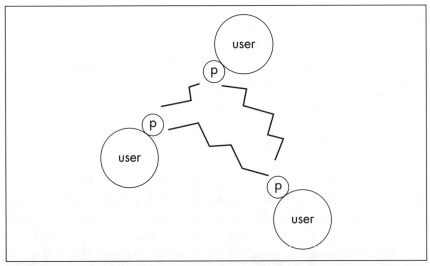

FIGURE 2-6. Mobile commerce users share trading strategies in portfolio rings.

The practice of portfolio peeking will naturally inspire an accompanying level of fraud, with particular stocks being pushed via fake portfolios. Community assessment schemes will be launched to check the activities of fraudsters, much as eBay's user ratings system allows auction customers to check the probity of sellers. Attempts to manipulate markets are nothing new, but the hugely increased scope of financial markets in the mobile commerce era will mean that many more people will be tempted to sin, and larger numbers of consumers will fall victim to fraud. The widened market will also create other social problems, as more people start to play the financial markets, and at a younger age. The ability to make intra-day trades cheaply and conveniently already exists with the fixed Web; mobile commerce introduces an extra dimension of secrecy, since people can use mobile services quite unobtrusively. Short-term financing to support mobile day traders will target vulnerable users. Consumers trained to gamble on state lotteries will transfer their attention to the mobile casino of the stock markets.

Mobile stock trading is an inevitable move for established brokerage companies, and a potential lifeline for retail banks looking to cement real-time relationships with customers. Competition amongst stock trading firms will be fierce. They will also need to fight the flow of information and disinformation produced by the mobile population itself, since adding reliable intelligence to the market is one way that firms can prevent their brands being devalued and their services being commoditised into simple, undifferentiated transactions. Building and defending a mobile stock trading brand will be a major challenge. Carpet-bomb advertising of the kind we have seen in fixed B2C e-commerce will be less effective in the face of more motivating hot-tip alerts and offers of discounts on commission. The ability to suggest that a particular brand's customers are more successful than those of rivals, while at the same time not falling foul of industry codes of practice and advertising standards, will be key to brand builders. Marketing aimed at prompting customers to switch brands will consume much of the attention of brokerage firms.

For players who want to get involved with the exploding mobile stock-trading business but who are not brokerage firms, the opportunities for building trader communities are clear. As well as providing chat areas and Napster-style portfolio-sharing facilities, companies may also create "dream team" properties by signing up star traders. The convergence of information, entertainment, and transaction creates a new world of media opportunities, particularly around live narrowcasting.

At a more general level, mass market mobile stock trading will generate the characteristics of entirely novel classes of business. If we genericise mobile stock trading, we can see service opportunities exist wherever three criteria are met. The first criterion is the service be concerned with personal ownership of a bundle of resources whose composition can be changed at any time. The second criterion is the resources are affected in some significant way by real-world events for which credible information streams exist. Finally, there must be an addictive quality to the owner's active management of the resource set. These criteria fit mobile stock trading, but they would also fit Tamogatchi farm management. Wherever groups of customers maintain holdings in a class of items, conditions exist for a live market.

News and Sports: Addicted to Events

The traditional voice-based cell phone is, amongst other things, a news device. Consumers who carry cell phones make themselves available to inbound news messages from their personal contacts. In Europe, where calling parties pay charges to cell phones, junk calls are rare. This means that users rarely resent their phones ringing, knowing that the call is almost certainly meant for them and from someone they care about. Carrying a phone is a natural way of staying in the social swim.

News, in the more general media sense of the word, is a form of social glue. News connects us with the life of the world around us, making us participants in the unfolding story of our age. Although elements of the news are outwardly disturbing – in that the news focuses on violence, misfortune, and deceit – the overall effect of the information stream is one of comfort. We recognise themes in the news we consume and are thereby reminded of our fears and beliefs. The news creates an intellectual and emotional agenda for society, an agenda that is continually renewed yet constantly recognisable. To deny knowledge of mainstream current events is to put oneself beyond the pale. The individual citizen may be powerless in the face of events, but ignorance of events is not a socially acceptable response. Communities need news to tell them who they are.

The role of news in our lives is an essential consideration for organisations offering mobile commerce news services. The mobile channel offers a direct, live, and personal connection to users superior to every pre-existing channel. Consumers dip into rolling news channels on TV and radio as and when they have the opportunity, whereas mobile commerce makes every moment an opportunity for information access and interaction. In other words, rolling news shifts from being a niche application to a broad service. The task of setting the news agenda acquires greater momentum as the news shifts from being "on the hour" to *of the moment*.

While mobile commerce causes the renewal cycle for news generation to accelerate, mobile commerce also challenges existing presentation modes for news. How should news items be addressed to nonsedentary users? How does a mobile user's quality of attention differ from that of a fixed user? How should levels of depth be treated and complex stories conveyed to users with differing levels of interest, patience, and background knowledge? These issues are beginning to be tested in mobile commerce news services for cell phones and PDAs.

The first emerging lesson of mobile commerce news is that brand has a leading role to play. A valuable news brand imbues a mobile commerce news service with credibility, making the transition to the mobile channel relatively easy for established news media players. This is not to say that new brands are barred from the mobile commerce field. The effectiveness of a news service in the mobile channel will have greater value in the long term than initial brand loyalty derived from traditional channels. Whether a news brand is well established or novel, the brand creates a *format* essential to success in the mobile channel.

Format is crucial to mobile commerce news services because the mobile channel is stingy with contextual information. Users require highly intuitive access to core content, and will not (or can not) negotiate complex site structures. Users of the earliest WAP services are essentially restricted to short scrolling sections of text, and although simple links can be navigated, site designers are unable to produce any kind of visually efficient navigation device such as a button bar or tabbed notebook. PDA users enjoy more sophisticated user interfaces, with browsers such as Microsoft's Pocket Internet Explorer interpreting standard Web pages with acceptable fidelity, and Palm's Web-clipping technology performing a similar function. Yet even when equipped with a reasonably sophisticated handheld version of the fixed Web experience, mobile commerce users are unlikely to navigate complex sites to find the content they seek. Display size is an obvious factor in users' unwillingness to pick and choose in complex menus, but usage context is also influential. Accessing news on the move is a convenience offer: fast food, not cookery.

A mobile commerce news service has to communicate its offer rapidly and transparently. The easiest way to achieve this effect is to present headlines as quickly and clearly as possible. The current headlines then form the menu, with each being a link to fuller stories. However, headlines alone do not create a format. The user has to decode the headline style in order to understand what the story is about and how it is being treated by the news supplier. This matter can trip established news brands in their transition to the mobile channel.

Compare the Web-clipping versions of the *New York Times* and the [British] *Guardian*. PDA users can access a mass of up-to-date content from both sources. Both services use headlines adapted from their paper products; and here's where the first hiccup occurs. The *Times* uses headlines that are immediately meaningful, written with the crisp clarity for which it is famous. Each *Times* headline is accompanied by a short lead-in text to further explain the underlying story. The *Times* user can quickly absorb the paper's agenda and decide which items she wants to pursue. The *Guardian* has also transferred its trademark headline style to the mobile channel. But in this case, established excellence fails to be a virtue. The *Guardian*'s headlines – shorn of full-story text, unaided by the photos that might appear in the print version and not supported by lead-in text – are often simply cryptic. Quirky story titles chosen to attract attention in the print version of the paper have the opposite effect when used in a stark list on a mobile device's window.

The suitability of the *Times*' headlines for the mobile channel is a bonus for the organisation, whereas the *Guardian*'s established style transitions poorly. Both titles have sophisticated structures for their paper offerings, with separately styled sections and regular features. The *Guardian* ships most of this structure into its Web-clipping version, whereas the *Times* restricts its selection to *Business, Technology, Book Reviews,* and *Page One Plus*. While limited, the *Times*' selection is coherent and simple. The *Guardian* offers much more content, but the user has to be familiar with the organisation of the print version to use it effectively. Even the loyal reader of the print *Guardian*, who will know that the menu item *G2* refers to the paper's second section, will have a hard time recognising the item in G2 headlined by a simple number is, in fact, the daily installment of *Passnotes*, the paper's jokey question-and-answer guide to a current live topic. Note that even if *Passnotes* were used as the headline rather than the serial number, the user would still have little idea of the feature's content. Habitual readers of the print version may recognise the feature by its distinctive layout and its position in the paper's physical running order and may not even know the official title of the series.

The flaws in the *Guardian*'s early mobile commerce services show once again that mobile commerce is not a simple matter of directing existing content to a novel platform. The difficulties with using the *Guardian*'s print-based format in the mobile channel in comparison to the efficiency of using the *New York Times* also suggests that news organisations need to be ruthless in distinguishing between news and entertainment services. The *Guardian* seems to have taken the view that its online activities should serve to expand the associations of its core brand rather than limit them: its Web and mobile commerce activities are branded using the *Guardian Unlimited* name and logo. The paper sees itself as more than a supplier of news, positioning itself as a daily component of a user's lifestyle. While this is broadly laudable, in the case of content delivery to mobile devices, the strategy is questionable. The key issue is bandwidth – not wireless bandwidth but consumer bandwidth. The user's ability to construct a mental world consonant with the *Guardian*'s input differs between usage contexts. Breakfast-time consumption of a broadsheet is somewhat leisurely and ritualistic, whereas on-the-go consumption involves pressured or stolen time and competing distractions.

Mobile commerce news services clearly benefit from legible and robust formats. Such news services also win when they prioritise memorable nuggets of information over complex presentations of information. Mobile users are looking for facts and opinions to use in the combat of daily life. They seek information to deploy in their work and conversations. Access to in-depth articles allows users to learn more about headline items, so the presence of links to full stories provides utility and also a level of comfort: a user may never dig deeper into a particular subject, but the fact that he *can* may make him more confident about adopting the news item in his current mental model.

Our characterisation of mobile commerce news services as delivery mechanisms for rapid "fixes" may seem bleak in tone and restrictive in business opportunity. The nuggets model of news delivery chimes with the advocacy of those developing services for low-bandwidth networks. As such, news is a flashpoint for players on either side of mobile commerce's great divide: the gulf between those who see mobile commerce as a simple extension of fixed e-commerce awaiting higher-bandwidth networks and better mobile devices and those who regard mobile commerce as a new species of business. We argue throughout this book that mobile commerce *is* different than fixed e-commerce, but our reasons centre on user desires, behaviours, and goals rather than technology constraints. In backing the nuggets model of news, we do not mean to suggest that the future of mobile commerce services eschews ambiguity, complexity, or diversity. News-based commentary, opinion, and interaction services will emerge in the neighbourhood of pure news-delivery services and offer content and communication opportunities to complement those of other channels. News – in this larger sense – has the potential to create new kinds of relationships with consumers, creating virtual spaces where users can discuss news topics, argue political points, and help shape the developing agenda.

Branded news services will therefore develop as competitors to overt mobile portals. Players who brand themselves explicitly as portals tend to position their lifestyle relevance around personal services such as recommendations and online shopping, with news a component of the offering. News brands can exploit the greater intellectual value and emotional affinity of their content to capture customer attention, adding typical portal components as peripheral benefits of their services. News services build loyalty through constant, reliable, and authoritative communication on issues that matter most to their users, such as politics, money, war, health, and sports. Their role as trusted messengers makes them successful conduits of commerce offers. Links to paid-for services will take over from static advertising's role in funding news supply for the mobile channel.

As news services expand their offers, they will need to protect the structural integrity of their core services. Without tight focus on the generation of solid nuggets, mobile commerce news services run the risk of degenerating into diffuse portal offerings reliant on the brand values of their continuing traditional media counterparts. Players must recognise and organise around two parallel principles: the *event stream* and the *community*.

The event stream is the core competency of any news organisation and forms a refined and standardised train of stories derived from raw inputs. Journalists write the first version of history; but for our purposes they also create the main information products of the online moment. Locating, defining, and packaging events is a skill set that extends to all areas of human interest. And everything that humans do is of human interest. Perhaps the most extreme form of news production is that associated with sports. Modern sports are wonderfully efficient at converting the physical and mental talents of a few into abstract data for the masses. We participate in sports through the consumption of numbers: the decimal-point science of batting averages, the broken-clock readings of tennis, the bird-language of golf. The progress of an event is as enthralling, if not more so, than its eventual outcome. Sports.com measured hit rates of some 100,000 per day on its WAP service during the Euro2000 soccer and Wimbledon tennis tournaments of Summer 2000[13] as fans kept up with the action.

Of course, sports fans consume more than simple data relating to ongoing events. They want to see actual games, hear commentary on tactics and incidents, replay key moments, and converse with other fans. These functions are served well by complementary platforms. The mobile channel adds the element of live scores, the feeling of being involved in an unfolding drama. Sports fans will continue to watch games on TV, read match analyses in newspapers, and search Web sites for statistics. Media brands that can cover all these platforms will capture the attention and revenues of fans for whom an interest in sports is a part of every waking moment. The mobile commerce component is the linchpin in any cross-platform sports media play. Mobile devices offer instant access to the action, regardless of the user's location. Mobile commerce sports services can be readily integrated with other services, so that sports news – like mainstream news or financial prices – can be consumed discretely and almost intravenously throughout the day.

---

13. John Cassy, "Net service is a winner for Wimbledon", *The Guardian*, 20 July 2000.

If event streams represent the processing of newsfeeds into news-drips, *community* is concerned with fostering a more sociable dimension for mobile commerce news services. If the news is our shared minute-by-minute myth, then community services attempt to weld together each disparate mobile device into a common hearth. A news service generating nuggets from sports events can also offer parallel services to the mobile commerce user that augment the user's experience and challenge (or cannibalise) offerings on other platforms. For example, the baseball-card size of the contemporary PDA makes the device an ideal conveyor of player photos, biographies, and statistics. Game-playing capabilities built into mobile devices allow electronic versions of games to be played by users, alone or with other players, so that users can play their own versions of tournaments in parallel with real events. E-tickets for events, replica shirts, and video compilations make natural sales opportunities alongside the live event stream. Audio chat rooms represent one of the most compelling potential community services in the sports sector, with the added possibility that fans could join in with player conversations in virtual locker rooms. Virtual newsreaders will add personality to news sites: Ananova, a newsreader who surely goes to the same clubs as Lara Croft, moved from her creators, the Press Association, to mobile network operator Orange in July 2000.

Today's mobile commerce news services rely on print-based precursors and are rapidly becoming experts in the creation of textual news nuggets. A neglected direction for news services is audio. Most commentary on mobile commerce is fixated on textual channels, and in particular on the evolution from fixed Web-based services to mobile delivery. Even those who stress the primacy of the cell phone above other forms of mobile device in the development of the mobile commerce market rarely address the phone's remarkable synergy with broadcast radio. But consumers are highly unlikely to want to carry more than one mobile device with them and will expect their phone or PDA to play all kinds of audio content. As mobile devices disintegrate physically and disperse around the body to form wearable personal systems, the in-ear component will stream audio content from phone conversations, disk devices, solid state memory devices, and broadcast channel sources as well as IP (Internet Protocol) sources. Mobile, personalised news will enter the mobile population's bloodstream through the ear as well as the eye. The audio content company Audible already offers spoken-word versions of newspapers and magazines as well as audio books for playing on mobile devices. Mobile portals offering one-touch audio bulletins combining news headlines, sports, and weather reports will be able to use the screen component of the mobile device as a pure control device rather than a content tablet, radically simplifying the user interface.

Gambling: Chips for Everyone

Gambling offers one of the starkest contrasts between the United States and European mobile commerce environments, with European players taking a clear lead in establishing services, building business models, and proving technology.

The legality of online gambling in the United States is in dispute and the proposed Internet Gambling Prohibition Act is journeying through the legislative process. The version of the act introduced to the Senate in 2000 excludes fantasy sports, horse racing, and state lotteries, so even if the act becomes law, U.S. citizens will still be able to place online bets in these categories. In the meantime, the existing Wire Wager Act does not cover wireless services, leaving the way clear for mobile commerce gambling services to target cell phones and wireless PDAs.[14]

Outside the United States, online gambling is legal in around 60 countries.[15] Online gambling is highly profitable, with sites taking commissions of 25 percent and upwards on transactions.[16] Gambling services were amongst the first WAP services to become available in Europe, with Sweden's CasinoDomain amongst the first and the

---

14. For a full treatment of U.S. law relating to online gambling, see *Internet Gambling Regulation* by Michael E. Hammond of the University of Kentucky College of Law, 17 April 2000: http://www.geocities.com/mehamm0/netgambling.htm.
15. "Mobile gambling set to hit the jackpot", *Mobile Internet*, 24 April 2000.
16. Ibid.

United Kingdom's Bet247 service from Littlewoods[17] amongst the leading mainstream companies. The developers of CasinoDomain, Net Entertainment, clearly see the service as a lifestyle-integrated offer:

> "You can imagine that you play your favourite game on Casino-Domain, say blackjack, at home on Sunday evening," begins Douglas Roos, Net Entertainment's CEO. "On Monday during your lunch break you login and play some more. Then in the afternoon you are on your way to the airport but your taxi encounters traffic problems. Then you can play blackjack on your cell phone. You just login to CasinoDomain exactly the same way as you do on your computer."[18]

Gambling, especially of the repetitive casino variety, is often seen as a time-killing activity. Roos's scenario shows how mobile commerce gambling services rush to fill the voids caused by dead time in users' lives. That Las Vegas slot-hall dream state can be summoned to paint over the drab lost moments of the day like some spiritual screensaver until real life kicks in again. Mobile commerce again shows its genius for wringing productivity (of a kind) out of consumers.

This style of gambling exploits dead time in users' schedules, but is itself time-independent. Other types of gambling are keyed to real-world events, and so time becomes a critical dimension in their construction, delivery, and consumption. Customers of mobile commerce gambling services can place bets on races at any time, check the outcome of the race as it occurs, and collect their winnings (or lose their stake) as the winning line is reached. Customers also benefit from added discretion by using the mobile channel to bet. They no longer have to seek out betting shops: every place with network coverage becomes a de facto licensed gambling venue.

---

17. Susan Dennis, "UK – Littlewoods Leisure moves onto wireless web", Newsbytes, 16 March 2000: http://www.emarketer.com/enews/032000_ukgambling.html.
18. Chuck Greene, "Gambling goes wireless", WINNERonline.com, 5 January 2000: http://www.winneronline.com/articles/january2000/wap.htm.

Whatever the moral status of gambling, there is no doubt that gambling is remarkably well suited to the mobile commerce channel. The data involved in making bets is simple and unambiguous, with the bettor choosing a wager, noting the odds and staking an amount. Outcomes are processed by a simple match of bets collected against a real-world measurement. Betting therefore makes efficient use of bandwidth, as well as making relatively simple demands on business system developers.

Aside from its friendly systems characteristics, mobile commerce gambling targets a large customer base. Gambling aggregates the small stakes of individual consumers into large revenue streams. Gambling also aggregates consumers' dead time into lengthy trading sessions, making each customer of greater potential value than the typical mobile commerce shopping user, whose purchasing behaviour is more typically of the hit-and-run kind. State lotteries and charity prize contests make gambling respectable, and as consumers find themselves equipped with pocket access to convenient, small-stakes online gambling, betting is likely to increase amongst all consumer groups. Few consumers will see much difference between betting on the fortunes of a fantasy sports team and investing in a stock market portfolio. Gambling will sit alongside stock trading on the mobile commerce user's mental dial.

Games: Playing to Win

The online games business is sometimes confused with the gambling industry. Older people tend to assume that any game played using a machine involves gambling. With the arcade-game–trained generation increasingly in power around the world, this misunderstanding is beginning to fade, especially as console and pocket games now occupy prominent positions in the domestic scene. To most people, "gaming" evokes images of piloting characters through imaginary environments, meeting challenges, and avoiding threats. However in U.K. law, "gaming" is still often used as a synonym for "gambling"; and the business plans of some mobile games companies suggest wagering is indeed a close neighbour of the gaming domain. For our purposes here, we will assume mobile game services are designed to offer players pure entertainment values and that opportunities to win money are related to skill rather than luck.

Our familiarity with computer games makes it easy to see how mobile games can act as personal time killers. Many cell phones come equipped with a number of simple games to divert the owner in their free moments. Users of some Nokia cell phone models can play games of Snake with each other using their infrared ports. Despite their apparent lack of sophistication, such games prove highly addictive. As standard features on mobile devices, games represent added value to the device owner and may help determine which device a user buys.

Game developers are busily revisiting the arcade classics of the 1970s and 1980s and redeveloping them for mobile device platforms. The low memory requirements, crude graphics, and restricted user input of early computer games are ideally suited to the constrained circumstances of PDA and phone platforms. Games such as Asteroids and PacMan move gracefully to these new homes. These classics also exploit the nostalgic feelings of a key consumer generation: people who have grown up investing in new technologies. The Korean company ToySoft is one such developer, creating games that can be embedded in cell phones, including for example a version of Tetris.

While embedding games in mobile devices can generate revenues through licensing deals with device manufacturers, a game company's greater interests lie in ways of making playing activity generate ongoing revenues. The game developer may choose to create games that are folded into a general mobile service and that generate revenue for a mobile network operator or portal or to create games services that generate revenue directly for themselves. WAP provides a means for service developers to forge enduring, connected, relationships with players. The earliest forays into this business echo practices in the non-mobile world. Gameplay, for example, offers the WapPet:

> a little creature that lives on your mobile phone! Your creature will hatch soon after you register as a parent and from that moment on, you'll have to care for your WapPet's every need . . .

As the WapPet grows up, you can watch it perform a vast number of hilarious and heart-warming animated actions.[19]

The real prizes in the games domain will be found in mass-participation games. Multiuser competitive and role-playing games have the potential to generate massive amounts of traffic. The established leaders in this area are the console games companies Sega, Nintendo, and Sony, who have already reoriented their primary business development strategies around online multiuser gaming. These companies represent significant threats to mobile device manufacturers and games service developers alike as they use their powerful brands and loyal user bases to penetrate the mobile gaming market. Sony and DoCoMo announced a joint project to allow users to play PlayStation 2 games on i-mode phones from late 2000, well ahead of the planned arrival of i-mode's broadband 3G (Third Generation) mobile network.

Other players are responding to the threat of the established games giants by exploiting key market differences controlled by the mobile commerce industry, particularly location awareness. For example, mobile game company In-Fusio[20] has developed the WAP game Katch'em as a location-aware, multiuser "tribal" game. The same company has also introduced In Spirit, a multiuser role-playing game set in the future, playable by users from all around the world. By using features such as location awareness and building global coverage through alliances with mobile network operators in different territories, mobile games companies can create compelling offers that speak directly to mobile players' imaginations and disrupt the smooth transference of existing games brands into the mobile channel.

Datamonitor forecasts that by 2005, four out of every five cell phone users in the United States and Europe will be playing mobile games, forming a market worth $6 billion.[21] Mobile gaming, and multiuser gaming in particular, sits neatly within the vision of a

---

19. http://www.gameplay.com/.
20. http://www.in-fusio.com/.
21. "The future of wireless gaming", *Datamonitor*, September 2000.

mobile population that derives most of its information, entertainment, and sense of community from personal wireless devices. Gaming will be seen by users as a type of community interaction, alongside functions such as chat rooms and buddy-list messaging. Games provide roles and structure for interaction amongst strangers, and therefore also act as a means of building communities as well as diverting existing communities.

Game builders can clearly generate revenues by selling games to device manufacturers, licensing games to portals or mobile network operators, or by running their own game services. Other mobile commerce players need not miss out on the gaming bonanza. Combining games with other content offers nongames companies a way of building highly sticky mobile commerce services. Retail brands, for example, often rely on static content to communicate their values, but are anxious to add action and interactivity to their content wherever possible. This is why so many retail brand Web sites offer downloadable screensavers. A screensaver not only acts as an ad for the brand, turning the user's display into a temporary billboard; it also puts some measure of life into the brand. Games offer an efficient means of engaging with customers and establishing a living presence for the brand. Just as soap companies hitched their sales messages to dramatic serials in the early days of commercial radio, creating the soap opera genre, so consumer goods and services companies will sponsor mobile games. Consumer companies may underwrite prizes for multi-user games, switching part of their sponsorship budgets from spectator sports competitions to this new type of player-spectator game.

Shopping: The Evolution of One-Like-That

Shopping is the first thing that comes to mind when we think about e-commerce, but we have chosen to cover it last in this survey of mobile commerce services aimed at consumers. This is because consumer retail is, perhaps surprisingly, the most radical aspect of mobile commerce from the point of view of its effect on current practice. Shopping in the mobile channel has great potential to disrupt existing retail models, threatening the recently established orthodoxies of online selling as much as those of entrenched physical retailers. Mobile commerce brings three distinct forces into the foreground of the consumer retail arena: *recommendation, comparison,* and *impulse.* We will examine each of these forces in turn in this section. As suggested in Figure 2-7, two of the forces act to rationalise product complexity for the user, and the third empowers the user to target purchases with great accuracy and instinctiveness.

Recommendation is a potent factor in most purchase decisions. The personal recommendation of products and services by friends and family reduces customers' perception of risk. A customer may follow a personal recommendation because he values the judgment of the recommender, having profited from following her advice in the past or experienced some other evidence of her success in purchasing. Customers who follow personal recommendations also benefit from reducing their emotional risk. If each purchase decision is a potential error, then a poor outcome following a decision modelled on that of an admired individual is less shameful than one made individually.

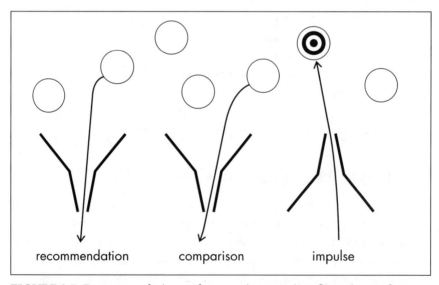

FIGURE 2-7. Recommendation and comparison services filter the product population, whereas impulse services apply point-and-click behaviour to the user's total environment.

Observers will be sympathetic rather than scathing when our purchased product falls apart in our hands.

The emotive power of personal recommendation is routinely extended to celebrities and to brands. Well-known faces are recruited to endorse products and services, lending their one-of-the-family status to the items they endorse. Whatever the degree of irony deployed in such celebrity campaigns, a celebrity's involvement injects an offer with the values he represents in the media. Would William Shatner agree to front a company that James T. Kirk wouldn't trust with his life? The thought is unformed, unarticulated in the mind of the consumer, but potent – possibly all the more potent for its inchoate nature.

Brands stand proxy to human personalities, encapsulating human values about companies, products, and services and communicating them economically. Some brands can be stretched to cast recommendation power over wide ranges of goods and services, while others specialise in niche endorsement. Virgin is a good example of a flexible and elastic brand, while Coke is a key example of a brand that sticks to a niche. The first type of brand is used to make recommendations. The attachment of the Virgin brand to a service suggests that the service will be innovative, good value, and non-stuffy.

Recommendation is a notable force in the building of online propositions. Consider properties such as Hotmail (a free Web-based e-mail service that was eventually absorbed by Microsoft) and Google (a search engine that prioritises results according to the number of links pointing to each of them). Hotmail grew its user base by inserting a linked ad to the service in every e-mail sent out by its users, making e-mail a viral carrier of its marketing message. Google grew through word of mouse as users told each other about it, but also through a relatively generous introductory affiliate program, whereby Web site owners could display a search box and earn three cents for each query submitted to Google.

These are automated recommendations: recommendations stitched into the fabric of e-mails and Web pages. The more explicit, and more human, dimension to online recommendations appears in those sites dedicated to finding and promoting the best products and services in a category. The mainstream granddaddy of them all is Amazon, which makes general recommendations for books (and other products) on its category home pages, and personal recommendations based on the customer's buying history. Mobile commerce is generating its own analog of these services. They tend to be stripped-down and ultra-focused.

The service 10Best.com illustrates how recommendation services can migrate to the mobile channel and maintain a harmonious relationship with their fixed e-commerce sites. It does what its name suggests: the service selects the ten best offers in a range of categories, organised by city. The categories range from *Dining* and *Lodging* through to *Sight Seeing* and *Personal Services* via subcategories of *Shopping* such as *Men, Women, Antiques,* and *Gift Shops*. Choosing a city on the fixed Web site leads the user to a home page for that city, complete with four-day weather forecast, random facts about the city, pictorial views of the city, a text backgrounder, and links to the recommendation categories.

The mobile commerce versions of 10Best.com take the base concept and hone it for mobile devices. The user can create an AvantGo channel, allowing the service to be delivered on her PDA. She can access the recommendations about cities she has selected on the fixed Web site, as well as add new cities. Information for newly chosen cities appears on the device on the next synchronization. The details of each 10Best-listed item are excellently matched to the PDA's display constraints, matching to-the-point brevity with attractive hooks, as in this excerpted entry for antiques store Curio-a-Go-Go in Columbus, Ohio:

> A delightful assortment of leather furniture, antiques, gift ideas, curiosities, tempting bath indulgences, and random beautiful and interesting items. Look for the dangling red monkey on the awning and watch out for the owner's cat, who enjoys reclining among the unique inventory.[22]

Here the customer has a recommended destination in her hand, together with its address and the quirky details that might make up

---

22. 10Best.com, 28 June 2000.

her mind to visit. The recommendation service is out in the world with the user, positioning its influence as near as possible to the point where a purchase decision will be made.

The AvantGo service is an ideal way of delivering this kind of information to organised travellers. 10Best.com also has a WAP version of its service,[23] offering a pared-down experience that does not rely on the customer being a user of the fixed Web site. Anyone with a WAP-enabled phone can access recommendations for a city without having any kind of long-term relationship with 10Best.com.

How does 10Best.com ensure its own position in the ten best lists of customers? The company's name propels it to the top of search engine result sets, and gives it a pole position in a PDA user's alphabetically organised AvantGo home page. Ultimately, the quality of the service's recommendations, its coverage of cities around the world, and the freshness of its content must act as magnets for repeat visits.

Services like 10Best.com help customers narrow their shopping searches and provide a level of comfort as to the quality of the resulting narrowed shopping space. MySimon is a company that goes beyond the narrowing effect of recommendations to the pinpoint accuracy of *comparison* shopping. MySimon To Go, the company's mobile commerce offering, lets customers compare products and prices from online and offline stores, wherever they happen to be – even within a physical store. While 10Best.com augments and simplifies the shopper's task, MySimon To Go arms the shopper with price intelligence and bargaining power.

Initially available for wireless Palm devices, and subsequently ported to WAP, MySimon To Go is a true online shopping application. The service launched with coverage of 500 products in fifteen categories, compared to the 170 categories and ever-expanding mass of products covered on the fixed Web site.[24] The user selects a product

---

23. http://wap.10best.com/.
24. "New game: MySimon Says", *Context Magazine*, November 1999: http://www.contextmag.com/setFrameRedirect.asp?src=/archives/199911/Virtual-Horizons.asp.

from the service's menu, and MySimon scours the Web for prices. Competitor IQOrder, launched in mid-2000, operates across a range of mobile devices including cell phones. Mobile phone usage gave IQOrders CEO Michael Bates the idea for his company's service. Shopping for a computer monitor, he called a colleague from the store and asked him to run a search on the Web for the product he was considering. His colleague found a site offering the same monitor for $100 less, so Bates left the store.[25]

Leveraging the customer's presence in a physical store as the basis for completion of an online transaction with him is the chief aim of comparison shopping services. These services allow customers to "browse in the physical world, then buy in the virtual world".[26] Physical stores, malls, and entire cities become reference libraries for products, freely open to a browsing population who may find inspiration there, but complete their purchase elsewhere. The U.K. company Scan.com offers a service whereby cell phone users can send the company a text message containing the barcode identifier of a product, and receive a set of offers complete with prices and delivery lead time. Users registered with the service can then accept any of the deals by entering their PIN number. BarPoint.com offers the same kind of service in the United States and delivers offers via cell phone, Palm, two-way pager – and a device with a built-in barcode scanner. BarPoint added the PocketPC platform to its offering in the fall of 2000. Info-Space and E-Compare also compete in the comparison services space.

Comparison services are attractive to consumers because they empower them with real-time price information that can be used to

---

25. Chris O'Brien, "Companies weave wireless Web, try to make a case for signing on", *San Jose Mercury News*, 5 March 2000.
26. Adam B. Brody and Edward J. Gottsman, "Pocket BargainFinder: A handheld device for augmented commerce," in *Proceedings of the International Symposium on Handheld and Ubiquitous Computing (HUC '99)*. Brody and Gottsman are with the Center for Strategic Technology Research (CSTaR) of Andersen Consulting, whose original BargainFinder project of 1995 heralded the emergence of online shopping robots.

avoid bad deals or negotiate better ones. Their value in the shopping process derives from their ability to make the user a virtual member of a well-informed group. The logical next step for such services is to act as organisers of buying clubs. We can imagine a mobile commerce service creating a virtual union amongst a store's visitors as each browsing shopper learns of better deals on the store's merchandise. The retail partners of the comparison shopping services could negotiate prices for aggregated groups of mobile shoppers, arrange nearby delivery – and dispatch e-tickets granting the buyers free coffee in the store's café.

There is something wrong with this subversive scenario, despite its attractive glow. First, why should brick-and-mortar stores tolerate this kind of invasive competition? Second, how many retailers – in whatever channel – can allow their products to be sold on price alone before margins become unsustainable?

To answer the first question, there is little doubt that development in the retail sector is leading rapidly to erasure of the distinction between traditional, physical retail, and e-commerce. Established retailers have extended their businesses to the online channel, whereas Net retailers have linked up with physical players. In time, every physical store owner will have a complementary online offering, either as an own-branded site or, for smaller players, within a portal. Offers in physical stores and e-commerce sites may be equalised to ensure that a price in a physical store is at least not beaten by the same company's online service. On the other hand a store may choose to reduce a price in a physical store, in order to avoid packing and distribution costs, and to encourage the customer to start filling his basket. A store could also choose to raise the store price above the online price in order to place a value on immediate availability of the item.

As comparison shopping services become popular, retailers will use the same services to monitor all their in-store prices for competitiveness. Electronic shelf labels would enable retailers to change prices in real time to respond to the competition. Checkout systems could be programmed to ring up the best price allocated to an item in the previous half hour. This would neutralise the effect of the comparison shopping services within the store.

Physical stores can also take the initiative in the comparison wars by taking the responsibility to arm customers with mobile shopping devices in the store. A customer entering a store could be issued with a handheld wireless device to take around with him, accessing product information about the items on the shelves and even acting as a mobile self-checkout. Leading U.K. supermarket Tesco introduced the Scan-Magic device for its Web-based shopping service as early as the spring of 1999. This device is a modified Palm PDA incorporating a barcode scanner. Customers can use it to add products to their shopping list by scanning product packages or a printed catalog of barcodes.[27]

Smart retailers will emulate banks in giving their customers full-function mobile devices with store-branded home pages – devices that are theirs to keep and use beyond the store. We can imagine a branded retail device that lives in the kitchen for much of its life, sharing seat space in the family car on trips to the store, and attaching itself to the handle of a shopping cart while the family shops. Customers will be able to order products at home, on the way to the store, and as they walk around the store. The journey to the store then centralises the fulfilment role of the physical location, with the processes of checking prices and paying for products neatly integrated into the customer experience.

Physical stores will continue to stress the nonprice elements of their offers in order to distinguish themselves from pure online rivals and mobile commerce comparison shopping services. Stores become more like entertainment destinations than fulfilment nodes as greater floor space is devoted to product demonstrations, themed multimedia events, live action shows, and game areas. Some retail spaces may explicitly convert from stores that display goods to exhibitors who also sell goods, charging an entry fee to browsers. Convenient fulfilment will remain a strong motivation for customers to continue to patronise "real" stores, despite possible price disadvantages.

Fulfilment of the customer's order is the primary reason why comparison shopping will not eradicate physical stores. In everyday lan-

---

27. *The Guardian*, 22 April 1999.

guage, a "store" is where something is kept, whereas a "site" is often a blank space where, one day, an artist's impression will be realised. When we go to a physical store, we are likely to walk away with something, even if our purchase is not exactly what we were looking for. IQOrder's Michael Bates traded productive working time for $100 when he walked away from that expensive monitor.

Gratification is delayed on the Web, although instant-delivery companies such as Urbanfetch and Kozmo.com reduce the disconnect between order and fulfilment, at least for metro area residents. A mobile population is by its nature difficult to ship to. A mobile commerce service provider may allow users to shop on the move and promise to deliver at a convenient time; yet the same company is part of a movement educating consumers to disregard time planning. Impulse, the great missing component of the fixed e-commerce experience, is only partly served by comparison shopping services.

Recommendation and comparison shopping services are clearly mobile commerce forces which escalate the arms race between shoppers and retailers. Retailers can manage their positioning in recommendation services by building alliances with such services, much as they must do with mobile portals. As we have seen, there is a range of strategies for competing with and neutralising the effects of comparison shopping services. Mobile commerce's encouragement of impulse behaviour is a greater challenge to retailers. The consumer's ability to buy anything, any time, anywhere, will lead to further investment in supply chain systems as retailers rise to the challenge. The key to a retailer's success will not necessarily lie in his ownership of every system component in an efficient supply chain, but in his ability confidently to make promises concerning delivery.

If, for example, a customer buys an appliance she has examined in a store display, she may have several options for fulfilment. The first would be to take a boxed appliance from an open shelf and tote it to the checkout. The second would be to pay for the item, then collect it from the customer pickup bay of the store. This option might introduce some delay, but will allow her to shop for other items in the interim and pick up all her packages on the way to her car. A third option would be for the store to promise her a home delivery of the paid-for item at a convenient time. Stores particularly anxious to remove local competitors could even promise to have the delivery waiting for the customer when she reached the house.

Retailers are also starting to build neighbourhood drop-point networks to serve customers better. Local stores, post offices, and dry cleaners are being recruited as terminating nodes for e-commerce fulfilment companies. Delivery to the customer's place of work is a successful e-commerce strategy practised by, amongst others, Waitrose@work in the United Kingdom. The Waitrose supermarket began its WAP service in spring 2000, trialling chocolates, flowers, and champagne with its existing fixed e-commerce workplace customers. The company plans to extend the service to include barcode scanning of products for automatic ordering.[28]

Commitment to a faster supply chain with a greater number of end nodes is not just a matter of technology spend or canny alliance building. Servicing the supply chain also puts pressure on backend manufacturing processes. Manufacturing technologies that enable build-to-order at the point of purchase will allow retail players to respond to the heightened impulse ethic of the mobile commerce user. Clothing, for example, may be built much as burgers are, with Net-connected cutting and colouring systems producing components for rapid hand-finishing in the store.

Taken together, the forces of recommendation, comparison, and impulse distort our established models of consumer demand. Just as increased informality and year-round international travel have undermined seasonality in the apparel business, mobile commerce erodes retailers' ownership of the product universe. This effect has begun with fixed e-commerce, but will be magnified hugely by the wider consumer participation inherent in mobile commerce. We can already see, in the fixed e-commerce world, how record company control of the music business is slipping away in the face of customer access to content. Personalization – a force strongly allied with the mobile

---

28. Bill Goodwin, "Waitrose to offer mobile shopping service", *Computer Weekly*, 16 March 2000.

commerce movement – allows infinite product differentiation, making the retailer a mere conduit to sophisticated manufacturing and logistics capabilities.

The majority of early mobile commerce shopping services concentrate on price, but the next generation of services will focus on satisfying impulse behaviour through creative fulfilment. Other opportunities in the mobile commerce shopping services sector arise from integrating shopping with the user's lifestyle. We can trace a trajectory from one of today's mobile commerce services to a future situation in which purchasing goods and services becomes completely instinctive.

The existing service in question comes from Snaz.[29] Snaz provides a mobile shopping cart that allows users to shop at any mobile commerce site and make purchases with one click (or tap or squeeze). The customer does not have to maintain separate relationships with each of the merchants or make individual transactions with them. His account is with Snaz, who is acting as the mediator. Snaz works across the Web, Palm devices, and cell phones.

Extrapolate from the one-click purchasing functionality of Snaz to an environment in which every object is a target for purchase. Mobile commerce sites are places to shop, but as we have seen, the barcoded products in physical stores provide another online shopping space overlaid on physical space. Products in our homes act in the same way: most packaged goods that we buy are barcoded, and all of them are describable to a system in some way, if only by name, size, and colour. TV shows provide another world of product and service illustration. In other words, the mobile commerce user will be able to buy anything that his environment suggests to him, with great ease and minimal interruption to the flow of his day. He will be able to buy the song playing on the radio, the dinner jacket James Bond is wearing in the DVD movie, the shoes the guy next to him in line is wearing. We will move from convenient one-click shopping to intuitive *one-like-that* shopping. We will point and confirm, and our mobile devices

---

29. http://www.snaz.com.

will order up the goods, adding stored personalised clauses such as "in my size" and "in my price range" to the "one like that" instruction. The online and off-line worlds will finally blend in an all-pervasive, commerce-enabled intelligent environment in which shopping becomes the sixth sense of the mobile human.

MOBILE COMMERCE SERVICES FOR BUSINESSES

Before we look in depth at mobile commerce business services, we need briefly to deal with the phrase "wireless B2B", if only to ask whether it is a better name for this section of the mobile commerce map.

B2B (business-to-business) has joined the general business lexicon and acted as a rallying cry for those aiming to haul e-commerce investments away from the overcrowded B2C (business-to-consumer) space. The mainstream media helped make B2B a talisman for nervous investors during the market correction of spring 2000. As "Internet stocks" fell, commentators began to acknowledge the wide differences amongst technology infrastructure companies, content companies, consumer retailing ventures, and business process improvement companies. The term "B2B" became a symbolic life raft as investors bailed out of over-valued consumer propositions and redirected their energies – mostly toward the crowded shallows of business-to-business exchanges. At the same time, the growing importance of wireless technologies started to make an impression on investors, commentators, and business planners. Inevitably, the phrase "wireless B2B" began to emerge. Take two fashionable terms, weld them together, and surely you have a new industry?

However, "wireless B2B" is a chimera. The virtue of wireless networks is they allow users to be mobile. B2B e-commerce allows companies to achieve savings in procurement, efficiencies in intercompany transactions, and transparency in collaborative projects. Certainly, wireless networks can enable B2B system users to operate from any location. Wireless adds convenience to the use of systems in all categories. But wireless does not create a fundamental change in the nature of B2B e-commerce. B2B e-commerce is not a naturally mobile sector. B2B is characterised by functional interrelationships: connections between task-responsibilities in member organisations. The mobility of the organisations involved or their active representatives is irrelevant to the purposes of B2B solutions.

The impact of wireless technologies outside the consumer sphere is, in fact, of greater profundity than the phrase "wireless B2B" could ever suggest. The capability to add mobility to business – to free the human components of a business from desktops and sockets – signals the unravelling of many established business practices and threatens cherished functional hierarchies, management techniques, and performance expectations. This section focuses on mobile commerce's effect not on business-to-business but on business itself. We focus on three specific places where mobile commerce makes its biggest impact on business: agent operations, distributed teams, and management tracking.

The common theme in each of these focus areas is *time-shortening*. Mobile commerce reduces latency in business processes, effectively speeding up a business's metabolic rate. By making systems usage more convenient and more personal through mobile commerce, companies can get more done, more quickly. Just as the Web interface has erased unnecessary variation in user interface design in favour of a reasonably standard and intuitive style of design and removed the need for expensive and time-consuming user training sessions, so the mobile channel removes the miserable uncertainty previously associated with remote systems use. The tiny elite of global road warriors equipped with every species of phone plug under the sun is being replaced by a massive army toting simple wireless connectivity. We have some way to go before every device will negotiate every environment and locate a robust means of communication, but cell phones and pagers are already entrenched as trusted go-anywhere devices. As wireless network options grow in power and reach, mobile working becomes second nature. When, for example, e-mail can be easily netted from the air, e-mail suddenly becomes a must-have personal application. There is no reason to be outside the loop when the loop extends to every spot on earth. Now that stimuli can reach every part of a business at any time, the business's reaction time reduces. The result: business time shortens as business space collapses.[30]

This acceleration in business metabolism is accompanied by an increase in the organisation's ability to inform and enable its people, but a reduction in its ability to mould their attitudes. Companies gain access to more of their people's time, while losing the captive audience for nonverbal corporate communication. Companies therefore have to meet the challenges arising from freeing their people, as well as embracing the acceleration that mobility brings. The local focus for this issue lies in the concept of workflow: the orderly progression of work items from one station to the next in a white-collar factory.

Workflow is a classic example of a *designed* approach to business. Any example of workflow stems from analysis of a business process and the resources that can be made available to satisfy the process. For example, the workflow associated with processing an insurance claim will concentrate on conveying a claim document through successive stages of assessment, with each stage equated with a growing level of risk for the insurer. Checking the claimant's policy number and premium payment history is less important than establishing whether he is covered for the incident cited in the claim, for example. Automated workflow systems will take claim documents through simple record-checking stages to the in-boxes of staff members qualified to deal with each stage in the process, routing documents around blockages and incidentally measuring the productivity of each node.

Classic workflow is challenged as decision-making ability streams to workers in the field. As appropriate tools and information are put in the hands of customer-facing staff, they become empowered agents, busy outside the walls of the factory. Factories do a marvellous job of concentrating workers, equipment, and processes and of regulating time. Mobile commerce inverts these factors. An insurance claims agent, for example, may be able to log and process a claim at the scene of an incident, agree a settlement, and sell a follow-on product all on her own. With the knowledge resources of the company available to

---

30. With apologies to physicists everywhere.

her in the field, the agent has no need of the conveyer-belt design ethic of the factory.

By dispersing their people, established companies can shrink their central facilities, thereby becoming more like virtual companies. Companies can do away with the artificial delays introduced to align inputs to make best use of fixed production resources. In other words, they can perform in real time. But as their people begin to live life outside the protective, normative walls of a concentrating physical location companies need to make greater efforts to foster employee loyalty, performance standards, and company values.

The nature of mobile commerce arguably works in favour of the company's ability to maintain corporate identity and purpose in the face of a distributed workforce. This is because, as we have noted, mobile commerce blurs the boundaries between work and private life. As people interleave work and personal interactions throughout the day via their mobile devices, work that satisfies is more and more work that fits naturally into the flow of life. Employers no longer own their employees' attention: "face time" in the office stops being a measure of dedication. Mobile employees expect to be measured on their productivity rather than seat occupancy. At the same time, they receive news and entertainment through the mobile device. The employer becomes one of the media presences in the mobile channel and is positioned to be the user's leading brand. We are already seeing corporations evolve their intranets into blurred work/life employee portals, so that workers can access shopping, information, and entertainment alongside their work tools. Smart companies will do the same with mobile portals, ensuring that they have 24-hour visibility in the employee's life.

The era of mobile business promises to change business practice forever. In the remainder of this section, we concentrate on specific opportunities for mobile commerce business services. These opportunities are by no means definitive. They form a starter set for decision-makers and entrepreneurs. Many of the opportunities have been generated from experience in mobile commerce consumer services. The strategy of adapting learnings from the consumer area to business practice has been immensely productive in the area of fixed B2B e-commerce. The e-procurement sector, for example, arises from the marriage of online shopping with corporate workflow. We set out here to apply early experiences from consumer mobile commerce to the world of work – and discover a series of services poised to add the thrill of speed to business.

Mobile commerce services for business users share the chief characteristic of consumer services in the mobile channel: they are best conceived as *services* rather than *applications*. One way of determining valuable mobile commerce business services is to break down familiar enterprise applications and examine which functions can inform and energise a mobile usage situation. Dan Taylor of systems integrators Proxicom calls this *tweezing*: the act of extracting – as if with tweezers – those functions that add most value to the mobile user.[31] Each of the service areas treated here triggers examination of existing business systems, generating an agenda for redevelopment.

Free Agents: Mobile Markets and the Independent Professional

WirelessRealty was launched in July 2000, targeting the 1.2 million U.S. real estate professionals with a mobile commerce service tailored to their needs. The service collaborates with Web service Realtor.com to serve real-time real estate data, including property details, photos, and prices. The service folds in e-mail and Web browsing functions and is available to realtors as a hardware-plus-software-plus-connectivity package.[32] But mobile assistants for realtors predate the rise to dominance of the Web: Mobile REP, a wireless PDA realtor package, was first introduced in San Diego in 1994.[33]

---

31. Mel Duvall, "For B2B, time to cut the cord: Wireless technology holds promise for business applications as well as consumer", *Inter@ctive Week*, 19 April 2000.

32. "CreSenda Wireless launches WirelessRealty, the first in a series of handheld solutions for mobile professionals", mobic.com, June 2000:http://www.mobic.com/news/2000/06/cresenda_wireless_launches_wirel.htm.

33. Patti Zullo, "Getting to 'Sold' in the wireless mode: accessing multiple listing service data 'on-the-fly'", *PCIA Journal*, Sept./Oct. 1994.

Real estate agents make a useful starting point for our exploration of mobile commerce business services. They live and work out and about in the physical world. They run people-oriented service businesses in a tangible world of atoms, not bits. They are amongst the least sedentary workers of our time, yet they are fuelled by information, and their output is transactions.

The real estate agent's day is taken up with communication-intensive tasks, all ideally performed on the move. She spends a lot of time on the phone, talking with existing and prospective buyers and sellers, so she is likely to be constantly connected via her cell phone and used to working from her car. Many of her phone conversations – and her pager/SMS and e-mail messages – will relate to meeting arrangements. Her schedule is in constant evolution, with client meetings and home viewings consuming most of her available slots. She will arrange times and locations for any agencies she uses in the course of her business, such as housecleaners and decorators. She needs to make time to schedule administrative tasks as well, such as preparing offer documents and checking incoming signed agreements. Her carry-around office must accommodate large information sets for each property in her current portfolio: inspection reports, financial data, and legal papers. At the very least, our realtor needs a handheld device just to cope with her schedule, contacts book, and property files. Her device is truly mission-critical.

Wireless connectivity extends the utility of the realtor's PDA by recognising the high mission value of the device and adding relevance on the time and location dimensions. On the time axis, a mobile commerce service can offer timely, up-to-date property information. This information includes properties for sale, their type, layout, age and condition, their addresses and, of course, prices. With a service such as Mobile REP, the realtor enters her criteria for target properties, and receives a result set containing the current best matches from the backend database. This ensures that the realtor is always working with current information and saves her from performing complex searches or carrying printed listings.

A further benefit is the realtor can use the service to provide price guidelines for prospective sellers. By entering details of the seller's house into the device, she can produce an on-screen report showing the spread and consensus prices for the seller's property type and location. Instant and authoritative comparison data can be more persuasive in a client meeting than bland assurances from the agent concerning realistic pricing.

Yet another time benefit of the service for the realtor is the ability to update her knowledge of the local market instantly. If she sees a for-sale sign on a property that interests her, she can enter the address on her device and immediately see the property details.

Real estate is famously all about "location, location, location". Even long-time residents of their patch need maps and directions for properties. Mobile map and direction services can help with route and schedule planning, feed into business mileage calculations, and replace outdated printed maps. Such services can also be used to prepare tailored route plans for prospective buyers, either as additional printed aids or as sections within a bound brochure.

Mobile commerce realtor services clearly make an efficient job of wrapping up mission, time, and location. They make excellent use of services developed with the consumer market in mind, such as scheduling functions and mapping services. They also demonstrate the "killer app" is not the appropriate quarry in mobile commerce, but rather the appropriate blend of targeted, relevant, atomic services.

But are real estate agents the exception or the rule? Most business people seem to spend their days locked inside buildings, chained to desks rather than flitting between properties. Is mobile commerce only for the blessed free? And does the suitability of mobile commerce services for real estate professionals suggest that vertical applications will reign supreme in the business sector of the mobile commerce industry?

These are fair questions for a business culture that has developed a largely static and constrained operational apparatus. We assume that people occupy set locations when they work and that they occupy analogous career streams. But these simplifications – if they were ever true – are under increasing pressure.

First, white-collar workers spend less and less of their time visiting the same location for work. Hot-desking, or hotelling, disconnects employees from permanent home sites within a building and communicates the flexibility required of most workers today. Increasing time in meetings, workshops, and presentations shifts attention away from solitary, deskbound labours. Admittedly, the rise in volume of corporate e-mail is magnetising some workers to their desks. However, mobile systems allow e-mail to be forwarded to personal devices, and dealing with e-mail on a small form-factor device may encourage users to be more decisive about deleting unwanted inbound e-mails and more selective about generating outbound e-mails.

As the service sector grows and focus tightens on customer relationship management, businesses are determined to engage customers in more frequent and more productive conversations. Sending their people out into the market is the natural way of ensuring that such dialogues occur. Ads for business banking services, for instance, stress the consultative person-to-person nature of the client-bank relationship, with bank managers depicted outside of their offices, on the shop floor with business owners – perhaps ingenuously failing to get to grip with the heavy-lifting part of a customer's manufacturing process, but more than making up for it in wise, practical financial advice and speedy delivery of banking services. Businesses that deal with other businesses don't win contracts unless they visit prospects, and they don't get their contracts renewed unless they invest in an ongoing relationship. This used to mean the occasional corporate entertainment event, but increasingly the purchasing company expects the selling company to place people in the business on a recurrent or even permanent basis. After-care service becomes part of the product package: a business buys a process, plus an expert in the process, or it buys a supply line of material plus an expert in the material's implementation in the manufacturing process.

The business-to-business world – that is, the whole world of intercompany commerce, not just the sometimes restricted senses of B2B e-commerce – is a fluid market: a market in products and services, certainly, but also a market in ideas, responsibilities, and skills. These latter qualities are all attributes of people and cannot be abstracted or packaged in the absence of their human carriers. Commerce is a communicable disease, and it needs contact to thrive. We constrain commerce if we constrict intercompany contact to formal communications between separate organisations. Mobile commerce empowers individuals to represent in the fullest sense the interests of a company, to create dynamic intercompany markets characterised by frequent, well-informed communications.

For businesses dealing with customers rather than other businesses, retail locations are traditionally used as contact zones. Storefronts and showrooms create spaces where the two tribes can meet. E-commerce creates an additional channel whereby buyer and seller can meet and transact. E-commerce sites are becoming more sophisticated as bandwidth improves, adding voice and video capabilities to product catalogs. Yet no consumer-oriented e-commerce site has successfully created an online space that improves upon the commercial potential of a well-designed, locally replicated physical retail space. The virtual worlds imagined by online designers have largely failed to click with consumer sensibilities. A three-dimensional shopping space with tailor's dummies to dress? Fun for a few minutes, but nowhere near as good as shopping in a real store with a best friend. Co-ordinated online shopping with a group of friends? Surreally sterile.

Perhaps surprisingly, given their low graphic capabilities, monochrome displays and truncated text space, consumer services designed for cell phones actually make a better fist of generating believable virtual retail space. With the impoverished "special effects" layer of these early services, the user's imagination works harder – and more willingly, more instinctively – to fill in the missing emotional components. The terse but well-chosen words of services like Breathe or 10Best.com suggest vibrant personalities – living brands – with more clarity and less machinery than multimedia confections such as the late, lamented Miss Boo, the animated shopping assistant at boo.com.

Consumer-oriented businesses continue to re-evaluate the role of their physical retail space. E-commerce challenges the store's role in selecting merchandise and explaining product features, whereas mobile commerce is set to create efficient, intuitive, and intimate relationships with customers. Yet the need to put people with people will continue to propel consumer ventures. If anything, the explosion in mobile commerce usage and mass market acceptance of the mobile channel will clear the way for creative businesses to focus the bulk of their competitive effort on real, live, person-to-person interaction. Stores may become more like clubs than guarded warehouses: places where people come to learn about products and services, enjoy the attentions of retail consultants, and try out new lifestyles. Our stores are already awash with coffee, so it's only a short step to their transformation into theme parks, palaces of the imagination, places of refuge. The joke term "retail therapy", used sardonically to dismiss the uplift most of us feel when spending money, will lose its satirical edge as retail encounters join with sports attendance and family gatherings as guilt-free sources of convenient sociability. And, of course, those retail consultants – mixing in the party, spraying clouds of lifestyle sample – had better be equipped with the latest thinking of their employing organisation: product and service data, commission rates, competition coverage, corporate expertise.

So, if we accept that most people live productive work lives outside the confines of a corporate building, playing roles in the midst of their markets rather than supplying them from distant bunkers, what happens to our assumption that vertical applications will win in the mobile commerce arena? The idea that people fulfil a distinct, preordained work role fades rapidly in the light of mobile commerce. Our imaginary realtor, for example, may be operating several other businesses as well as her real estate stream. Any service package that we design for her must not disable other types of professional service. Even within the property sphere, she may operate a rentals business or be involved in property development deals. On the other hand, she may run other services concerned with people moving into the local area, perhaps finding schools and health clubs for incomers or arranging storage facilities for those moving temporarily to other cities.

In addition to the many potential business streams in which she may engage, the realtor is also a private individual in her own right. Because mobile devices are personal tools that accompany us everywhere, mobile commerce cannot seek to assign users to exclusive functional roles. When we no longer need to attend a sacred location in order to perform work-related rituals, we are free to interleave business and personal concerns. We use the same equipment to check our work tasks, access business documents, order gifts, and talk to our loved ones. We may not all want to process e-mail on the beach, but neither do we want to be denied access to business systems just because we are out of town. As the elite besuited professions swap city shoes for loafers and extend dress-down Friday throughout the week, so business and personal culture merge in our habitual use of the mobile channel.

Exclusively vertical applications are consequently less compelling propositions to the user. In the past, systems designers did not need to worry too much about the headline acceptability of a system, only its functional and presentational details. A system intended for store merchandise buyers, for example, had to serve a notional, idealised store buyer with efficiency, transparency, and immediacy, but it did not have to persuade its user community to *be* store buyers. Traditional business systems satisfied the needs of captive audiences: user populations that checked their souls at the door of the company building and grabbed a role-based mental coverall. In the mobile commerce age, our understanding of role permanence and functional productivity changes dramatically. Users switch in and out of roles during the waking day. Systems are no longer developed and owned by companies on behalf of static, passive workers, but insinuated into the daily fabric of users' lives. Such service sets need to fight for the user's attention alongside all the other demands and distractions being streamed to the personal device. An employee's potential productivity improves because he is equipped with relevant information and the tools to manipulate that information, and then released into the marketplace. He is empowered, and hopefully has incentive, to make better use of his time and the company's resources in pursuit of added value for his employer. The employer becomes a true ally and companion in the user's life, playing a supporting role via its mobile commerce services and helping the user to win in his work role, rather than imposing a rigid and constant role definition upon him. The concept of the "vertical application" seems somewhat quaint in this context. Users will grab specialist tools from their mobile kitbags and tap task-specific information sources to meet work goals as they arise and will show little interest in casting functional boundaries consonant with ideas of a vertical application.

Vendors of vertical business applications like to talk of selling "seats" when they discuss volume licensing of their products, but the user population has now stood up and walked away. Sedentary activities such as product design or contract appraisal can move out into the world of use. A designer of industrial equipment can spend her time visiting installations, seeing the machines in action and talking to the people who run the processes. A loan officer may be better off hanging out in a mall than hiding in a back office, making appraisals in coffee shops or cars, devoting valuable "face time" to interacting with prospects and merchants.

Mobile commerce therefore encourages the trend towards employee empowerment and the related trend towards conversion of customer service roles into consultative relationship roles. Corporate rhetoric defining management's role as the support infrastructure for front-line staff is being realised in the spread of wireless networks in organisations, as data and services are relocated to the time and place of real commercial opportunity – the hands of the company's people. We are all becoming free agents. Mobile commerce makes us free to mix business with pleasure by multitasking our responsibilities, multiplexing our time, and multilocating our fields of action; free to raise our games through convenient access to up-to-date, context-relevant business services.

Team Play: Mobile Collaboration in Action

Our exploration of free agents as actors within the mobile commerce landscape puts the informed, commerce-enabled individual at the centre of concerns. The realtor, for instance, is a highly mobile and highly independent worker, dependent on timely supplies of quality information, but ultimately reliant upon her own powers of discrimination, organisation, and salesmanship. Although she works with other professionals, she maintains sole responsibility for each sale activity from inception to completion. As we have seen, there are many other work roles of the free agent type, and all of them can benefit from mobile commerce business services.

But the business world is also alive with players who rely upon more than their own efforts in order to achieve their goals. Such players have interdependent roles, complementing each other's contributions, transforming each other's outputs, and building outcomes that are more than the sum of their parts. These team plays extend to all areas of business, but they are particularly visible in "outdoor" sectors, and especially in architecture, construction, and engineering (ACE) projects. We can use one branch of ACE as an example of mobile commerce services for teams, namely, the reimaging and repurposing of physical retail sites.

Retail outlets require frequent reconsideration of their functionality and presentation. In the case of a consumer goods store, display areas need to be refreshed, redesigned, or reconfigured depending on changes in product lines, visual design fashions, and store policy. A low-level intervention may demand the replacement of display boards to include images from a TV advertising campaign. A more fundamental project could involve the extension and reshaping of a retail department to give it more floor space and a better traffic position within the store. At the extreme end of the scale, a company may change its corporate identity, or even its core line of business, triggering fundamental changes in retail space functionality.

Whatever the level of intervention, retailers with many branches need to replicate standard transformations across estates that will exhibit greater or lesser diversity. Few multiple stores can claim identical units across an entire property portfolio, and even those that manage to restrict the variability to key measures such as floor plan and building height will have to contend with local variations in building codes and safety regulations. Most retailers with branches have considerable diversity within their estates, making the replication and maintenance of a common look and feel quite a challenge. In addition, many retailers do not own their branch presences, but work with franchisees or co-owners.

Consider how a retail site might be transformed as part of a global intervention by the parent company. The site is to receive a new visual design in line with an update to the company's identity. The site is at some distance from headquarters, perhaps in another country. Despite the comprehensiveness of the reimaging project and the need for limited construction work, the site must remain open for business during the transformation. The reimaging of this site is an instance of a repetitive process, since many sites will be treated to achieve a common look and feel. At the same time, the reimaging of this site is a unique challenge, carried out at a specific time and place and by a specific team of specialists.

Clearly the site-transformation project will use a number of blueprints or templates. Before and after plans of the site will communicate what needs to be done in overview. Detailed work plans containing tasks to be undertaken will orient and direct the team members. Technical manuals containing the project's component types and their characteristics will also be required, containing everything from the fonts to be used in signage to the bolts required for attaching signs to walls. If we could put all of this information in the team's hands – make all those manuals truly manual – then we would be assisting the project greatly. Construction industry professionals have in fact been early and enthusiastic adopters of handheld devices, especially PDAs and GPS (Global Positioning Service) devices. Work plans are particularly well suited to the PDA format, since the device's native "to do" feature may be sufficient to present work tasks and record their completion.

The real benefits of the mobile channel kick in when we start to consider the interdependent nature of the transformation project. In the first place, the project's goals, tools, and methods will evolve during the project. In particular, lessons learned in successive site transformations will feed into the adjustment of site components and their methods of use. A team at one site may discover that new secondary signage will not fit existing brackets in 20 percent of cases and present a workaround using standard hardware store components. When the workaround is approved by the central coordinating team, the knowledge must be spread to the other sites in the transformation project in order to forestall wasted time or invention of alternate workarounds. The central team may also consider redesigning the secondary signage itself, depending on the cost/benefit profile of doing so. In any case, feedback from the field affects the overall project from now on.

Using wireless devices, the field teams can have continuous access to the latest resources and wisdom of the entire global team. Field teams don't need to be recalled for retraining or bombarded with update notes. There is no need for representatives from headquarters to tour the estate communicating new details, allowing those with coordination, safety, and quality roles to concentrate on their primary issues during their visits.

Just as the mobile channel allows the team to share best practice and methodology updates, wireless connectivity allows the work plan to be more plastic. Plans can be adjusted during the project, taking into account progress across a range of projects in a local area. Team members can be redirected between sites as work slots open and close. Live critical path management using the mobile channel can optimise completion rates and minimise wasted time. In this scenario, everyone working on the global project is assumed to be mobile, and mobility is a distinct asset to the company. Any team member can find his work schedule altered from day to day and may visit a range of sites with little prior warning. The functional specialists in this team combine their engineering and craft skills with the flexibility of taxi drivers or delivery agents.

The chain of command in real ACE projects is rarely as simple as the one in this example. We have assumed a central, coordinating role whose judgement is never questioned. In reality, complex ACE projects make more intelligent use of the massed expertise they apply to projects. Responsibility for subprojects is handed to subcontractors. Each subcontractor is hired not to follow bite-size orders but to exercise his best efforts in the delivery of a defined outcome. At the same time, the subcontractors must meet each other's requirements for timely delivery and the project owner's requirements for quality, safety, and cost. The electrical contractor, for example, must negotiate with the building contractor to clear access for cable installation while meeting the retailer's power specification for the building. Negotiations between subcontractors need not impinge on the project owner's consciousness so long as the overall work plan and project standards are not jeopardised. In this example, electrical and building contractors could share a planning session on their mobile devices, much as desk-based facilities like Microsoft's NetMeeting allow fixed workers to collaborate. On the other hand, both parties could simply use one device to input the result of their negotiations.

The mobile device's role in ACE projects therefore spans from that of knowledge repository to negotiation mechanism. As such, his mobile device becomes the ACE professional's most important tool. With the device established in this central position, opportunities for mobile commerce services begin to proliferate. First, users can exploit mobile commerce's real-time, real-place characteristics to shave costs. Contractors can buy materials and labour on a just-in-time basis, ordering supplies as they are needed in the field. Supply companies that can commit to short delivery times while maintaining quality will stand to secure this business; many will be mobile companies themselves, sending their supplies out on the road with wireless-enabled drivers just as Cemex has done in the cement business.[34] Short-notice suppliers should be able to charge premium prices, but buyers will still benefit from improved cash flow, reduced overbuying, and stock elimination.

Second, the growing population of mobile devices amongst ACE professionals creates a potentially lucrative market for associated commerce services. Project-related services that can be streamed into this market include project management and financing offers. ACE projects represent opportunities for those with management expertise to sell consulting and recruitment services, and the need to cover materials and labour costs makes the sector attractive to those selling finance packages. Perhaps the largest prize in this sector will be contract procurement services, whereby intermediaries match project owners with suppliers and perform the necessary nuptials.

These follow-on services are reasonable extrapolations from fixed e-commerce. The sale of related services such as project financing is analogous to advertising credit cards on consumer retail Web sites. The concept of mobile commerce contract procurement services has its parallel in the many online business-to-business exchanges that are organised by industry. ACE is a sector that benefits rapidly from the evolution in form factor represented by mobile commerce. The mobile channel allows this distributed, time-dependent industry to share in

---

34. For a discussion of Cemex's 20-minute delivery model, see Paul May, *The Business of Ecommerce: From Corporate Strategy to Technology*. New York, Cambridge University Press, 2000, pp. 142–143.

the commerce benefits established for the deskbound population. As such, we could simply see ACE as an illustration of the low-impact theory of mobile commerce: the theory that mobile commerce is just the Web on wheels. However, although the mobile channel allows ACE to act more like stationary industries, mobile commerce also allows stationary companies to act more like ACE players. In other words, the true impact of mobile commerce flows in the opposite direction. Mobile commerce unfreezes deskbound organisations and encourages free agency. As employees are liberated from white-collar factories to rejoin humanity, they will collaborate with each other more, not less. They will also find themselves interacting with the personal systems of workers in other organisations. Just as e-ticket-holding moviegoers beam their virtual tickets at cell phone-equipped ushers, mobile employees will exchange credentials with each other. They will also work together on describing common requirements and selecting solutions. An insurance appraiser, for example, will interact with the driver of a damaged car and a garage mechanic to specify a repair job and establish its cost, logging details of the arrangement and digital photos of the vehicle as he goes.

How many jobs can safely be returned to the wild? Is there a practical limit on the evacuation of our office blocks? We can make independent free agents of many business roles and support interdependent teams with well-designed mobile commerce services. Only those with a need to use a specialised resource, such as an expensive piece of fixed equipment or a laboratory, need be tied to a single location. While retail outlets evolve into leisure meeting spaces, office accommodation will continue its ongoing evolution into business meeting space. People will continue to visit "office" spaces in order to work with each other on common projects that require private interaction space. They will still need and want to work together in this way. We are used to the minority of mobile employees opting out of fixed-space meetings, but business is evolving towards an opt-in culture for meetings. In other words, when everybody is assumed to be mobile, presence at a fixed-space meeting acquires more significance. When all meetings can be virtual, "real" meetings take the highest status, being reserved for important decisions and concerted actions.

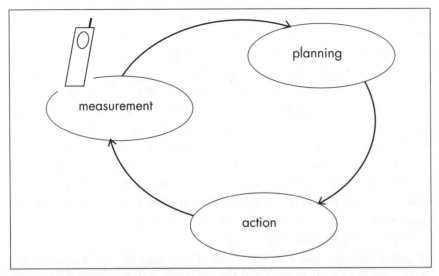

FIGURE 2-8. The management cycle.

Reality Check: Mobile Commerce Closes the Management Loop

Active business management is concerned with three main activities, as shown in Figure 2-8. Many diagrammatic versions of this cycle exist, with different terminology and numbers of stages. Top-down approaches to management tend to assume that the cycle begins with planning, although few managers are brave enough to formulate a plan without using measured data as input; and all measurements presuppose prior actions, which themselves suggest pre-existing plans. Wherever we choose to break into the cycle, the important message of this visualisation of the purposive management process is its dependence on feedback. Without closure, the cycle does not function. Without a tie back from measurement to planning, an organisation's actions might as well be random, because it will hear nothing of its success or failure.

Much trial and error, training, and literature has been devoted to the planning and action phases of the cycle. These are without doubt complex challenges, making demands on the creative, analytical, organisational, and motivational talents of team members. We tend to put less emphasis on the measurement phase of the cycle. Measurement appears to be a mechanical process in which we collect data values against an agenda we have set earlier in the cycle. In one respect, business measurement is a simple matter of checking an external number: the company's valuation. We had a plan, we executed the plan, and the market now scores us on our ability to execute the plan, or on its opinion of our plan, or a mixture of both. In reality, such vehicles are one-shot ventures unless they use the market's feedback to adjust their plans and submit new actions to the market's consideration. The ambiguity of market valuations and their incorporation of adjacent factors into stock prices makes the connection between measurement and plan difficult to unpack.

Elsewhere in business, the focus of measurement is less challenging semantically, but fraught with practical difficulties of collection. Mobile commerce brings rapid improvements to measurement situations that are fragmented and fast-changing. This is especially true for product distribution, where the auditing of product placement and pricing completes the promotional management loop.

A branded beverage company, for example, contracts with local stores and licensed premises to stock certain quantities of bottled drinks. As part of each deal, the beverage company requires the retailer to place the stock in favourable shelf positions. The deal includes support of the retailer's margin, requiring him to keep the retail price of each beverage within agreed parameters. The beverage company also supplies in-store promotional materials to attract customer attention: freestanding cardboard figures, flyers and posters. Rules concerning the placement of promotional materials are also included in the package.

Once the beverage company has signed an agreement with an outlet and supplied the product, promotional materials and rules of the scheme, the company needs to police the agreement's implementation. Similar agreements are signed with outlets throughout a sales territory. At the same time, outlets are making deals with other companies. Deals concerning the promotion of other beverages and snacks compete for the customer's dollar and the retailer's attention. Unless our beverage company polices the deals it makes, its bottles may not remain at the front of the prime shelves for long, and its cardboard figures may languish limp and forlorn in the stockroom. Most importantly, retailer pricing might soften, thus undermining the beverage company's brand positioning efforts.

Wireless devices make an important contribution to the policing function required for effective product promotion schemes. An agent in the field can visit participating outlets according to the schedule and route displayed by her mobile device. The device can be preloaded with details of each agreement, or retrieve this information from a backend database as and when required. Barcode scanning allows the agent to collect data on the products at the outlet, including those of rivals. Digital images of shelf layouts can be captured and appended to the log for each outlet.

Most importantly, the mobile channel allows integration with backend ERP (Enterprise Resource Planning) systems. A store audit transmits live, accurate data about stock levels to the company's supply systems and may thereby trigger changes to forthcoming delivery schedules. Since the mobile device is in the ownership of a company representative, the device can also be used to capture new orders or changes to existing orders. The company's core systems acquire a real-time presence in its retail network while enhancing the productivity of its agents.

Mobile commerce may go even further in streamlining the management loop for product distributors. Intelligent price tags, capable of communicating the identity of the items to which they are attached, have begun to make inroads in supply chain systems. Electronic Article Surveillance (EAS) tags, Radio Frequency Identification Devices (RFID), and contactless smartcards are all electronic tagging solutions that allow products to announce their existence to listening systems. These throwaway, no-battery-required devices are still too expensive to deploy in massive numbers, and variations in technology and standards present a fragmented market for would-be adopters. The concept of intelligent tagging is broadly accepted within the retail industry, though opinions differ as to the time horizon for widescale viability.

The management of service delivery also benefits from mobile commerce. Any employee carrying a mobile device that assists with part of his duties can become a passive informer on his own performance. An engineer, for example, may need to use his PDA to access job details and log fault reports. Each time his personal system connects to a back-end system, the engineer's time and location can be recorded. If the support systems he uses via his mobile device are designed to mirror his work pattern, then the engineer's productivity can be measured automatically. As he completes one task, and asks the device to prompt him with the next task he passively punches the clock.

This kind of passive collection of performance data helps to automate the measurement stage of the management loop for service businesses, though its implications for employee morale are less beneficial. Mobile commerce promises its users liberty, convenience, and control: close surveillance isn't supposed to be part of the deal. In any case, the ability to take measurements transparently should force management attention to the significance of the measurables. Anecdotes abound concerning measurement follies in our most automated service sectors, particularly phone-based customer service centres. Some service centre teams are given incentives according to the number of inbound problems they solve. Where this policy prevails, a team has no economic interest in reducing the level of reported incidents by, for instance, suggesting a design change to a product or a textual amendment to a user manual. Call logging, classification, and timing are simple by-products of contemporary phone equipment, and the ease of data collection quickly obscures the larger purposes of the company. The purpose of any measurement, as suggested by our management cycle diagram, is as corrective input to the ongoing process of improving the business's function. Measurement should promote organisational coherence rather than internal goal conflicts.

3 Technologies

This chapter examines the enabling technologies of mobile commerce. The emphasis is on providing a coherent overview of the mobile commerce technology landscape and on suggesting where the service developer can best exercise choice.

The dominance of Internet technologies in software development has restricted developers' choices in such matters as presentation layer styles and system modalities. In other words, developers have become habituated to developing user applications that use HTML for the user interface – perhaps with some Flash animations for extra interest – and that take the user through single-routed, step-by-step procedures. The result has been a massive increase in developer productivity and an accompanying reduction in development risk. The Web has brought computing to the mainstream masses, but it has also narrowed our sense of what computing can be. Although plug-in technologies such as Flash and Java applets allow Web pages to become interactive, most Web experiences (and certainly the majority of e-commerce experiences) remain exercises in form filling.

The mobile commerce technology landscape is a good deal less stable, uniform, and predictable than Web development territory. Though WAP was hailed as an Internet-equivalent development and delivery environment, doubts persist as to whether WAP (in its present form) will survive as mainstream technology on the phone platform or acquire a significant role on the nonphone platform. The client devices engaged in the growth of mobile commerce show little of the conformity evident in the PC-dominated deskbound world.

Furthermore, there is a bewildering array of wireless network technologies competing for attention in different market segments and geographical territories.

The diversity of the technology landscape opens up choice for service developers, but also creates greater opportunities for developers to back the wrong options. All the technologies discussed in this chapter are at least candidate members of the emerging, simplified mainstream. We have omitted many mobile network types, device types, and application development tools from the survey in favour of those that are garnering most support from developers, service providers, and customers.

The chapter's section on *Network Technologies* explores the types of wireless networks that underwrite the mobile commerce vision. Some types of network complement each other, contributing to an invisible patchwork of connectivity and providing a virtually seamless communications environment. Other network technologies compete with each other to offer enhanced performance, capacity, and coverage – particularly in the transitionary phase between today's networks and the new Third Generation (3G) services. We find that choice of network technology is often dictated by regional considerations.

The section on *Mobile Devices* describes the types of mobile devices currently available to users and how these are evolving. We give a flavour of the diversity and innovation on display in the mobile device market, first to suggest how variation in the delivery and consumption of mobile commerce services will drive service developers to discover new ways of making their offers compelling and also to convey a sense of the excitement building in this genuinely new field of consumer products.

The section on *Service Development Technology* provides an introduction to WAP, an exploration of content management issues, and a discussion of the roles for XML in improving service development productivity and flexibility. We also survey the three main operating systems for data-centric mobile devices, and the role of the Java platform in relation to mobile devices.

The final section of this chapter is devoted to *Mobile Commerce-enabling Standards* – in particular the standards that enable security and payments for the mobile channel.

The breadth of the mobile commerce field and the speed of developments make it impossible to mention every single network technology, mobile device, or application development tool. This chapter focuses on the leading technologies where these are obvious, such as WAP (Wireless Application Protocol), and on representative products in areas where leadership is less obvious, such as in mobile device development.

We have tried to emphasise the key points of each topic rather than present exhaustive coverage of every one, and to reduce the acronym count to a bare minimum. We have also tried to relate the technologies to each other in the context of their roles in everyday use rather than their fundamental technical characteristics. The undeniable ingenuity of the individual technologies therefore takes second place to their contribution to the development of viable mobile commerce services.

NETWORK TECHNOLOGIES

In this section we look at a range of competing and overlapping wireless network technologies. We look briefly at the global, local, and personal network technologies seeking to claim ownership of the mobile channel by virtue of their coverage characteristics. We then turn to the cellular networks, which have the most convincing claim as the universal suppliers of ubiquitous connectivity. Next we explore how the current generation of cellular network technology is evolving towards the capabilities of the promised third generation of networks, with their ability to deliver full multimedia content including streaming video images.

Global, Local, and Personal Networks

The world's first commercial, global wireless communications network is already history. Iridium, a system of 66 satellites costing $5 billion to build, opened for business in November 1998 and ceased service in March 2000. Iridium had around 55,000 subscribers using brick-sized devices and an $8-per-minute call tariff. Conceived as a world-shrinking service for high-worth global travellers in the early

1990s, by the time of its roll-out Iridium had been eclipsed by the worldwide growth of the GSM network standard and the availability of lightweight, low-cost dual- and tri-band cell phones. The ubiquitous connectivity promised by Iridium – and still promised by satellite networks Teledesic and Globalstar – has been stitched together from a patchwork of commercial terrestrial systems.

The growth of the wireless environment and its extension into the close personal sphere of the body continues to display this piecemeal, market-driven character. The unfolding fortunes of IrDA, Bluetooth, HomeRF, and LMDS hint that technical excellence in specific environments will eventually yield to the realities of device penetration in the general population. In short, product choices made by consumers in equipping themselves for the mobile lifestyle will dictate the morphology of the wireless environment.

Many discussions of mobile network technology begin with the efforts of existing wireless network operators and device manufacturers to improve connectivity and performance for cell phone customers. Before we turn to these activities in the next section, we can gain some different insights by starting with the mobile device and considering how it might make communications contact with its immediate environment. In other words, we can consider a world fitted for mobile commerce but not necessarily reliant on the intermediary services of phone companies.

We begin with IrDA (Infrared Data Association), a standard for infrared communications. IrDA uses light pulses in the range of 850 to 900 nanometers to transfer data. IrDA devices have to be aligned so that each can "see" the other, and such devices have a typical operating distance of 1.2 metres. IrDA transmission speeds can reach 4 Mbps or 16 Mbps with the VfiR (Very fast infra Red) standard. IrDA is well established in portable devices including laptop computers and cell phones, and services for IrDA components are generally built into the motherboards of relevant equipment. This helps to make IrDA relatively cheap to add to a device, adding around $1 to $3 dollars to the build cost.[1]

---

1. "Bluetooth at home with infra-red", Peter Fletcher, *IT Week*, 26 April 1999.

The Advanced IrDA standard enables infrared devices to communicate on a multiparty basis rather than on the basis of peer-to-peer relationships between pairs of devices. Advanced IrDA uses more sensitive receivers and exploits reflectivity, so all the communicating devices must be within the same room.

Although IrDA has achieved significant penetration of the device market, attention has turned to the promises of Bluetooth technology for communications in the personal space. Bluetooth communicates via low-power radio, using the unlicensed 2.4 GHz frequency. Bluetooth signals can penetrate obstacles, so Bluetooth-enabled devices do not need to be in line-of-sight with each other as IrDA devices do. The system uses 80 communications channels, hopping from channel to channel at the rate of 1,600 channels per second. This frequency-hopping strategy allows Bluetooth to avoid detectable interference, which could otherwise be plentiful in some environments as the 2.4 GHz band is shared by other devices, including wireless LANs, cordless phones, and baby monitors. Hopping also makes it hard for any uninvited device to log a message. The power of a Bluetooth transmission is automatically choked back to the optimum requirement for any connection, which helps to insulate transactions from external monitoring. Bluetooth has a standard operating distance of 10 metres, which can be extended to 100 metres using booster components, and a practical data transmission rate of up to around 725 kbps.

However, Bluetooth components are not yet common enough to warrant inclusion in motherboard design, pushing their marginal manufacturing cost to between $25 and $30.[2] Bluetooth chip costs were forecast to fall to around $5 each by 2004.[3] Bluetooth has generated jargon as exotic as its name (the sobriquet of a tenth-century Danish king), with terms like *piconet* (a Bluetooth network of between two and eight devices) and *scatternet* (two or more separate piconets); yet for users – and applications software developers – Bluetooth performs anonymously in the background.

---

2. Ibid.
3. "Bluetooth devices yet to bite", Antony Savvas, *Computer Weekly*, 23 March 2000.

Bluetooth was originally scheduled to launch commercially at Christmas 1999, but Bluetooth products have been slow to emerge. By the middle of 2000, the only Bluetooth consumer products slated for release were a wirefree headset and accompanying T36 cell phone from Ericsson, while Axis Communications' Axis Point wireless LAN was the first announced infrastructure product. Ericsson predicts there will be one billion Bluetooth devices sold annually by 2005.[4] Bluetooth's chief role may well be in the office environment, enabling users to synchronise their mobile devices with desktop machines without attaching cables. If Bluetooth's future lies as a simple wire replacement at the desktop rather than as an enabler of PANs (Personal Area Networks), then it may have a very short lifetime. This is because prominent IrDA windows fitted in target equipment allow users to synchronise their devices using channel-changer gestures while keeping device costs low.

Bluetooth is often cited as an ideal technology for mobile commerce transactions between users and fixed points such as cash registers, vending machines, and ticket readers. However, these scenarios centre on point-to-point transactions where line-of-sight may even provide a useful psychological component of the user's experience. Being silently recognised and debited by an unseen point-of-sale terminal might be unnerving, whereas pointing at an identifiable terminal and beaming an authorisation to it retains some sense of human action for the customer.

Bluetooth has a more convincing part to play in ad hoc conferences, where a number of business users come together and establish temporary co-working arrangements. Bluetooth will effectively create an instant wireless LAN for such an event. With users becoming less tied to workstations and more committed to field work, ad hoc face-to-face meetings with shared computing resources will prove highly attractive. Business users currently beam contact details between PDAs and cell phones, but these are very much one-to-one transac-

---

4. "Ericsson's Bluetooth to spark mobile war", Neil McIntosh, *The Guardian*, 6 June 2000.

tions. Bluetooth's instant wireless infrastructure will allow temporary teams to share documents and applications in real time.

Devices equipped with either IrDA or Bluetooth can enable person-to-person mobile commerce services without the need for an intervening full-scale wireless network. Where such devices are brought into communication with a node of another network – for example, when a user beams cash into his device from an automated teller machine – they also enable generic mobile commerce services. Yet the majority of mobile devices containing IrDA or Bluetooth capabilities are likely to be cell phones. The wireless network operators may not earn revenues from sessions conducted via IrDA or Bluetooth, but if customers are destined to carry only one mobile device about their person, the wireless network operators would like it to be a cell phone – whatever else it might be.

On the domestic front, wireless LANs such as Proxim's Symphony and Intel's AnyPoint have started to appear in homes, usually where the owner wants to share a high-speed Internet connection among many machines within the house. These solutions conform to the HomeRF Working Group standard, which uses the 2.4 GHz frequency (as does Bluetooth). Such networks connect up to ten PCs together, using PC cards or USB units, and deliver maximum data transfer rates of 1.6 Mbps. Range in these networks is officially cited as 150 feet, though this distance can be greater in practice. HomeRF networks also allocate unique identifiers to each device in the network to ensure security. HomeRF's data and voice communications protocol is known as SWAP (Shared Wireless Access Protocol), a possible point of confusion with WAP (Wireless Application Protocol), which we discuss later in this chapter.

The proliferation of wireless solutions is likely to cause consumer confusion and retard the growth of some wireless technologies. While wireless as a generic concept is touted as the death knell of incompatible plug and socket dilemmas, the various wireless solutions raise their own compatibility and applicability problems. Take, for example, the use of the 2.4 GHz band by both the HomeRF and Bluetooth standards. Both systems will operate side by side, although devices need to be separately equipped for each system. Neither should interfere with the other. Consumers may be reassured by the explanation for the existence of two technologies apparently competing for the same market: that HomeRF is designed for home networks while Bluetooth is designed for PANs. Yet this is a supplier's distinction and has little relevance to the consumer's decision-making process, which will be driven by convenience and cost rather than demarcations of his personal space. Mobile commerce requires transparent mobility; if the wireless industry demands consumers recognise invisible boundaries between network technology spaces, then the industry will greatly impede market growth.

The likely beneficiaries of such confusion will be the cell phone networks, which have already proved to consumers the transparent mobility of their technology. If cell phone manufacturers privilege Bluetooth functionality over IrDA components, then Bluetooth will become the de facto communications network for in-room use. In this case HomeRF will suffer simply because it is being sold by fixed phone companies. Consumers will regard their mobile devices as tools for use in every environment, and readily eject the fixed phone companies from their traditional incumbent ownership of the home connectivity market. Today's young adults own telecommunications accounts at an early age, and take their equipment from location to location, often choosing not to install fixed line equipment in their homes.

Traditional connectivity suppliers are responding with wireless offers that stress big-carrier performance benefits to domestic users. LMDS (Local Multipoint Distribution System) is a broadband wireless alternative to the copper-wire "last mile" connecting subscribers to the world's telecommunications networks. LMDS uses channels between 25 GHz and 32 GHz. The FCC allocated the US's reserved spectrum for LMDS (28 GHz to 31 GHz) in 1998 and the United Kingdom allocated its 28 GHz channel in 2000. LMDS is a wireless technology, but it is by no means a mobile network technology. As a means of widening access to the market for broadband installations in the home, LMDS has an important role to play in improving the connectivity of our environment. Yet its appearance may be too late – the technology's benefits lost on a population that has invested in ever-improving devices for cellular networks.

Cellular networks are likely to prevail as the primary transport mechanism of mobile commerce, partly because the cell phone industry will provide the largest segment of the mobile device market, and partly because existing and projected investment in cellular networks brings wireless connectivity to the largest markets at the greatest speed. The world's landmasses are already overlaid by cellular networks; our homes are not blanketed in HomeRF.

Consider the situation in which a user wishes to buy a late-entry ticket to a theatre. One scenario has an IrDA- and Bluetooth-equipped turnstile guarding the entrance: the user can negotiate for a seat with the turnstile using her mobile device, and beam payment at it. The second scenario has both user and turnstile communicating via the cellular network: an intermediary system communicates with both components via WAP.

The first scenario requires specialised equipment, as well as special client and server software. The second scenario uses mass market equipment, exploits existing service commitments – and generates revenue for a network operator. With neither theatregoer nor theatre required to make significant investment in specialised technology, the toll to the network operator represents good value to all parties. Cellular networks will be the path of least resistance for the majority of mobile commerce services.

Cellular Networks

Cellular telecommunications relies on a network of radio receiver/transmitters, organised in cells. The cells are arranged so that each uses a different radio frequency from its immediate neighbour. As a user moves from one cell to another, the call is passed onto the frequency of the new cell. A cellular network is itself connected to the ordinary PSTN (Public Switched Telephone Network).

Cell size and transmission power are designed with reference to each other so that cell phone transmissions cannot travel far beyond the current cell. This allows the network to reuse the same small number of frequencies throughout the network. Analog cellular networks such as AMPS (Advanced Mobile Phone Service) in the United

States and Total Access Communications System (TACS) in the United Kingdom are now labelled first-generation systems. Analog networks use the 800 MHz band in the United States, where service is almost universally available. AMPS uses frequency modulation – the principle used in FM radio. The FDMA (Frequency Division Multiple Access) model simply divides the allocated spectrum into separate channels, exactly like radio bands on the audio dial.

Digital, or second-generation, networks have three principal advantages over analog systems. The first is that digital networks are data friendly. As we shall see, not all digital networks are packet based, but every digital network is designed to ship zeros and ones rather than auditory signals. The second advantage – and the primary benefit for the general consumer – is the improved transmission and reception quality of digital cellular phones over analog phones. Calls are clearer and interference is reduced. The third main advantage of digital networks is their security: to all practical purposes, digital wireless calls cannot be tapped.

Digital cellular networks operate alongside analog services in the 800 MHz band in the US. Digital signals are transmitted using several incompatible schemes, with Code Division Multiple Access (CDMA) and Time Division Multiple Access (TDMA) the leading types (Figure 3-1)[5]. CDMA splits calls into fragments, which are each labelled with an identifier and then transmitted over several frequencies at the same time. CDMA's use of multiple frequencies gives the system effective protection against interference and lost calls. With TDMA, each device using the network is allocated a time slot in a channel. TDMA effectively slices calls into time periods and interleaves them on the same channel. Both techniques allow multiple digital calls to be aggregated for transmission and disaggregated at the receiving node.

The standard digital network in Japan is Personal Digital Cellular

---

5. Adapted from *CDMA Technology & Benefits: An Introduction to the Benefits of CDMA for Wireless Telephony*, Product Management, Advanced Cellular Products Group, Motorola, Version 1.3, March 1996.

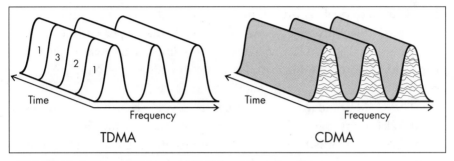

FIGURE 3-1. How CDMA and TDMA carry user calls.

(PDC), a TDMA system operating on the 1,500 MHz band. The standard digital cellular network in other areas outside the United States is GSM (Global System for Mobile communications), another implementation of the TDMA model. GSM started life as an initiative of the European Community; in fact, GSM was originally the French abbreviation for the standard's development team, "Groupe Special Mobile". GSM is a key example of government pump-priming. In this case, national European authorities recognised that developing a successful digital wireless standard would be beyond the resources of any individual state. At the same time, prior to the deregulation of the telecoms industry in Europe, national governments made up the industry's handful of customers. By mandating a world-beating standard, the nations working together could achieve both economies of scale and technological innovation.

Although GSM and other European telecoms initiatives were launched well before the rise of the Internet, the vision behind such projects was entirely concerned with building an information-based economy and encouraging the convergence of computing and telecommunications. GSM plays a symbolic role in the European technology scene similar to that of the Internet in the United States. Both technologies establish universally applicable networks, and both derive from government initiatives. The Internet is a component of the post–cold war peace dividend, while GSM is a gift from the old dirigiste Europe to the new free-market Europe. Most noticeably, GSM is often said to give Europe a two-year lead over the United

States in matters of mobile commerce – a conscious echo of the familiar dictum that Europe lagged America by a similar period in usage of the Internet. Today, GSM networks are common in Asia as well as throughout Europe. GSM has also made inroads in the North American market.

The GSM standard was designed as a voice-bearing system that would also carry data. The basic data transmission rate is 9.6 kbps. Some GSM networks have been modified to use an enhanced encoding scheme, which allows bandwidth up to 14.4 kbps. GSM operates on the 1,800 MHz and 900 MHz bands outside North America, and on 1,900 MHz in North America. A GSM cell phone user with a dual-band phone can shift effortlessly between networks as he moves from one area to another, as long as a roaming arrangement exists between his contracted network operator and a partner in the new area. Roaming agreements in Europe allow European travellers to use their phones for voice and data services throughout the continent. The same freedom is available to prepay customers as well as contract customers.

GSM's basic data functions allow mobile commerce transactions via SMS messaging and WAP. GSM cell phones can also be connected via cable or infrared port to laptop PCs and PDAs to enable Web browsing and e-mail access. GSM is not a packet network, and the tardy 9.6 kbps to 14 kbps data transmission rate renders most functions beyond simple text messaging fairly unattractive to consumers. European GSM users with WAP phones access mobile commerce services as a matter of course, but early implementations of WAP fail to convince consumers that WAP is an experience equivalent to full Web access. Anecdotal evidence suggests consumer disappointment is not with WAP's lack of screen pyrotechnics and most WAP phones' lack of colour, nor with the brevity of the information that can be presented on each card of a WAP service. Consumers are much more likely to complain of the time required to set up a call, the frequency of transmission failures, and the time taken for cards to arrive at the device. The better the device's user interface, the larger the disappointment seems to be. The user may be able to scroll and click with ease, but the time lag in the system's response has that my-first-modem tinge of déjà vu.

Third-Generation Networks

Third generation (3G) is a generic name for the wireless networks that will supersede those currently in place around the world. The aim of the 3G movement is to bring faster data transmission rates to the wireless population and to introduce multimedia capabilities to wireless services. While enhanced data rates and the potential for video services rightly capture much of the industry's attention, 3G systems will also impact the utility of mobile commerce devices by enabling multiple concurrent services.

Concurrency is highly significant for mobile commerce service developers. The ability to offer online shopping facilities alongside continuous audio and video programming will be key to the development of instinctive mobile commerce behaviour. 3G networks will also allow users to discuss live content and offers with each other in real time through a single device. The advent of 3G networks will see dispersed fans sharing the excitement of a sports match and customer service agents talking individual customers through product trouble-shooting procedures. True multimedia applications involving the engagement of all our communications skills will cement the mobile device's role as the most vital tool in our personal armoury.

In the formal world of standards bodies, 3G is synonymous with International Mobile Telecommunications 2000 (IMT-2000),[6] an initiative launched by the International Telecommunication Union (ITU) in the mid-1980s and standardised by regional bodies such as the European Telecommunications Standards Institute (ETSI) in Europe, Telecommunications Industry Association (TIA) in the United States, and the Association for Radio Industry and Business (ARIB) in Japan. IMT-2000 attempts to harmonise the various regional efforts under way to create 3G networks and provides a technical base for standardisation efforts.

---

6. Originally known as Future Public Land Mobile Telephone System (FPLMTS). See http://www.itu.int/imt/.

The specified data rates for IMT-2000 networks are 384 kbps for pedestrians and users in vehicles travelling up to 120 km/hour in urban environments, 144 kbps for mobile users in vehicles travelling over 120 km/hour in rural settings, and 2 Mbps for services to stationary devices. The 2 GHz band was chosen for IMT-2000 networks in 1992. In practice 3G systems will use other spectrum in the United States, and the GSM Association argues that further spectrum will be required elsewhere to ensure true global rollout of 3G services.

The air interface for 3G networks is wideband CDMA (Code Division Multiple Access). There are two main implementations of this technology: cdma2000 in the United States and WCDMA in Europe and Japan. The two implementations share basic technologies but adopt different parameters for the construction of their systems. WCDMA marks a break in technology for GSM network operators, whereas cdma2000 is a logical development for CDMA networks.

Existing CDMA networks are true packet-switching networks, and they use standard Internet protocols in the transport layer (TCP/IP). CDMA devices include proactive power management, varying the power of each call and so optimising battery lifetime. The technology makes very efficient use of spectrum, creating capacity triple that of comparable TDMA networks. This is because CDMA splits all traffic into packets and tags each packet with an identity code, rather than using time slots.

CDMA is undoubtedly a superior 2G technology to GSM, but its growth has been limited by regional regulatory decisions. GSM is the de facto (and originally state-encouraged) standard for European nations, and typically several network operators compete for customers using the same technology. CDMA has no European market, but the greater openness of the U.S. regulatory environment has allowed GSM to exist there alongside CDMA. CDMA competes with GSM for digital markets around the world and also with analogue markets in the U.S. 2G CDMA is undoubtedly a better choice for new markets eyeing the 3G future, since cdmaOne networks can evolve gracefully into cdma2000 services without further spending on infrastructure. Starting with GSM as the choice for 2G commits network

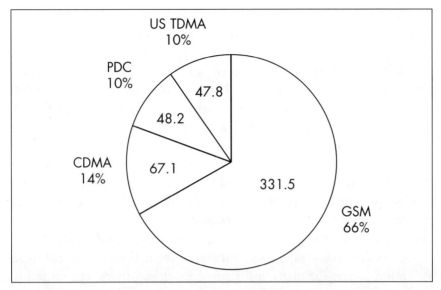

FIGURE 3-2. Global digital subscribers at end June 2000 (in millions).

operators to expensive network equipment refits during the transition to WCDMA. As Figure 3-2[7] shows, GSM has the largest share of digital subscribers.

The rollout of cdma2000, or IMT-CDMA Multi-Carrier (1X/3X) in its official ITU terminology, is split into two phases, which respectively implement the 1X and 3X capabilities of the standard. The 1X phase (also known as TIA standard IS-2000) enables data transmission speeds of 144 kbps for packet data for mobile users and faster rates for stationary implementations. 1X also improves power efficiency in the mobile device, leading to longer battery life. Further enhancements to phase 1X will allow burst data rates of 614 kbps. 1X is effectively an evolutionary path for cdmaOne, parallel to the 2.5G evolution in the GSM world described below.

---

7. EMC World Cellular Database / GSM Association. There were also 82.8 million subscribers to analog networks at this time.

A variant of CDMA 1X called 1XEV (where EV stands for "evolution") delivers very fast data rates for single connections. Data transmission rates of 5.3 Mbps can be achieved in a 1.25 MH channel.

While 1X implementations of cdma2000 are designed for use with CDMA systems' existing 1.25 MHz channels, the 3X phase will work with a bandwidth of 5 MHz (thus "wideband cdmaOne"). 3X enables data rates up to 2 Mbps and represents cdma2000's completion of the 3G goal.

The European version of 3G is also known as Universal Mobile Telecommunications System (UMTS). European network operators tend to present UMTS's break with existing 2G technology as a logical development. UMTS was conceived as a packet-switched network that would also carry voice calls, as opposed to GSM's origins as a voice system that could also bear data. With GSM the incumbent technology type for many millions of European users, the option of evolving an enhanced CDMA environment simply does not exist. Despite the media attention given to 3G in Europe, the first WCDMA 3G services will actually debut in Japan. DoCoMo of Japan plans to introduce the world's first 3G services in 2001, offering data transmission speeds around 300 kbps. The company plans to offer 2 Mbps service by 2003.

The Generation Gap

As the telecommunications industry speeds toward the introduction of third-generation networks, network operators are taking steps to derive better performance from pre-3G networks. Just as fixed network operators have been motivated to develop DSL technology to improve the performance of copper wire in the face of competition from cable operators, so mobile network operators need to defend and extend their existing customer bases as the demand for mobile commerce services increases.

HSCSD (High Speed Circuit Switched Data) typically uses two 14.4 kbps GSM channels to deliver a 28.8 kbps service. Supported by Orange in the United Kingdom but so far ignored by other players, HSCSD is being positioned as a card-modem solution for mobile laptop and PDA users rather than a cell phone service. HSCSD is championed by Nokia, which makes a Type II PC Card HSCSD device. Although Ericsson and Siemens are also supporting HSCSD, the relative narrowness of HSCSD's support will likely condemn the solution to a niche role in prepackaged offers. A corporation with field staff who need access to Web applications running in real time may welcome an application comprising laptop, PC Card, and network subscription. But with few sources of supply, prospective purchasers are unlikely to learn of this potential solution unless they have a strong need for guaranteed-bandwidth applications such as streaming video.

Other suppliers are harmonising their sales messages around packet-based solutions such as CDPD (Cellular Digital Packet Data) in the United States and GPRS in Europe. These strategies are sometimes known collectively as 2.5G ("generation two and a half"). CDPD and GPRS exploit existing analog and digital networks respectively to create packet-switching systems. From the strict technological point of view, CDPD is not a 2.5G solution because it does not use a digital network. However, as a market-building wireless data solution and a means of introducing mobile commerce services in existing network areas, CDPD is an important bridging tool for developers of mobile commerce services.

CDPD was originally designed as a packet-switched system superimposed on AMPS networks. CDPD uses idle voice channels to carry data, improving the performance of existing networks. The system coexists with the voice network and does not require any changes to the existing voice service. CDPD effectively hides from the voice network, acting like an opportunistic parasite. The system listens for power changes in antennas, sensing incoming voice calls and hopping to nearby channels in search of clear space. CDPD services are available in more than 3,000 U.S. cities and offer data transfer rates up to 19.2 kbps. Connections are protected with 128 bit encryption and users are charged by data traffic rather than time online.[8]

---

8. The CDPD specification is controlled by the Wireless Data Forum at http://www.wirelessdata.org.

GPRS (General Packet Radio Service) is an enhancement to GSM networks that introduces packet switching behaviour. Rather than maintaining a switched circuit for the duration of the connection, GPRS combines packets of data from different calls to make optimum use of capacity. Bandwidth up to 170kbps is theoretically possible with this technique, though expectations of commercial performance have been regularly downgraded from 115 kbps to 56 kbps, equivalent to existing fixed-line modems. In practice, even 56 kbps service will not become common until late 2001. By fall 2000, initial speeds of 20 kbps to 40 kbps for data reception and 10 to 20 kbps for transmission were being forecast.[9]

GPRS uses multiple frequencies to boost throughput, with each "slot" used adding bandwidth. Services using four slots and achieving around 56 kbps are now commonly quoted as the practical ceiling for GPRS data rates, with 26.8 kbps quoted for double-slot solutions. The main technical problem manufacturers have experienced with GPRS at high speeds is power consumption, with components overheating and battery life reducing. The reduced practical speeds expected for GPRS have the effect of prolonging WAP's independent life, reaffirming the need for efficient use of bandwidth.

BT Cellnet launched its GPRS service for business users only in June 2000, offering the PocketNet Office service as a means for corporate users to access their intranets via a laptop and cell phone or GPRS card. BT Cellnet estimated that a company would typically need to invest £5,000 connecting a corporate intranet to the mobile network[10] and £200 on each GPRS cell phone, with subscription fees of between £35 and £70 per user month.[11] GPRS services to consumers were delayed until the end of 2000, and rival U.K. network operators continued to hold fire on their own offers.

The main benefit of GPRS to the mobile commerce user is its

---

9. "Tooling up for wireless", Antony Savvas, *Computer Weekly*, 17 August 2000.
10. "BT Cellnet launches always-on mobile service", Guy Campos, *Computer Weekly*, 1 June 2000.
11. "An office in your pocket", *The Guardian*, 1 June 2000.

"always-on" status. The user is always connected either to an ISP or company network and does not need to set up a call. As with a CDPD network, users can be billed according to measured data usage rather than time online. GPRS devices also buffer data for up to one hour, so that sessions are not lost when a user moves out of the network coverage area or momentarily loses her network connection. IP streaming, which will allow network-delivered radio, may be introduced with GPRS or deferred until 3G networks are in place. Delivery of acceptable quality video content will certainly require the greater bandwidth of the 3G networks.

EDGE (Enhanced Data Rate for GSM Evolution) layers enhanced modulation[12] over GSM (and other TDMA systems in the 800, 900, 1,800, and 1,900 MHz bands) to take channel capacity to the 384 kbps promised by 3G networks. EDGE also dynamically manages channel quality to improve overall network capacity. In order to provide the same services as true 3G networks, EDGE also enables packet switching, IP (Internet Protocol) connectivity, and access to the Internet. These Internet-like elements overlay the existing services of the network, protecting the operators' existing investment in infrastructure. EDGE was first proposed in 1997; the first commercial implementations are expected in 2001.

The first EDGE-enabled mobile devices are likely to provide data rates below the 384 kbps mark. The rationale is that high data rates are required from the server to the client, but not usually in the opposite direction. A mobile user surfing the Web will benefit from a high data rate on incoming data, but outgoing data will be restricted to relatively short and infrequent commands. A two-speed EDGE implementation will allow network operators to concentrate investment at the network side, while keeping costs down at the mobile device side. In effect, EDGE's enhanced modulation technique would not be applied by the mobile device.

This description of the evolutionary routes from second- to third-

---

12. EDGE's 8-phase shift keying (8-PSK) modulation scheme encodes 3 bits per modulated symbol.

generation wireless networks is by no means exhaustive. All the evolutionary efforts under way at the current time attempt to emulate the capabilities of 3G without implementing standard 3G technical architectures. Systems developers need to track the solutions defined for their target markets – not so much from the point of view of the solutions' technical bases but with regard to the compromises inevitably made in commercial deployment. The erosion of expectations for GPRS and the likelihood of two-speed EDGE implementations show that defining a 3G service for today's premature network environment is a risky activity. Service developers must take into account the practical limitations of 2.5G deployments when responding to business requirements, and they have a duty to pre-empt business modelling with clear statements of performance constraints and the timescales – subject as they are to constant revision – for improvements.

This period of transition is above all marked by an apparent contradiction centring on resource availability. On the one hand, we are moving towards an environment where the Internet is pervasive, its abundance liberated from fixed desktop applications and integrated in consumer lifestyles. On the other hand, the fundamental technical characteristics of wireless communications impose constraints on the abundance of the mobile channel. Fixed e-commerce business can count on incremental actions in order to achieve scalability: more boxes, more wires. Mobile commerce must rely on improved ingenuity in the exploitation of spectrum: sending more information through the same channels. We would need a lot of fibre optic cable to choke the Atlantic Ocean, but the airwaves are quickly saturated.

Mobile Devices

Any survey of mobile devices risks citing device types destined for obscurity. Yet rapid product obsolescence is a key driver of this market. Mobile devices occupy crossover territory, uniting computers with phones, encroaching on the market space of other consumer electronics goods such as personal stereos, and even invading territory previously reserved for clothing and jewellery manufacturers. The creativity unleashed in the personal equipment market by the mobile commerce movement is beginning to shape the mobile lifestyles of the future as consumers gravitate towards product types that best serve their needs and preferences.

Developers designing mobile commerce services need to consider the capabilities of the devices their target users are likely to be carrying, and how those devices have been designed to service particular user behaviours. Mobile device types express theories about mobile commerce usage, and these theories may clash or chime with the service developer's model of desired customer behaviour. For example, a mobile commerce service focused on alerts will want to prioritise delivery to pagers and cell phones, because these are devices that are always connected to wireless networks, always carried by their owners, and designed to attract the attention of their owners when specific events occur. In other words, pagers and cell phones are not only provisioned for text-based alert services but they are *permissioned* for them as well. The same service delivered as a Web page, a WAP deck, or an AvantGo channel may miss its primary market. At a deeper level, a service developer may note that the majority of mobile devices carried by his target population are equipped with audio output, and as a consequence choose to prioritise speech output. A frank assessment of device types and their popularity in different markets can radically alter the character of a mobile commerce offer.

The convergence of device types, and in particular the continuing cross-pollination of cell phones and PDAs, may suggest that mobile commerce service designers are best advised to ignore device type diversity, secure in the knowledge that at some point everybody will be carrying something that connects them with everything. Such a strategy ignores the fact that consumers regularly allocate specific device types to particular roles and jealously defend those boundaries once they are established. If the pager remains the majority's preferred means of receiving, say, stock market alerts, then separate pagers will continue to coexist with other device types. As devices continue to become smaller and more power-efficient, ownership of multiple devices will actually become a stronger force than convergence. As products compete for attachment to the user's personal space, they will no longer need to build alliances in order to storm the user's pocket: there will be sites of mobile commerce functionality dotted around the user's person, adorning his body and infesting his clothing. We examine hybrid devices in this section, but we have not attempted to predict an all-purpose, all-people's mobile device.

Manufacturers will continue to position new mobile device products as the only device the customer will ever need, but in practice each of us will be carrying or wearing a range of products. Mobile commerce is currently perceived as an initiative of cellular phone manufacturers and computer manufacturers. However, as the device market continues to build, mobile commerce becomes a legitimate site of activity for all kinds of companies. Consumer electronics companies such as Sony and Matsushita are already active in the space. Companies positioned on the cusp of consumer electronics and fashion – notably Swatch – are poised to enter the fray. With continual falling costs of computing power, rising expectations about mobility, and widening access to wireless connectivity, companies concerned with outfitting consumers – in many senses of the word "outfitting" – will be drawn towards the mobile device space. Apparel manufacturers are beginning to design clothes with devices built into them, reasoning that consumers might as well don their personal connectivity options as load them into their clothing or luggage. Levi's and Philips launched their range of e-jackets in September 2000: the collar contained microphone and headphones, and a chest pocket pad controlled the attachable cell phone and MP3 player. Designers of jewellery and other personal furnishings such as spectacles and buckles are adding "intelligence" to their products, effectively exploiting such products' ownership of footfall in and around the ultimate customer site.

If this vision seems farfetched, the earliest manifestation of the mobile device as personal outer covering is the smart car, a mobile commerce device type making a rapid transition from the concept stand at motor shows to the auto construction line. Although a large part of the mobile commerce industry worries about which mobile devices people can be persuaded to carry, cars are fast becoming mobile commerce devices that carry people.

We also consider in this section two component-level technologies that are instrumental to the success of mobile commerce: smartcards and power-efficient processors.

Pagers, Phones, and PDAs

The stripped-down take on electronic commerce makes e-commerce an efficient means of ordering goods and services online. In this view, e-commerce is no more nor less than paperless catalogue shopping. We can port this no-frills definition to the mobile commerce dimension by picking up a device such as Motorola's Timeport Wireless Communicator. This smart pager receives and transmits pager and e-mail messages, vibrating when new items arrive. Motorola's PageWriter 2000X is another example of a smart pager. The hand-sized device opens to reveal a small screen and keyboard and can be used to send and receive both pages and regular e-mail. The popular BlackBerry from Research in Motion (RIM) also lets users send and receive e-mail, duplicating their desktop-based e-mail in- and out-boxes. The same company's RIM 957 adds a BlackBerry-style QWERTY keyboard beneath a Palm-style screen, creating a PDA-format device with added WAP browser and built-in wireless modem.

If consumers are happy with text-based communications, then two-way paging is a suitable platform for delivering basic mobile commerce services. However, pagers have two drawbacks. First, pagers do not have the processing power to offer any interesting additional functionality to users. Second, pagers are not phones. Pagers' limited functionality condemns them to niche roles in environments with poor alternative connectivity.

Europeans regard pager use as a curious facet of American life: a sudden reminder that daily life hasn't become completely homogenised across the western world. European and American messaging behaviours have been dictated by systems availability. Paging creates a near-universal text communications system for North America, while SMS is a built-in text messaging capability incorporated in GSM services. Neither is inherently superior to the other, and both are likely to coexist with enhanced e-mail capabilities on other platforms. Cell phones incorporating pagers are starting to become common in the U.S. market.

Messaging capabilities tend to drive the ownership of mass market mobile devices, but such capabilities do not represent a complete framework for conducting mobile commerce. Phones enabled for WAP (described elsewhere in this chapter) are becoming the de facto platform for mass market mobile commerce services in regions where GSM predominates. Although WAP is a standard, the term has variable meanings in the commercial setting. A WAP service developed by a European provider may be accessible by WAP users in the United States as well as Europe. However, some services labelled as WAP services by U.S. providers are inaccessible to European users because these services actually use HDML (Handheld Device Markup Language), a predecessor to WML (Wireless Markup Language) that is not supported by most WAP browsers in the European market.

Many WAP phones look little different than standard GSM cell phones, though they often sport larger LCD displays. The four function keys of the GSM phone are used to control WAP functionality, with the up/down scrolling keys allowing the user to read WAP cards and choose from menus.

Europe's fascination with WAP phones rapidly spread to the United States in the first half of 2000. However, Sony's CMD-Z5 cell phone, first shown in mid-2000, includes Microsoft's more-than-WAP Mobile Explorer browser. Mobile Explorer renders HTML sites and also supports XML, begging the often-asked question whether WAP's WML has an independent future of its own.

Contemporary cell phones pack a range of features alongside WAP functionality, including calculators, calendars, alarms, and games. Such capabilities have been borrowed from the world of PDAs (Personal Digital Assistants), or pocket computers.

PDAs have long been considered toys of the professional crowd, at home in the shirt pockets of engineers and lawyers. The PDA's need to dock regularly with the PC mothership to suck down fresh content gave the PDA an early position as an office add-on rather than a consumer item. Users might buy them as personal equipment, but PDAs flourish more noticeably in office-based roles than in consumer situations. The sight of a shopper patrolling the aisles of a supermarket while receiving spousal purchasing instructions on a cell phone is more common than the sight of a shopper tapping on a PDA-stored list. PDAs have become more mainstream with the addition of Web-style features, orienting them more towards the computing/entertainment/management convergence characterised by the Web.

Perhaps more importantly, the PDA market has been constrained by relatively high product costs. Perceptions of price disparities between PDAs and cell phones have been greater in Europe, where full-function GSM phones continue to be cheaper than PDAs. European users are more likely to regard an address book as a free feature of their cell phone than a motivation to buy a PDA. In the U.S. market, where Palm has enjoyed phenomenal growth, the introduction of cheaper Palm clones and other Palm-inspired products has helped to fuel the market further and broaden the ownership base. Handspring's Visor range of PDAs using the Palm OS come in the now-obligatory spectrum of fruit flavours, signalling fun and approachability. Further out of left field comes Agenda's VR3, a utilitarian-looking Palm-style solution that runs the Linux VR operating system. The user is shielded from Linux by a user-friendly tap-activated front end. The device weighs 4 ounces and costs under $150, putting the Agenda neatly in an acceptable price band for both home computer peripherals and personal equipment expenditure.

The future for cell phones and PDAs as mobile commerce devices was misread in Nokia's 9000 Communicator, a phone wedded to a QWERTY-keyboard PDA. The bulky and expensive Nokia did not chime with trends towards lighter, cheaper phones and stylus-activated PDAs. Qualcomm's PDQ made a better reading of the future. Equipped with the Palm OS, the device acts as a typical Palm device; the flip-down cell phone keypad restyles the device as a phone. Continuing imitation will flatter PDAs and phones alike, and lead to further hybridisation as functions from other device types are married to voice and information management capabilities.

Hybrid Devices

How many personal electronic devices can a traveller carry? Today's executive needs a laptop to access corporate systems, a PDA containing her schedule, and a multiband cell phone. She may also want to take her MP3 player with her, as well as an audio notetaker and a camera.

The urge to meld these different device types into single packages is producing a generation of device hybrids. In the absence of a single device to perform every imaginable function, mobile device manufacturers target novel feature additions in their attempts to gain market share. The principal sales driver is currently felt to be the LAT factor: industry argot for "look at this!"[13]

3G videophones have the highest LAT value, allowing owners to share their sense of live connection with non-owners. Prototype 3G devices from manufacturers such as Sony, Panasonic, and Ericsson twist the phone format to create music-phones, still-camera-phones, and PDA-phones as well as videophones. Ericsson's prototype Communicator of early 2000 is visually similar to a PDA, the earpiece-and-bead plug-in being the only reminder of a conventional cell phone. The Communicator promises WML and HTML Web access, GPS location finding, and PDA functions such as address book and calendar. Built for the EPOC operating system, the Communicator will be launched in the GPRS timeframe. Motorola's Accompli A6188 phone looks like a PDA with added antenna and integral cover and has typical PDA functions, including PC synchronisation as well as a WAP browser.

The current period of device evolution is generating a wide variety of product types, many of which will inevitably fail to reproduce themselves. While the PDA strikes many contemporary observers as the natural format for mobile devices, more innovative designs such as Lernout & Hauspie's Nak – a mobile device designed around speech recognition rather than button pushing and screen tapping – may set new standards.

Targeting the music consumer, Matsushita joined forces with network operators in the United Kingdom and Japan to trial a mobile commerce music service in both territories in late 2000 with commercial launch planned for late 2001. Consumers will be able to browse

---

13. "This is the future calling", *The Guardian*, 20 April 2000.

music tracks and download content to a Secure Digital (SD) card contained initially in an add-on unit and subsequently built into the phone device. Capacity of early SDs was 64 Mb with capacity expected to climb during development of the technology. Media for music storage is an area of intense competition amongst consumer electronics companies, with Compact Flash and Sony's Memory Stick already battling for market share. Competing storage formats will hinder uptake of multifunction mobile devices as consumers balance the attraction of new services with the possibility of being left holding an unsupported storage technology.

Simple devices designed to empower the customer's desire for "one like that" are also beginning to appear. Sony's eMarker and Xenote's iTag come in the guise of translucent plastic keyfobs, and each has a single integral button. Pressing the button won't open your car; but the action will record a timestamp that can be uploaded to a PC. The timestamp data is then used to check the playlists of radio stations, so that the user can see the name of the record that was playing when they tagged it – or an offer associated with an ad.

As we noted in Chapter 1, a favourite site for personal technology is the wrist. Motorola's prototype WatchTac series is intended to grow from an early (February 2000) GSM 900 model to a tri-band WAP phone. Watch-based formats have the benefit of display: owners can casually reveal their ownership of the latest technology without appearing to draw attention to it. At the same time larger displays, led by Sony's Airboard device, are breaking loose from their traditional product homes and finding new roles as wireless components. Larger wireless devices such as displays and keyboards will tend to live in houses and offices, co-operating with personal devices worn by people.

Smartcards: Security and Identity in Hand

Originally promoted as substitute mechanisms for cash, smartcards have failed to find a role in everyday commerce in the United Kingdom or the United States. The Mondex electronic cash card, first trialled in the United Kingdom in 1994, was intended to reduce cash handling costs for businesses as much as improving convenience for consumers. At the time of its conception, few consumers carried cell phones, and fewer still had encountered the Internet. While smartcards are popular in Europe in the guise of credit cards as well as electronic purses and are successfully used in transport systems such as Hong Kong's, they have not completely displaced cash in any market. However, mobile commerce offers the smartcard a further lease on life, as – and alongside – the SIM card.

The SIM (Subscriber Identity Module) card is a tamper-proof microprocessor buried in a sliver of plastic. Effectively a mini-smartcard, the SIM card provides the network identity of a GSM cell phone. The SIM card is most noticeable to users as the place where her personal phone book is recorded, but the SIM card also stores a PIN number that can be used to enable or disable network services. Most SIM cards in use today are 16 kb or 32 kb devices, with 64 kb devices due in 2001.

International standards govern the size of smartcards and the positioning of the chip on the card, but operating systems and applications are not standardised. There are some fifteen electronic purse smartcard systems in Europe, while England is rolling out incompatible smartcard systems for transportation networks in London and Manchester.[14] The Visa-backed Common Electronic Purse Specifications (CEPS) standard has received support from many European players, yet interoperability among smartcards in different European territories is only likely to become an issue when notes and coins denominated in Euros become available. Multipurpose smartcards, offering cash and ticketing features, are usually targeted at city neighbourhoods, allowing users to use a form of virtual local currency with participating businesses – and these are intentionally not interoperable with other smartcard systems in other places.

The lack of a true universal standard for smartcards would seem to be a factor in their failure to take over from cash, identity cards, and season tickets. But while smartcard system developers have sought to introduce smartcard-based applications in discrete territories and for

---

14. "We're not so smart", Richard Sarson, *The Guardian*, 9 March 2000.

separate business cases, consumers have begun to solve the interoperability problem by taking personal ownership of the data-reading device. Premobile commerce smartcard systems assume that the smartcard is the smartest piece of technology a user will carry. The disconnected consumer must insert his card in a reader, or wave it near a dedicated radio receiver. Now that people tote their own wireless equipment there is less need to make the data-bearing component of the system explicit in a separate card. The smartcard chip can migrate from its home in the user's wallet to the slot in his mobile device.

The strength of the smartcard – and of other chipped devices such as Sun's Java ring – in the mobile commerce era derives from the card's ability to bypass human comprehension while communicating identifying information. Credit card numbers are readable and recordable by owners and interlopers alike, whereas smartcard identifiers can be encrypted and never exposed as messages legible to the human world. Assuming consumers can be persuaded to trust in PKI technologies, then the smartcard's lack of an exposed key makes it an ideal commerce-enabling component.

From the technology developer's point of view, Microsoft's belated entry into the smartcard world with the release of Windows for Smart Cards in June 2000 will give comfort to developers working with Microsoft technologies, and creates further competition for the better established smartcard platforms MultOS and Java Card.

Cars: The Sit-in Mobile Device

With Scandinavia the commonly acclaimed nexus of the wireless Internet age, the announcement of the WirelessCar[15] project by Ericsson, Telia and Volvo in February 2000 is a prime example of cross-industry collaboration to promote mobile commerce. Ericsson and Telia specialise in equipment and networks respectively, while Volvo is one of Europe's biggest truck manufacturers. WirelessCar aims to provide services for all kinds of road users, including breakdown and

---

15. http://www.wirelesscar.com/.

remote diagnostics services. Eventually WirelessCar will merge the user's driving experience with his experience of the pedestrian and stationary world. The WirelessCar venture is easily assimilated into contemporary northern European business culture as an example of the inexorable pervasiveness of the mobile channel. WirelessCar directs its marketing messages at vehicle manufacturers and fleet operators rather than consumers, but its approach is clearly market led.

The lifestyle-service approach to in-car mobile commerce seems to be a more compelling story for consumers than the alternative car-based approach, where auto manufacturers attempt to imagine the car of the future bristling with multimedia and Internet functionality and somehow isolated from the daily life consumers recognise. For example Ford's 24.7 concept car for the 2000 Detroit Motor Show was criticised for its boxy, utilitarian exterior and cream plastic cabin. The design team's concept of users carrying their normal computing and communications behaviour from the stationary world into the car was lost amid the shine and cupholders elsewhere in the show. Yet cars like the 24.7 are conceived not as cars with added features but as workstations that happen to function as road vehicles. The most noticeable features of the 24.7 are the LEDs replacing conventional lamp clusters and the tiny video cameras it uses instead of side mirrors. More relevant to the mobile commerce experience is the 24.7's replacement of the fixed dashboard of dials with a back-projected screen and the addition of voice activation. The driver can add e-mail or satellite navigation information to the display alongside the speedometer and status light, saving his preferences in the car's computer, in exactly the same way as he would personalise his desktop computer in the office.

The Ford 24.7's reception perhaps indicates the extent to which the fixed Web has been normalised as a part of daily experience, but the mobile lifestyle is still seen as a little bizarre. Daimler-Benz displayed a Net-enabled concept Mercedes in May 1997, incorporating a screen, voice control, and that most European of accessories, a smart-card slot. Dubbed "Internet Multimedia on Wheels", the Mercedes's Net features seem charming but unthreatening. By January 1999, Oldsmobile's concept Recon was positioned as an office on wheels, with the reconfigurability of the interior a key benefit alongside Internet access. The Ford concept car of 2000 concentrates on providing for in-car working, including video-conferencing – a prospect likely to jar with motor show visitors.

Ford has since created the Wingcast joint venture with Qualcomm, aiming to bring wireless connectivity to more than a million cars by 2002. Jac Nasser, the company's president and chief executive officer, is clear that Wingcast is concerned with "transforming the automobile into the next mobile portal".[16] Other auto manufacturers have similar plans.

Drivers will find new production cars equipped with wireless connectivity as a standard feature during the next decade. The motivating factor will not be consumers' excitement at formalising the car's role as a mobile workplace or a mobile portal but a mixture of commercial and regulatory pressures. As road congestion continues to climb, the wireless channel will offer drivers and passengers mobile commerce services to exploit dead time lost in traffic, while providing traffic management systems with precise real-time data. Each connected vehicle becomes a peripheral of the traffic system, reporting on the location, orientation, speed, and even planned destination of the vehicle. Traffic authorities can use such data to program lights at intersections. The data could also be used to implement tidal routes, temporarily switching the direction of unused lanes in response to traffic demand. Such systems can be justified on their optimisation of road space, traffic speed (and hence emissions), and journey times. Wireless in-car stool-pigeons of this kind will also mesh with some authorities' desires to collect tolls more efficiently, facilitate emergency services' access to incidents on and off the road, and allow police forces to isolate fleeing criminals rapidly. At the same time these systems conflict with citizens' rights to privacy in their movements and with the economic and political role of the car as an instrument of freedom.

---

16. "Ford, Qualcomm to Create Telematics Venture", Ford/Qualcomm Press Release, 31 July 2000.

Backfilling the Mobile Population

The design and production of new styles of device suggests consumers will be happy to replace their equipment at intervals as mobile commerce capabilities grow. What of the many consumers who will be reluctant to change machines, for reasons of cost or simple inertia? SIMalliance is an initiative that will ensure that consumers with pre-WAP GSM phones need not miss the WAP wave. The SIMalliance Toolkit, released as a specification in August 2000[17], builds on the SIM Toolkit platform for GSM to bring WAP functionality to around 100 million suitable existing GSM phones. A network operator can send new SIM cards to subscribers through the ordinary mail or make them available at retail outlets, giving customers a low-effort upgrade path to WAP. SIMalliance Toolkit servers will appear alongside WAP servers to provide WML-based services to large user populations.

The SIMalliance approach has advantages and disadvantages over pure WAP implementations. SIMalliance Toolkit phones offer a greater level of security than phones built for the WAP 1.1 standard, because the underlying SIM Toolkit allows the application developer to incorporate a PIN number in addition to the subscriber identifier. WAP services are packaged in SMS messages, which can be encrypted using the PIN number. This allows true end-to-end security between the customer and the mobile commerce service without any "clear text" period in the network. On the other hand, the Phase 2+ phones with which SIMalliance Toolkit works cannot display images. Clearly, the SIMalliance approach will be most useful for those offering lean mobile commerce services that rely on secure transactions, such as banking and stock trading, and where rich content is not an issue. Cell phone customers may find themselves using mobile commerce banking services via SIMalliance Toolkit without ever considering

---

17. The full specification is available at http://www.simalliance.org/. The members of SIMalliance at the launch of the Toolkit were Gemplus, Giesecke & Devrient, ORGA, Schlumberger, and Oberthur Card Systems.

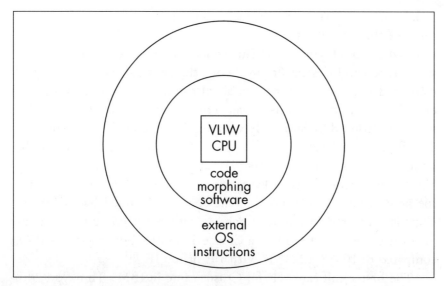

FIGURE 3-3. How Transmeta chips work.

they are using "the wireless Web": such services will arrive as replacement SIM cards rather than requiring customers to commit emotionally to a new era of technology.

A Longer-Life Lifestyle

While organisations of all kinds analyse the mobile commerce landscape for opportunities, one company has focused on a key vulnerability of the mobile device and proposed a solution. The problem is power, and the company is Transmeta. A legend before its own lifetime, Transmeta was founded as a "stealth" company in 1995 and revealed its Crusoe processor in 2000. Linux inventor Linus Torvalds is the highest-profile member of the Transmeta team which also includes several leading computer science gurus from hardware and software disciplines.

The Crusoe processor uses a strategy known as VLIW (Very Long Instruction Word), which packages up to four RISC chip instructions together and executes them in one cycle. By using a technique called code-morphing, Transmeta translates instructions written for other types of chip into Crusoe instructions, and optimises them for execution by Crusoe (Figure 3-3). This collaboration of software and hardware responsibilities results in a chip that is small and cheap when compared with competitors, capable of running software designed for other chips and mean in its power requirements. Power consumption is further reduced by on-the-fly variation in the chip's clock frequency. The first commercial Crusoe chips used around one quarter of the logic transistors needed by a traditional chip.

A happy coincidence of language lets Transmeta describe the Crusoe processor as "cool": much of the energy consumed by traditional chips is converted into heat. Transmeta quote a maximum chip temperature of 48° C (118° F) for a Crusoe TM5400 chip playing a DVD, compared to 105° C (221° F) with a Pentium III.[18]

The first significant role for Crusoe came in IBM's Thinkpad 240, first demonstrated in July 2000; the device's battery life was around eight hours. Three-pound Web pads with battery lives of eight to ten hours were planned for release later in 2000, and Sony chose Crusoe for the Vaio C1 subnotebook family released in 2001.

A Thinkpad without an "Intel Inside" logo may raise some eyebrows amongst corporate and professional buyers, but microprocessor brands are not usually a live issue with most buyers of mobile devices.[19] Cell phone customers buy on device looks and functionality, or take whatever phone comes in an acceptable billing package. PDA users have tended to prioritise storage capacity and battery life ahead of chip considerations. If Transmeta can acquire a solid reputation as a life-extending component of mobile devices, then the company stands to have as influential a position as Intel enjoys at the desktop.

---

18. *The Technology Behind Crusoe Processors: Low-power x86-Compatible Processors Implemented with Code Morphing Software*, Alexander Klaiber, Transmeta Corporation, January 2000.
19. IBM dropped its plans to use the Crusoe chip in the week prior to Transmeta's IPO in November 2000. Whether this decision was taken for technical or commercial reasons remains unclear.

SERVICE DEVELOPMENT TECHNOLOGY

We have already noted some service development issues relating to the network environment and to the device environment. In this section we provide an introduction to WAP, examine content management issues, and explore roles for XML in improving service development productivity and flexibility. We also survey the three main operating systems for mobile devices.

WAP Basics

The term WAP has made a remarkably rapid transition from the technology lexicon to the mainstream vocabulary. WAP stands for Wireless Application Protocol, an evolving collection of specifications managed by the WAP Forum. The WAP Forum was formed in 1997 by phone.com (formerly Unwired Planet), Ericsson, Motorola, and Nokia. By 2000, more than 200 companies were members.

WAP has been used sloppily as a synonym for "the wireless Web", as if it were a purely technical means of transmitting Internet content between the fixed and mobile worlds. But WAP was born of a specific moment in the convergence of fixed and mobile technologies: when the capabilities of mobile devices and wireless networks demanded a constrained treatment of the Web experience. The small size and low-power characteristics of mobile devices mean they have less powerful processors, less memory, smaller displays, and restricted input devices when compared to desktop machines. Mobile networks are inherently less stable than fixed networks because of their lower power and the movement of users around and between cells. The scarcity of wireless spectrum means that network operators will always need to squeeze as many users as possible into the spectrum they have available, leading to bandwidth reductions. While bandwidth is set to increase with the advent of 3G networks, chances are applications will grow in their data transfer requirements, undercutting the advantages of enhanced wireless networks in much the same way that "application bloat" in the fixed world ensures disk and working memory space are consumed as quickly as capacity grows. WAP has therefore been designed for use with slow network connections, including 9.6 kbps and 14.4 kbps GSM networks, and with handsets built around currently available technology. WAP is also likely to evolve as a technology alongside the rollout of 3G networks.

These technical considerations provide much of the motivation for WAP, but market considerations also play a part. The telecoms industry is marked by a diversity in device and network types. A mobile commerce service operator cannot predict what types of equipment his customers will use, so standards that allow all kinds of devices to interact with all kinds of services help to ensure broad potential user populations.

WAP has two main aspects: an application framework and a set of network protocols. An important principle of the WAP effort is the commitment to use and enhance existing technologies wherever possible, rather than inventing new ones from scratch. WAP specifies a layered architecture similar to that of the Internet technologies, as shown in Table 3-1.

TABLE 3-1. WAP and Web Architectures Side by Side

LAYER	WAP	WEB
Application	Wireless Application Environment (WAE): WML, WMLScript	HTML, JavaScript
Session	Wireless Session Protocol (WSP)	
Transaction	Wireless Transaction Protocol (WTP)	HTTP
Security	Wireless Transport Layer Security (WTLS)	TLS (formerly "SSL")
Transport	Wireless Datagram Protocol (WDP) User Datagram Protocol (UDP)	TCP/IP
Bearer	eg SMS, CDMA, CDPD	

WML (Wireless Markup Language) will look familiar to anyone who has worked with HTML. An implementation of XML, WML uses tags to instruct the browser to render text, images, input forms, and styling instructions such as those for line breaks and bold text. WML has no concept of style sheets or frames, nor does it currently include colour tags. However, WML does include tags for linking to

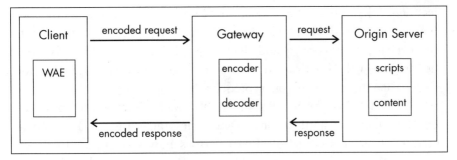

FIGURE 3-4. How WAP delivers.

other resources, inputting values from the user's keypad or pointing device, and displaying monochrome bitmap images.

WML introduces two new terms of relevance to application designers. These are the *deck*, which is a WML "page" (the unit of content downloaded to a WAP browser), and the *card*, which is the unit of content browsed by the end-user (a unit of navigation). WAP sites are therefore delivered as decks, but the user experience is designed using cards. WMLScript is an extended subset of JavaScript that allows service designers to add simple client-side functionality to WAP sites, including arithmetic, string, and URL functions, allowing client-side data validation and manipulation.

WAP adds an intermediate piece to the familiar client-server model of the Web: the gateway, as shown in Figure 3-4.[20] The gateway, a proxy server by another name, sits between the WAP client and the "origin" HTTP server, and has two responsibilities. The first responsibility is to translate requests from the WAP protocol stack to Web protocol stack to allow the WAP device to communicate with a standard HTTP Web server. The second responsibility is to pack outgoing content into a smaller data size for transmission over the wire-

---

20. Adapted from "Figure 2: WAP Programming Model", *WAP Architecture Version 30-April–1998*, WAP Forum.

less network, and to inflate incoming data into its natural "plain" format for the fixed Web. These complementary processes are known respectively as encoding and decoding. The term "coding" is used here to mean the application of a coding scheme to data and does not imply that the content is encrypted.

Version 1.2 of the WAP standard also includes a generic means of enabling backend applications to push messages to users. The associated Push Access Protocol (PAP) defines how content is delivered from push initiators to push proxy gateways for onward delivery to the mobile device. The Push Over-the-Air (OTA) protocol specifies how underlying session services are used to deliver push messages.

There are many ways of implementing the push concept, so requirements will vary across mobile commerce services. Services that emit marketing offers to users in particular locations may choose to push messages blindly without checking for their receipt, whereas a stock-trading service may need to prove a customer received an alert on his device at a recorded date and time.

Content Management

WAP arrives in many software development organisations as an additional responsibility – an extra layer of functionality that must be created, maintained, and improved alongside systems designed for delivery via the Web. Since the first WAP sites are primarily concerned with presenting static information, many developers have turned to HTML-to-WML conversion tools in order to generate informative WAP sites in double-quick time.

Products such as Aether's ScoutWeb and IBM's Websphere Transcoding Publisher dynamically translate pages to WML, but automatic generation of WML from HTML is hampered by the variable quality of existing HTML resources. Web pages exist in versions of HTML through to 4.0, with some optimised for particular browsers. Many Web pages contain remarkably little pure HTML content, using graphics for menu options and text alike or using Flash to present an animated show. HTML-to-WML converters fail when presented with such sites as raw material.

Automatic translation also ignores the original intentions of the site designer and often undermines the coherence of the content. The home pages of many sites contain a large number of links to other areas of the site, with portals containing the highest number of links. A designer may organise the wealth of available options into a legible and attractive whole by using columns, different font sizes, and graphic links. An HTML-to-WML converter will fail to detect or respect the design integrity of the page, reducing the content to a long strip of information, sliced into a sequence of cards. Automatic converters produce particularly unfortunate results with pages that carry significant amounts of advertising. Parsing the page from top left to bottom right, the converter is likely to fill the first card with placeholders for or links to ad banners. The user needs to click 'Next' at least once in order to arrive at any primary content. Since every user click is an opportunity for the site to lose a customer, this is a poor outcome for the site owner.

WML tags have been added to leading content development tools such as Macromedia's Dreamweaver, allowing the developer to design a WAP site without learning individual WML tags. In any case, mobile commerce offers are rarely straight translations of existing sites. The communication of the offer needs to be redesigned to fit the new consumption context of the mobile user, and this is often more easily accomplished by starting with a clean sheet – or a clean deck of cards.

However, developers inevitably find "pure" WML development anything but pure when it comes to testing WAP sites on multiple devices and networks. Different WAP servers and WAP phones interpret WML tags differently, with particular problems in the areas of link listing, table formatting, and implementation of bold and italic text. Products such as Escape Velocity (from the company of the same name) generate different WML decks depending on the capabilities of the device requesting content. This means that tables can be presented to phones which can render them, such as the Ericsson R320, but suppressed or reformatted as lists for other phones.

Unless XML clients become common in the mobile channel, developers will face an explosion in the diversity of target user environments. WAP developers already need to test WAP sites on every available WAP phone, with every known release of the WAP browser, and with every mobile network operator's WAP gateway. To add to their woes, there are a number of WAP emulators available for the desktop. Such tools should help the process, but they also interpret WML in different ways. Many users' first experience with WAP is via an emulator running on a desktop rather than via a live cell phone, so a WAP site that performs competently on every known real phone and network can still create a poor impression in the market.

At the server side, discrete WAP servers will be less visible as WAP functionality is bundled with new releases of application server products. BEA agreed to integrate Nokia's WAP server with the BEA Web Logic application server in May 2000, making WAP a service-delivery option for many mainstream businesses. By aligning WAP functionality with transaction processing, BEA and Nokia are emphasising WAP's role in enabling mobile commerce, rather than its use as a publishing mechanism for static information. Tools to assist developers in creating WAP services include applications architectures such as Reuters' Wireless Infrastructure Services (WIS), a toolkit designed around WAP infrastructure, content management, and customer billing and announced well ahead of the WAP hype in Europe.[21] Other tools include Microsoft's Airstream initiative, announced in Summer 2000, which will translate data from Windows applications for WAP phones. Airstream services will be hosted by network operators, further reducing the separate visibility of the WAP element of mobile commerce services. Specialist wASPs (wireless Application Service Providers), such as Livemind and Poqit, aim to take translation and infrastructure concerns away from mobile commerce service providers, using combinations of automated site translation and hand-finishing.

Moving away from the WAP world, the SyncML protocol will enable users to synchronise data between different device types, removing the need for the separate synchronisation software currently

---

21. "Deal is big news for mobiles", Shan Kelly, *IT Week*, 19 April 1999.

used by PDAs. The SyncML group includes Ericsson, IBM, Lotus, Motorola, Nokia, Palm, Psion, and Starfish, but not Microsoft.[22] SyncML is designed to be independent of the underlying connection mechanism, so SyncML products will negotiate fixed, infrared, cable, or Bluetooth networks. Implemented using XML, SyncML is an example of an application service layer component for mobile commerce services. SyncML has a valuable role to play in content management for services that do not rely on the thin-client paradigm and will be particularly prominent in services designed for corporate users equipped with different types of mobile device.

Current tools and frameworks for mobile commerce service development concentrate wholly on content management issues. There is a distinct absence of reusable code for the provision of functionality. At the business components level, mobile commerce services differ radically from their fixed e-commerce cousins, as we have seen in Chapter 2, reducing the potential for existing software components to participate in new mobile commerce services. While some core data objects are reusable across channels – prices and product names, for example – more function-oriented objects are less likely to make the transition. Services delivered via WAP will sidestep some of these issues by necessarily retaining the bulk of the processing burden at the server side. But as more sophisticated devices and higher-bandwidth networks become available, client-side functionality will grow accordingly. Software for the presentation layer will differ between channels and between platforms in each channel unless developers restrict themselves to Web-style applications.

Roles for XML

If developing services for WAP is fraught with so many difficulties, why not dispense with WAP altogether and design mobile commerce services in traditional HTML? The data-transmission speeds of 2.5G networks and enhanced CDMA networks seem to negate WAP's focus

---

22. http://www.syncml.org/.

on efficient use of scarce bandwidth. Web browsers for handheld devices already cope efficiently with full-blown Web pages via wire-line modems, so the client-side software is in place. Using the Opera browser on a Psion handheld, connected to the Internet via an IrDA link to a GSM cell phone, a user can already experience the full wire-less Web experience at a slow 9.6 kbps. Add GPRS to the equation, and WAP seems to have lost its rationale.

Applications development teams, contemplating the investment they have made in building HTML-based systems and refacing legacy systems for the Web, naturally want to reuse their HTML applications set. When the same developers consider the availability of Web browsers on PDAs, the growth of the PDA market, and the timetable for introduction of enhanced data rates for wireless networks, they can quickly conclude that WAP is a dead end.

In reality, the greatest market for mobile commerce services in the foreseeable future will not be owners of PDA-type machines but cell phone users. These customers will acquire WAP phones at low prices and will access WAP mobile commerce services for the benefits those services bestow rather than the technology they use. WAP browsers running on SIM chips will rapidly bring existing GSM phone users into the WAP-user community. At the same time, 2.5G networks will not become available at the same time in all areas or with the same level of subsidy that has been designed into the WAP phone market.

Service developers are therefore stuck with WML for some time to come, for better or for worse. As we have seen, translating existing content into WML can be an attractive but not wholly automatic or complete solution. Developers need to generate content in HTML *and* WML, and their best recourse is to define and store information in the scheme that prefigures both markup languages: XML.

XML stands for eXtensible Markup Language, but thinking of the X as standing for *anything* is helpful. XML documents can be processed by applications, including Web browsers. Unlike HTML, XML can be made to represent and preserve any type of coherent knowledge structure. So while HTML is limited to describing the lay-out, styling, and linkage of documents, XML can also take a view on what the elements of a document *mean*. Of course, no piece of data means anything without a defining context, so XML provides that, too.

XML documents are associated with their own specially designed information contexts, or Document Type Definitions (DTDs). We can then define our own document tags, which have meanings within that context. Whilst the HTML tag <b> is silently understood to refer to the meaning "render the following text in bold weight", we can define XML tags whose meaning can be looked up in a explicit dictionary. For example, we could define an XML tag <customer>, and define it within a related DTD as a piece of character data of a certain maximum length. We can even define XML elements that contain other XML elements; so our <customer> could contain an <address> with its own definition in the DTD. Elements can also contain attributes, so we could define "name" as an attribute of <customer>.

When an XML-equipped browser meets an XML document, it can use the associated DTD and an XSL style sheet to render the document as HTML. So, our browser might choose to replace XML

```
<customer>
  <name>Paul May</name>
  <contact>555-1000</contact>
</customer>
```

with HTML

```
<b>Customer</b>:<tt>Paul May, 555-1000</tt><p>
```

The same source code could produce WML code that wrapped the customer entry in a single card, placed "Customer" in the title bar of the card, but did not add any text styling. In this case, the XML document would be processed at the server side so that WML was delivered to the WAP phone. Developers can choose always to process XML at the backend, delivering HTML or WML resources as necessary and never exposing client devices to the full XML implementation. XML is then being used purely as an in-house common storage and document generation facility rather than as a medium of ultimate delivery.

A further advantage of separating the underlying data from the presentation style is that the developer can offer different WML style sheets as well as HTML style sheets. This means that when, for example, WAP phones request a resource, the backend system returns a WML deck containing bold face tags to phones that can process bold text but not to phones that cannot.

The developer can also specify variant HTML style sheets, with the standard desktop browser version joined by a layout optimised for PDA users. While PDA Web browsers like Microsoft's Pocket Internet Explorer make brave efforts at rescaling and reformatting standard Web pages for the smaller PDA window, no client application can recover the complete design *intent* of the original user interface development team.

For example a horizontal tabbed-book navigation bar, such as those used at multidepartment online stores such as Amazon, is reassembled by Pocket Internet Explorer as a grid of tabs. This avoids the user having to scroll horizontally, but the navigation device now takes up most of the window on the PDA. What used to be a handy device parked at the top of the frame of reference, near the desktop browser's buttons, has become an unwieldy and obtrusive collection of buttons, displacing the page's contents and forcing the user to scroll vertically. A style sheet optimised for PDA Web browsers could render the tabbed-book as a simple vertical list of text links, or a smaller set of buttons set in a frame at the foot of the PDA window – near the buttons of the target device rather than anchored to the layout characteristics of a nonexistent desktop browser window. Such strategies can be built into style sheets and lodged in the backend application.

Since XML retains meaning within documents, XML documents can also be thought of as transferable, self-describing data sets: databases that carry their own schemas as hand luggage. Although the primary use of XML in mobile commerce delivery is for content management and generation at the backend, developers may choose to convey actual XML documents to mobile devices for some applications.

This is a particularly attractive option for services based around the purchase or exchange of products. A mobile commerce auction service, for example, might define sale notices and bidding procedures within an XML DTD. The service provider might generate appropriate HTML and WML resources from the associated XML documents on request from browsers. However, the service could also deliver pure XML documents containing items for sale, and client applications could process these as they see fit. A developer could write an application that polled the auction site on a regular basis, probing elements of the document structure relating to item type, age, and price. The user of the client application could then personalise the feature to specify that she was interested in model trucks up to fifteen years old offered for less than $50. The probing agent would alert the user only when it found a match, firing up her mobile device's Web or WAP browser and pointing it to the relevant product at the auction site. With "always-on" access, this kind of regular monitoring will become an attractive feature, and one that is readily implemented using XML.

Device Operating Systems

There are three leading operating systems in the mobile device market: Palm OS, PocketPC, and Symbian. Each has a different heritage and its own strengths. However, as wireless network technologies complete the task of creating an apparently seamless computing environment, and device types mutate in competition for the limited pocket space of the individual user, each of these operating systems is racing to become the de facto platform for mobile commerce services at the client side. Meanwhile, the Java programming language and deployment environment continues towards its goal of allowing developers to create mobile commerce services to run over any operating system, on any device.

Palm OS

The Palm series – originally called the PalmPilot – established the classic PDA form factor and features: a hand-sized machine with a portrait-oriented screen, four function keys, and built-in applications for an address book, calendar, notebook, and calculator. One of the least intimidating computing devices ever launched into the mainstream market, and with easily comprehensible life-enhancing functions, for many users the Palm *is* the PDA. The Palm OS runs on 78.4 percent of the world's handheld computers,[23] and the population is set to grow further with the availability of the low-cost Handspring range of expandable Palm-alikes.

The Palm was conceived as a complementary device to the PC. The hardware cradle and HotSync software are the functional expression of this symbiotic relationship. Palm application developers strive to minimise the amount of heavy-duty data entry that will be performed on the mobile device, relying on the user's synchronisation behaviour to carry the brunt of data entry over from the PC platform. The Palm OS was designed to work without a conventional keyboard – although plug-in keyboard accessories are amongst the most popular add-on gizmos in the Palm market. Palm users can enter data using the Graffiti pen-stroke recognition system or peck from a keyboard layout shown on the PDA's screen. Palm stresses that typical users employ their device many times during the day, but for brief operations. Speed of delivery is therefore very important in the PDA environment. In fact, Palm OS has no "wait" cursor.

The Palm's roots as a satellite device for straying PC users are further reinforced by its meagre use of power and memory. Palm devices use standard batteries, so while owners of some mobile devices such as cell phones and PocketPCs use their cradles as charging devices, Palm owners need to dock only when they have to refresh their data. With memory capacities ranging from 512 kb to 8 Mb, Palm devices are unfriendly hosts for bloated applications.

Only one application can run at any time on the Palm platform, and all applications are single-threaded. Palm OS is designed with the assumption that applications will be event-driven, so all Palm programs contain an event loop. In-built functions allow programmers to sound alarms or utilise the infrared port for beaming information to other devices. The Palm OS does not use a conventional directory and file system; all data are held and manipulated as database records.

The biggest constraint for designers of applications for the Palm

---

23. Market share figure from http://www.palmos.com/platform/.

OS is the device's 160 × 160 pixel screen – though scrolling became available with Palm OS 2.0, allowing application designers to cater for long lists or content sets.

The main software development environment for the Palm OS platform is Metrowerks' CodeWarrior Interactive Development Environment (IDE). The IDE enables developers to create source files, run programs in a Palm emulation environment, and debug programs.

The addition of wireless capabilities to the Palm platform and the general reorientation of the mobile device industry around mobile commerce threaten to undercut Palm's traditional positioning as an information-management tool for the overloaded desktop user. Phone manufacturers, in particular, naturally stress the importance of a mobile device's role in instant data communications rather than as a temporary store of desk-oriented information. Technologies such as WAP promote thin-client applications, where the device acts as a window into a live application running on a remote server rather than the data-synchronisation model of the Palm OS. Yet an alliance with Sony in November 1999 saw support for the Memory Stick added to Palm OS and Sony committing to use Palm OS in new mobile devices. Sony's first such product, the Clie (pronounced *klee-ay*), appeared in the fall of 2000. The two companies also announced they would work jointly on future versions of the Palm OS, giving Palm a strengthened position in the consumer market. Nokia announced its commitment to Palm around the same time, despite the Finnish cell phone company's founding role in the Symbian consortium.

The wireless Palm VII introduced *Web clipping*: essentially a means of rendering Web-style content into a format suitable for the device. Web clipping uses a subset of HTML 3.2 to represent content, and proxy servers run as part of the Palm.net service. Although it uses different technologies, Web clipping is similar to WAP: the HTML 3.2 subset is functionally equivalent to the basic features of WML, whereas Palm.net's proxy servers perform a similar service to WAP gateways. Palm expects application designers to provide most Web clipping content from server-side processes such as CGI scripts or Java servlets. While static Web clipping content can be transmitted to the Palm device, the assumption is that most static content will be held within the Web clipping application on the device, with live updates restricted to relatively small data sets. The implication for developers of mobile commerce services is the need to cater for content translation into the Web clipping format as well as into alternative formats such as WML. The general technique for coping with this diversity of outbound content structures is discussed later in this chapter in the *Tools and Frameworks* section.

PocketPC

Launched in April 2000 and formerly known as Windows CE 3.0, PocketPC is a Microsoft operating system implemented initially in devices produced by Hewlett-Packard, Compaq, and Casio. The PocketPC operating system look and feel is a combination of desktop Windows theme and organiser simplicity. Microsoft refers informally to the PocketPC's "Windows affinity" feel, stressing that the platform is not a direct copy of the desktop Windows experience. In contrast to previous versions of Windows CE, PocketPC has a flat look instead of three-dimensional button and pane effects: the flat look works better on the smaller screen of a mobile device, and "3D is so . . . 95".[24]

The format of the first-generation of PocketPC devices makes it clear this product line is intended to challenge Palm as the lead PDA. The layout of screen and buttons gives the first clue as to PocketPC's outward inspiration. Handwriting recognition and a hunt-and-peck graphical keyboard add to the tribute. PocketPC's late arrival in the Palm space has its benefits: character recognition is achieved without recourse to a stylised alphabet such as the Graffiti scheme. The Peacemaker card-beaming feature from Conduits Technologies and smaller.com negotiates business card transmissions between PocketPC and other devices from other manufacturers; perhaps the name is a gentle sideswipe at the CodeWarrior development environment for the Palm OS.

PocketPC has clearly been designed to attract consumers with a

---

24. *Building Great Applications for the PocketPC*, Mobile Devices Division, Microsoft Corporation, presentation to Microsoft Tech Ed 2000.

wealth of features intended to give the product family dominance over the rival Palm series. The colour Palm IIIc has a 160×160 pixel screen compared to the HP Jornada 540 series' 240×320 pixels. The Palm device also only offers 256 colours compared to the HP machine's 65,536. With a built-in media player, the PocketPC doubles as an MP3 player, giving potential customers another powerful reason to purchase the machine. Pocket versions of Word, Excel, and Money emphasise the device's compatibility with mainstream desktop systems and reduce user fears concerning file translation between machines. Pocket Internet Explorer provides visual continuity with its deskbound sibling and automatically fetches Web pages from the Internet or from cache, depending on the availability of a network connection.

Expectations derived from the desktop Windows experience are frustrated by the lack of explicit save and close functions in applications, but satisfied by the appearance of a "wait" cursor – a colour-cycling segmented circle rather than the familiar hourglass. This is one example of PocketPC's compromise between PDA-style instant gratification and PC-style versatility.

PocketPC runs on a large number of processor types, but executables are not compatible between the different versions for the different chips. Microsoft's Common Executable Format (CEF) should solve this problem, allowing developers to ship the same version of their applications to every type of device running PocketPC.

For the developer, the prime benefit of PocketPC is its use of familiar desktop-class Windows features. The platform includes Message Queue and Transaction Server clients so that PocketPC applications can work easily with other Microsoft-based backend systems. Developers responsible for existing Windows applications can also provide access to these backend systems using Citrix's ICA (Independent Computing Architecture). This product set allows the mobile device user to access Windows and Unix applications despite having a different operating system on their device. ICA clients are currently available for Windows CE and PocketPC platforms and also for Symbian's EPOC operating system.

As well as spawning the PocketPC platform, Windows CE 3.0

also provides the basis of Microsoft's Handheld PC 2000 family, a class of devices with integral keyboards. The Handheld PC 2000 platform includes an integrated client for backend Windows applications, making this option a strong candidate for companies who want to make existing applications available in the mobile channel without redesigning their user interfaces.

Symbian

Symbian is a consortium formed by Ericsson, Matsushita, Motorola, Nokia, and Psion. Of these founding fathers, Psion is the least well known. A British company, Psion was founded in 1980 and supplies hand-held computers to the business and consumer markets. Psion devices are particularly visible in retail stock control applications and in their Series 5 PDA model.

Symbian's EPOC operating system has been designed specifically for mobile devices. The primary aim was to create an operating system with powerful features that would nevertheless occupy a small footprint. EPOC's goals make the technology a natural bedfellow for Sun's Java technologies, and Java is indeed a core element of the EPOC offer. EPOC is an object-oriented platform, enabling modular development from standard middleware and user interface components.

EPOC is rather more than a base operating system, as it ships with a number of features traditionally regarded as applications. These include a word processor, spreadsheet, contacts book, personal schedule, calculator, drawing program, database, spell checker, game ("Bombs"), and full OPL programming language and compiler. The fifth release of Symbian in March 1999 included features such as integrated e-mail, text messaging, Web browser, cross-platform synchronization, and an optimised Java implementation. Additions during 2000 included protocol stacks for WAP and Bluetooth and a WAP browser.

Symbian attempts to divide the device world into two broad classes, *smartphones* and *communicators*. A smartphone is a telephone device with added information processing features, whereas a communicator is an information processing device with added voice capabilities. As we have seen, this division is unlikely to stand the test of very much time as devices mutate in the consumer market. However, from

Symbian's point of view the smartphone/communicator split helps segment the early target market for the EPOC operating system. Phone manufacturers looking to add PDA functionality can consider EPOC, as can PDA manufacturers looking to add phone functionality.

The growth in diversity of device types is already evident in the bifurcation of Symbian's communicator category into "EPOC Release 5 form factor" devices and a separate reference design of the Web pad variety. EPOC was originally designed for text input from keyboards rather than for handwriting recognition. Symbian's Quartz reference design for communicator-class devices has a pen-based user interface, bringing EPOC into line with Palm and PocketPC solutions.

EPOC encourages user-centred user interface design, and promotes consideration of the user's situation.[25] For example, EPOC users do not have to save and close files explicitly, though separate save and close functions are provided for PC-trained users who expect to find them. This approach derives from the platform's heritage in the Psion PDA operating system. Ironically, Microsoft's PocketPC dispenses with save and close functions altogether, not even providing the comfort of redundant explicit functions.

Programmers can use C++, Java, or OPL (a Basic-like language deriving from the Psion family) to develop applications for EPOC. The typical approach to development is to develop in a PC environment and then test on the EPOC platform. This allows developers to use familiar development tools such as Microsoft's Visual C++. Memory-management disciplines are built into EPOC, with an exception handling mechanism known as trap/leave, which is similar to the try/throw strategy in Java. Symbian stresses that EPOC was designed specifically for mobile devices, so that issues like power management and memory management have been built into the platform's foundation. Symbian regards the lack of memory-management features in Windows CE platforms as a drawback of the rival platform, though

---

25. Symbian's excellent style guides include the informal *Making It Easy*, a set of guidelines worth reading by anyone designing a mobile service; see http://www.symbian.com/technology/papers/easyui/easyui.html.

development managers are likely to see the continuity between full-scale Windows programming and Windows CE development as a counterbalancing benefit.

At the strategic level, Symbian has formed a relationship with IBM to deliver enterprise applications. IBM is making MQ Series and DB2 clients available for the EPOC platform as part of this effort.

The Role of Java

Java 2 Platform, Micro Edition (J2ME) is one of three versions of Sun's programming platform, the other two being the Standard Edition (SE) and Enterprise Edition (EE). J2ME is aimed at every kind of device in the consumer environment except ordinary desktop computers. This category of electronics products covers devices all the way from smartcards and cell phones to set-top boxes for use with TV entertainment systems. The virtual machine contained in J2ME is naturally optimised for devices with small memory capabilities. This version of the Java execution engine has been specified to run in spaces measured in kilobytes rather than the megabytes available to desktop machines and servers.

In fact, J2ME includes two configurations of the virtual machine: one for devices with between 128 kb and 512 kb available memory, and one for devices with more than 512 kb to offer the Java environment. The first of these configurations is known as the Connected Limited Device Configuration (CLDC), while the second configuration is called the Connected Device Configuration (CDC).

Further tailoring of Java's capabilities for different types of device is achieved using profiles, which are collections of classes chosen to create complete application environments for specific types of device. Java's "write once, run everywhere" philosophy is therefore realistically constrained within species of devices. J2ME functionality developed for the PDA Profile (PDAP), for example, will run on any J2ME-capable PDA, but not on J2ME-capable phones, since phones require a different profile – the Mobile Information Device Profile (MIDP).

As well as allowing developers to target entire classes of device without rewriting applications for each product type in the class, J2ME leverages the wide availability of Java skills existing in the development community. Service designers using J2ME avoid the narrower skillsets associated with programming for specific platforms.

J2ME is set to take a commanding share of the mobile commerce service development business. The factors that might slow J2ME's progress include questions about its performance, given the environment's limited resources. A second factor affecting J2ME's success will be the speed with which new profiles are defined. Profiles are defined by industry working groups, which may not be able to stop individual players rushing out their own preferred API sets. The last factor in J2ME's potential dominance is the extent to which the user interface standards defined for each profile allow developers to exploit the functionality of different devices. Device manufacturers seek to differentiate their products through, amongst other things, innovative display and control features. Industry profiles may impose lowest-common-denominator user interface capabilities that negate such differentiators and turn developers away from J2ME.

MOBILE COMMERCE-ENABLING STANDARDS

Standards create markets. GSM created the digital cell phone market in Europe, but no existing technical standard creates either trust or currency – the two commodities vital to a functioning commercial environment. The linked issues of *security* and *payment systems* both require standardisation if stable markets are to be built, consumer confidence gained, and substantial migration of commerce activities to the mobile channel achieved. While wireless networks and mobile devices enable mobile relationships, serious mobile commerce also requires a measure of trust – security – and a means of exchange – payments.

Payment Systems

As we have seen, mobile commerce entails an explosion in transactions and a reduction in the average value of a transaction. In this fluid, transactional environment, content may still be king but cash is queen. Cash is a means whereby users trade with each other without the real-time presence of a value-exchanging intermediary.

Smartcards have long been promoted as an alternative to cash, or as a means of securing and transacting stored value. Smartcards have traditionally been tied to static networks of terminals that enable cash to be loaded into cards from checking or credit card accounts. The first commercial launch of a mobile commerce e-purse application was Gemplus's application for CashCard in Singapore. CashCard is a payment card operated by NETS (Network for Electronic Transfers) and used for settling small purchases and road tolls. From April 2000, users have been able to reload their CashCards using a dual-slot cell phone fitted with the 32k Gemxplore SIM card. As we saw in Chapter 1, dual-slot cell phones are helping to grow the effective point-of-sale terminal population of France.

The ability to load cash onto cards without visiting a fixed location may be a boon in territories where smartcard usage is entrenched, but for other markets the reverse process – beaming cash from cards into the ether – is a more compelling realisation of mobile commerce payments. This cash-equivalent is already gaining popularity amongst users of e-mail and is spreading to PDA users as well.

PayPal is the most successful of a number of Net-based person-to-person payment systems, and the main such service to be made available on PDAs. PayPal acts as an intermediary for small-value payments. Users send money by instructing PayPal to debit a credit card account, or they can choose to send checks, money orders, or direct transfers to PayPal. The user supplies an e-mail address for the recipient and fills in a dollar amount, all from a simple Web form. Recipients receive an e-mail informing them of the payment. The recipient has to visit PayPal's site and register there and can then choose to have the payment credited to her PayPal account or mailed as a check.

PayPal has a viral element to its growth. PayPal users can send money to anyone who has an e-mail address, but the transaction can only be completed by the recipient joining the PayPal family. Once joined, the new user is more likely to recruit further users by sending payments of his own.

PayPal is particularly popular for paying for items bought in

online auctions, and the service supplies a special form for such transactions including fields for the auction details. PayPal runs on devices
running PalmOS. Palm users can access PayPal services via synchronisation in the usual manner, but they can also beam payments directly
to each other. Palm users are already used to beaming business cards
to each other; with PayPal they can also borrow money from each
other and repay small debts. This PDA functionality makes PayPal a
potent form of live cash without requiring the relatively heavy infrastructure associated with smartcard e-purse solutions.

PayPal is ideally suited to a commercial landscape with no common standard for payments. The service uses the lowest-common-
denominator technology of the Internet – e-mail – to generate a
transparently simple cash economy exploiting established offline payment mechanisms. In the mobile commerce context, PayPal leverages
the PDA user's comfort with using the device as a controller, with the
device's infrared port acting as a kind of money gun.

Electronic cash of all kinds is underwritten by strong encryption,
with the mathematics of cryptography taking the role of guarantor
away from governments. In a hard cash economy, a government's
access to sophisticated stamping or printing technology allows it to
create monetary tokens that are hard to forge. The technology for
manufacturing electronic tokens is more freely available. But electronically minted money still has to be tied into real-world values, ensuring a continuing role for intermediaries. The British WAP company
Thyron, for example, offers ISPs a payment service infrastructure
known as YES.wallet. Users of YES.wallet register online, giving
their credit card details. They can then make purchases from WAP
sites by clicking a YES option and entering a PIN number.[26]

Many digital cash solutions have been trialled in the fixed Web
environment, but none has been successful in gaining a significant
user community. Digital cash systems require users to use special software. Any requirement for software installation above and beyond the
capabilities included in the most popular Web packages (Microsoft

---

26. http://www.yes-secure.com/.

Internet Explorer and Netscape Communicator) deters most users. Consumers have become steadily more suspicious of plug-ins and separate applications, partly through fears of introducing a virus to their systems, but also through an unwillingness to manage multiple applications, learn new terminologies and procedures, and deal with e-mails about upgrades. Consumers require highly compelling reasons to invest in new applications, even if the required investment is time and not money. MP3-sharing software has been the only class of application to gain widespread support since the acceptance of the Web browser suite. The ability to acquire free music is a much greater motivator than the opportunity to buy digital coinage that may or not be accepted elsewhere on the Web.

The de facto payment system for the Web today is the encrypted credit card number. Despite continuing consumer fears about credit card fraud on the Net, the card number remains the lowest-effort payment mechanism for consumer and merchant alike. The ability to secure credit card numbers for transmission over mobile networks – and ideally the ability to hide the numbers even from their owners – will create a simple transition to mobile commerce for millions of contented online shoppers and the stores they favour.

Security

The SIM card at the heart of a GSM cell phone's operability is designed as a single-purpose unit. SIM cards enable access to the GSM network and identify the wireless device to the network, and cannot run any other applications. Ideally, this "identity chip" would be expanded to hold more information about the phone's user. In fact the Multos smartcard operating system has been adapted to run on an upgraded 32 k SIM card, allowing GSM phones to contain digital signatures and credit card numbers.

Nokia, Ericsson, and Motorola launched a project to standardise security mechanisms for mobile commerce in April 2000, with the goal of producing an open standard by 2001. A mature, generic security environment for mobile commerce must await the full transition of PKI to the mobile channel.

Public Key Infrastructure (PKI) is an e-commerce architecture that combines specialist authorities, digital certificate management systems, and directory facilities to create secure networks on top of unsecured networks. PKI combines three aspects of security: confidentiality, authentication, and nonrepudiation. Confidentiality is the basic property of disguising a message's contents from an unintended recipient. Authentication refers to the ability to validate the identities of the communicating parties. Nonrepudiation means completed transactions cannot legally be denied by either party.

Confidentiality is provided by the technique of public key cryptography. With this technique, each party to a communication uses encryption software to generate a pair of keys, known as the public and private keys. The remarkable property of this key pair is that neither can be transformed into the other. The keys are generated by multiplying large prime numbers together. Finding the original factors of the resulting product is computationally intensive, whereas knowing one of the factors will reveal the other readily.

A user can publish her public key and then anyone wishing to send a message to that person uses the public key to encrypt it. Only she can decrypt the message, using her private key, which remains securely on her own machine. If she wants to send a secret message to another user, she can obtain his public key directly by e-mail or from a database dedicated to holding public keys.

Authentication in PKI is supplied by digital certificates. A digital certificate ties together a user's identity with his public key. The certificate, also known as a digital ID, is therefore an electronic artefact that relates the use of a key to a known individual. PKI generates credibility in identities through its capability to manage reliably and credibly the distribution of keys and certificates. This management system uses Certification Authorities (CAs) and Registration Authorities (RAs) to ensure nonrepudiation. A CA is a software service that creates and issues certificates to users who have been registered with the CA. Qualifying users must have been pre-approved by an RA. The PKI also manages the entire lifecycle of a certificate, from creation and issuing to revocation and archiving.

PKI can be implemented as a stand-alone function within a com-

pany's systems or as a distributed function shared with an external partner such as VeriSign. VeriSign's OnSite product locates the CA within
the enterprise, but links to VeriSign's secure data center for running
hardware-based cryptographic routines. This implementation avoids
using software-based cryptography – a potential target for attack – at
the enterprise's site and adds off-site archiving into the package.

Within an organisation, registration of users is reasonably straightforward. Approved users can be drawn directly from a human resources database, for example, and fed to the RA module. As soon as we reach the
e-commerce world, however, we can no longer rely on such a simple
source of preapproval. A Trusted Third Party or *TTP* is essentially an RA
that runs a CA on behalf of other companies. The British Post Office, for
example, offers an e-mail signature and encryption service called ViaCode,
which uses PKI software from Entrust. The backing of a postal authority
provides assurance that users have been adequately checked before they
are registered. The British Post Office is well known for its strict approval
processes, which require physical proofs of identity. Presumably, the
organisation hopes that customers' experience of its rigor in checking
identity will help its brand to stretch to ensuring electronic identities.

PKI is not yet a standard feature of most users' Web experience.
Legal recognition of digital signatures continued to cascade through
the world's nations during 2000, ensuring broader support for digital
certificates and therefore the entire PKI architecture. At present, credit
card companies are left holding responsibility for disputed payments
when an e-commerce customer claims that he did not make a billed
purchase. As individuals become certificated, transactional liability
will begin to flow more equitably through the electronic markets.

The WAP architecture includes a distinctive security layer: surely
WAP is therefore a secure environment for full mobile commerce
transactions? In fact, WAP's security model is fragmented and not
equivalent to security practice on the Net.

End-to-end security between customer and supplier is achieved
transparently in fixed e-commerce. On entering a secure site, the user's
Web browser requests the site's digital certificate and checks that the
site represents the identity that it claims. With this authentication
step completed, a pair of keys is generated for use in the session.

This direct relationship between user and commerce service provider is broken in the WAP world. WAP 1.1 includes a layer called WTLS (Wireless Transport Layer Security – sometimes unfortunately pronounced "witless"), which bridges to the TLS layer (formerly known as SSL [Secure Sockets Layer]) of the fixed Net. The server still presents digital certificates when queried, but these are fielded by the WAP Gateway component of the network rather than the end-user's mobile device. The WAP Gateway has its own cutdown digital certificate that can be processed by the client mobile device. The end result is an encrypted session between customer and mobile commerce service provider – but the session is actually composed of two concatenated segments with a nonencrypted junction.

WAP security is by no means an automatic feature of the mobile commerce scene, as SSL is in fixed e-commerce. In the first place, not all WAP Gateways and mobile devices are equipped to provide encryption. With the earliest WAP services focused on pure information services, and mobile network operators anxious to build market share quickly, most WAP-enabled networks launched without secure gateways. This situation was steadily remedied during the latter half of 2000.

Second, WAP phones differ in their support for security. Some early WAP phones have no encryption functionality. Of the most popular WAP phones with security features available in mid-2000, only Nokia's 7110 was able to process a WAP Gateway's certificate in order to authenticate it.

The third problem with WAP security has received the most critical attention and is the least amenable to simple improvements in network componentry or mobile device functionality. This is the "clear text" problem: the brief but nevertheless significant time when a message passing through the WAP Gateway is decrypted in one scheme before being encrypted in the other scheme. The security path is in reality two separate paths linked by the WAP Gateway, so the Gateway itself represents a target for abuse. A rogue WAP Gateway could provide perfect customer service while recording every item of clear text passing through it. The ability to change a WAP phone's Gateway settings via an SMS message now becomes a potential security loophole. Configuring a WAP phone's access settings is far from straightforward, so OTA (Over the Air) configuration is normally a benefit to customers. But if a user's WAP phone is reconfigured to use a rogue Gateway and the phone cannot process Gateway certificates, then the potential for data theft is immense.

From the point of view of application developers, mobile commerce services for WAP simply need to use HTTPS and authentication. The WAP Gateway must be in a secured environment, and the customer base must be instructed in the security issues of phone types and alternative gateways. Some mobile commerce service providers have sought to control every variable by operating their own WAP Gateways (that is, not using a Gateway in the network operator's system) and dispensing WAP phones to customers. This approach is a good way of creating an initial customer base, but it will no longer be workable as more consumers find WAP a bonus feature of their new devices. Amazon has sought to reassure mobile commerce customers by extending its "safe shopping guarantee" to the mobile channel, meaning that the company will cover any unauthorised credit card transactions arising as a result of customers using the service.

The key to improving WAP security lies in WIM (WAP Identity Module), an element of the WAP 1.2 specification due for rollout in WAP phones during 2001. The private key used for client authentication and digital signatures needs to be stored securely in the mobile device. The key also needs to be retained in the device for relatively long periods, so as to avoid the security system performing frequent authentication checks or handshakes. Each handshake demands processing effort and network traffic, so lessening these instances improves performance all round. The WIM (WAP Identity Module) is a tamper-proof component designed to meet these needs, storing private data – including key pairs, certificates and PIN numbers – in a permanent form and performing calculations and transformations on that data. All key operations are therefore performed within the WIM, and the private key itself never leaves the module.

Although a WIM could be implemented as any number of components, in practice WIMs are smartcards. A WIM can be incorporated within a GSM phone's SIM (Subscriber Identity Module) smartcard or implemented within a second smartcard. In line with their declared practice of leveraging existing technologies, the WAP designers have used generic cryptographic interfaces so that a WIM could also be used to implement schemes such as SSL.

WAP 1.2 also adds a function called SignText to WMLScript. This function allows a WAP client to add a digital signature to a transaction, and is an alternative to the SIM-based signature solution. The challenge of providing digital signatures at the client can be side-stepped by lodging the customer's certificate in an online repository. The certificate can then be full sized rather than cut down and can be processed by existing Internet security applications.

Certificate lifetime is one striking difference between PKI in fixed and wireless environments. In fixed e-commerce, certificates are issued for reasonably long periods, such as a year. Clients can check whether a certificate has been revoked by referring to a Certificate Revocation List or making a direct query to the issuing authority. Advertised revocation of certificates ensures that fraudsters cannot operate services using second hand certificates. Mobile devices do not currently have the processing power or bandwidth to carry out such functions. Consequently, certificates are issued on a daily basis for key generation during each day. A server's certification can therefore be revoked simply by cutting off the regular supply of daily certificates. The client device checks the validity date of the presented certificate, and rejects it.

A number of standards initiatives have been launched in the wireless PKI arena. The PKI Forum, founded in December 1999 as part of the Open Group, is driven by security and IT infrastructure players in the fixed e-commerce world but extends its interest to the wireless world as well as fixed networks. The group has a particular focus on ensuring interoperability amongst PKI products. Radicchio, founded in September 1999, is a group of companies organised to promote the use of PKI in the mobile channel. Meanwhile the Mobile Electronic Signature Consortium, formed in January 2000 by a group of wireless network operators and device manufacturers, is looking beyond WAP security to a security infrastructure integrating fixed and mobile security systems.

4 Live Issues

This chapter describes a number of live issues affecting the successful development of mobile commerce. These include distinctions between what is technically possible and consumers' desires and motivations, issues around security, trust, and privacy, and concerns relating to health. We also consider the impact of unequal access to the benefits of mobile commerce, the implications of the blurring of the dividing line between work and private life, the re-emergence of geography as a key factor in electronic commerce, and the problems associated with obsolescence in networks, devices, and systems. Lastly we look at the cost burdens on would-be dominant players in an often high-stakes game.

The Possible and the Probable

Technology-based visions of societal change often stretch the bounds of credulity. In extrapolating from today's technical possibilities technologists run the risk of imagineering a future with an inflated role for their current pet gizmos and a bias toward wholesale behavioural adaptations that have no precedent outside the somewhat peculiar habits of technologists themselves. The generic future according to e-commerce is, unsurprisingly, a twenty-four-hour society fuelled by intense competition, instant gratification, and home-delivered pizza. Mobile commerce is sometimes painted as an artist's impression of an accelerated Silicon Valley lifestyle, with distressingly few points of contact with a recognisable mainstream world outside of that subculture or – God forbid – on a foreign shore. We have deliberately avoided citing the twin clichés of mobile commerce in this book so far – but here goes. Concept Number One: Isn't it great to be able to order a soda from a vending machine using your phone?[1] Concept Number Two: Isn't it great to be told where the nearest pizza place is and offered a discount on your personal favourite topping? These are not questions destined to light a fire under a failing social gathering.

Mobile commerce is a technological inevitability, but its social expression will not conform to the convenient scenarios occupying the attentions of early promoters of the movement. The principal problems underlying the usual artist's impression of the mobile commerce era are the painter's focus on supplier benefits, and his characterisation of the mobile commerce user as a consumer-combatant.

The first effect twists operational or marketing effects into dubious consumer benefits. Thus a vending machine can be rendered less vulnerable to vandalism if it accepts electronic messages rather than hard cash, enhancing the effective life of the machine. Since the machine no longer caches cash, the people hired to restock it need no longer be monitored for theft, and the costs of the whole cash management cycle can be removed from the business. Phone-to-machine ordering makes vending machines portable across currency borders without modification, and such machines may have their pricing structures reconfigured remotely. But these added efficiencies are unlikely to result in more convenient, or cheaper, soda for the customer.

The second distorting effect enters as technology is shown colonising the interstices of daily life and converting every moment into a commercial opportunity. As we have seen, "dead time" is a prime target for mobile commerce service developers, and delivery of entertainment, games, and gambling to mobile users can be seen as legitimately enriching otherwise stressful or boring situations, including unavoidable transport delays. Yet the idea that people actively seek to play the role of consumer in every waking moment is at best

---

1. See, for example, the prototype Virgin Cola machine in central London's Virgin Megastore.

unproven. We try to blank out advertising messages in our environment; we put the phone down on helpful sales calls; we hit the remote when the ads come on; we refuse to use the sponsor's name when we talk about the local stadium; we stay away from over-hyped movies in crowds of Hollywood-epic dimensions; we choose to make heroes of the contestants on *Survivor* or *Big Brother*. We don't do everything we are told: we're not programmable.

The types of mobile commerce services described in this book are all practical business propositions, and all are being developed by various players according to their different theories of market success. While mobile commerce exploits the blurring of boundaries between work and private life, and may be said to be accelerating the blurring process, this does not mean that bland, homogenised services will dominate in the market. Mobile commerce is a quintessentially personal phenomenon that will frustrate broad-brush attempts to dictate user behaviour. The majority of mobile commerce players are today focused supremely on location-based services, a one-dimensional approach that leads to caricatured markets in which mobile users are manipulated through skeins of commercial offers like metal rats in a curiously magnetised maze. Unfortunately for such boosters, few people like to see themselves as "consumers", still less as consumers implicated in a continuous struggle to realise marginal benefits. We don't want to think we're part of some shoot-'em-up game cynically transposed to human-size space. We equip ourselves with mobile devices to make ourselves *free*.

During the United Kingdom's fuel crisis of September 2000, a relatively small number of protesters used mobile technology to immobilise the nation, blocking refinery plants and staging go-slow protests on the highways. Using cell phones to keep in touch with each other, the protesters created an informal networked organisation with no identifiable central control. The British authorities were forced to confront a movement without a leader: no union, no terrorist, no demagogue underwrote the action that brought the country to a standstill in less than a week. The drought at the gas stations and the dearth in the supermarkets stood as ironic testimony to the dominance of just-in-time logistics. Mobile technology may, in our plans, be converging with fixed technology, but here is a key example of the two forces clashing. Fixed information systems – the fabric of the just-in-time, optimised supply chain – are suddenly invalidated by the imaginative use of a widespread mobile technology. And the mobile applications driving the protest movement? A little bit of text, and an awful lot of voice.

Technology creates possibilities, but people create probabilities. To mistake possibilities for probabilities is to misread the market. Business developers seek to relate possibilities with probabilities through market testing. They trial devices and services with selected groups of users and solicit feedback on the utility and attractiveness of the offer under consideration. The early market for mobile commerce services is a distributed, heterogeneous, self-selecting trial group. The members of this group are not obliged to give detailed feedback on their experiences, so often a service provider's only clue to the viability of his offer is the sustained interest of users. Introducing new features to a service may risk losing users, making innovation a high-risk activity. Mobile commerce service providers naturally seek to min-imise customer loss by analysing whatever detailed feedback they do have, running more formal test groups selected from the user popula-tion, and educating customers ahead of new feature launches. Yet development of successful mobile commerce services will continue to be an iterative and uncertain process.

The unpredictability of mobile commerce development rests in the fundamentally fluid nature of the mobile channel. Each addition to the pantheon of services that can be accessed and actioned via the mobile channel has the potential to change the underlying communi-cations character of the channel. The introduction of anyone-to-any-one text messaging in GSM networks, for example, created a new form of mobile interaction which rapidly captured a sizeable propor-tion of the subscriber base. The cell phone *became* a text messaging device, and text messaging *became* something that ordinary folks do. No one ran focus groups asking potential users if they would be happy using both thumbs to compose messages on a 10-key keypad, and no one ran ads extolling the pleasures of swapping notes with other cell phone owners. The ability to play in a lottery or purchase a music track will have similar effects – as long as the associated services are simple, obvious, and under the user's control. In other words, successful mobile commerce services must be compelling and intuitive: if services speak to the desires and abilities of real people, then people will acquire the habits and skills necessary to enjoy the benefits of those services. Give them the tools, and consumers will refashion their world.

Security, Trust, and Privacy

The three interrelated issues of security, trust, and privacy are often bundled together under the single heading of security. From the technology point of view, each points to a partial common solution in cryptographic techniques. Cryptography, as we have seen, can be used to disguise the content of messages and to establish user identity. However, cryptography alone is not enough to implement secure transactions and is only a contributory step towards achieving trust and privacy.

True security is a combination of procedure and organisational framework. The finest password-protection function can be quickly invalidated in an organisation in which users are not discouraged from writing their passwords on sticky notes they attach to their monitors. In public systems, the PKI architecture establishes a guardian role in the RA (Registration Authority), which is tasked with approving the entry of players into the system.

The mobile commerce environment benefits from its telco origins by having strong authority players at its heart. Cell phone manufacturers and mobile network operators, in particular, control key pieces of infrastructure, allowing them to mandate security measures within the systems that enable mobile commerce. Phone manufacturers can ensure WIM-enabled WAP phones enter the market alongside the introduction of secure WAP gateways in the networks. Mobile commerce has a better set of initial characteristics for security than fixed e-commerce could boast in its early days. Since mobile devices are inherently personal, we can accept the notion of securing the device as an aspect of its personalisation. A desktop machine, on the other hand, is more like a piece of furniture, and is more likely to be used by more than one person. Desktop machines are never likely to be thoroughly secured at the personal level, certainly not to the extent of being inoperable without the insertion of a valid smartcard.

Security remains an issue for mobile commerce service developers because security acts as an acceptable catch-all objection for many consumers. Media concentration on security lapses at high-profile e-commerce sites and the parallel mythologisation of attackers, hackers, and crackers creates the impression that all systems are vulnerable. Wireless systems may appear doubly vulnerable to some consumers because thin air is an even better medium for invisible gremlins than wire. The suspicion that technology bites back can be an effective palliative for consumers who are reluctant to embrace a new generation of technology.

The dissuasive effect of the security issue is however somewhat lower-powered than its manifestation in fixed e-commerce. Consumers often cite security as a reason for rejecting e-commerce, but this often masks a more fundamental rejection of computing and the investments – in both time and money – and lifestyle changes computers entail. Business-to-consumer e-commerce companies often fail to reach their sales targets not because their offers are poor or sites badly designed, but because their business models rely on vast numbers of consumers converting to online shopping habits. Many such companies bet their businesses on mass behavioural changes that are proving slow to materialise. Not a few of such companies miss the essential problems of online shopping: online shopping is not an intuitive act, no matter how well a site is designed, and online shopping is not really fun, however many smiling faces are portrayed on the site.

Cell phone and PDA users don't need to be converted to the enabling technology of mobile technology: they already own it. The majority of mobile commerce users are consumers equipped with cell phones which just happen to offer transactional capabilities. Doubts concerning security are likely to be raised if users have to enter credit card numbers manually into the device, or if such numbers are stored in easily accessible features such as a phone's built-in address book. But once security mechanisms are effectively buried in the device's innards, security will become reasonably transparent to the user. Lingering worries about being observed entering a PIN number into a device may be dispelled by simple use of voice recognition technology to validate the identity of the user.

However, the ease with which security mechanisms can be encapsulated within the mobile device reveals a more basic, non-technological security threat for mobile commerce users: device theft. The smaller a mobile device, and the more often it is used, the more likely it is to be lost or stolen. The laptop heists that regularly occur in the bars of our major cities every Friday night may be a taster for more widespread attacks on mobile devices. Technologists who laud the mobile device's role as an electronic wallet seem to forget that the wallet is a prime target for thieves and a major point of vulnerability for travellers in unfamiliar environments. While software experts seek new means of full-proof authentication such as thumbprint-recognition features, hardware designers will introduce theft alarms and other repellent mechanisms into mobile devices. The combined cell phone, PDA, and media player of the near future may also detonate in a shower of indelible dye following a remote command from its distressed former guardian.

While security can be dealt with using mechanisms and organisational elements, trust is an issue of relationships. Consumers query whether they can trust a mobile commerce service provider to deliver the goods they have ordered or to give accurate information or to survive long enough to make the emotional and learning investment in interacting with the service worthwhile. The leading brands in the fixed e-commerce world have won the trust of their customers through consistent, open, and timely service. Mobile commerce creates opportunities for the development of new businesses and new brands, but the access characteristics of mobile devices dictate that mobile portal operators will be the agencies to bless a relatively small number of suppliers on behalf of the user. Even as improvements in bandwidth and device performance stream into the market, bringing the potential of a true wireless Web, mobile commerce service providers will need to bring themselves to the attention of users who will not be minded to search for them. The usage context of mobile devices seems to accentuate the user's need for instant gratification, and to reduce the user's patience with tasks involving sorting and selection. Working the Web from a desk, we forgive slow downloads, rusted links, and irrelevant resources because we imagine the force with which we are interacting as a gigantic book distributed around the world, anchored at strategic points to powerful backend engines. But double-thumbing through the mobile channel, we are neither at rest in a static, familiar environment nor fixated on an imaginary information companion. When we are mobile, we are shifting position in the location-time-mission space. We need answers, and we need them now. We don't want to be shopping around for a better opinion, a keener price, or a nicer tone of voice unless those criteria are well to the fore of our mission agendas. In most situations, we are going to go with the tried and tested suppliers who have delivered for us in the past.

Establishing trust is therefore partly a matter of efficient brand transition for existing e-commerce suppliers, and of rapid brand value establishment for new players. For the latter group, endorsement by mobile portals, bricks-and-mortar partner companies, and respected commentators are key considerations. Mobile commerce promises new billions for advertising agencies as billboards and media ads speak to potential customers armed with the means to respond at the very moment they see the message.

Privacy is perhaps the most serious of this cluster of issues. The ability of mobile network operators to track the activity and location of users facilitates more than just benign, if irritating, personalised marketing messages. In theory a mobile network operator could assemble a detailed narrative of any user's daily life, charting her movements and pinpointing her purchases. While theoretically possible, such detailed personal audits are expensive to produce. Proponents of civil liberties will have been cheered to learn of a French judge's dismay that wireless network operators were taking between one to five months to supply him with data on cell phone calls made by suspected terrorists.[2] Users of mobile networks tend to trust the mobile network operator to keep

---

2. Jon Henley, "Judge puts mobiles in dock" , *The Guardian*, 1 June 2000.

their promises of privacy, but consumers may not extend the same generosity to every mobile commerce service provider in the constellation of suppliers available to her through the mobile channel. Hardened by a lifetime of junk mail, spam, and unwanted phone calls, consumers will be rightly suspicious of mobile commerce service providers offering some types of service, especially services heavily biased towards the location component of our model, unless those providers put explicit privacy policies in place.

TRUSTe[3] operates a certification scheme for Web sites, enabling site owners to reassure their users as to their privacy policy and information usage practices. Site owners obtain the TRUSTe seal or "trustmark" by paying TRUSTe a fee to assess their privacy policies. Qualifying sites can then display the seal together with a link to the TRUSTe site. Users can click though to TRUSTe to check the site displaying the seal is indeed covered by the TRUSTe scheme. Extensions of such schemes to the mobile channel will help to reassure mobile commerce users, though the format of the seal will need to be revised to fit the characteristics of the mobile channel. This is a prime example of an opportunity for a company to develop an effective aural brand: a series of tones indicating a service provider's attainment of privacy certification would act as a rapid and intuitive indicator of probity.

The cleanest approach to respecting privacy is to invite users to opt in to marketing offers and mobile communities, and to state clearly how any member may leave. Service providers may need to pay users to obtain permission to acquire and use information about their whereabouts and habits. This notion may outrage those marketers who regard customer information as a natural resource, yet paying for permission to use such information has a number of benefits. In the first place, a paid-permission model establishes a value for the usage of a service above and beyond transactional value. A mobile commerce service may derive its primary revenues through selling specific goods and services, but any information that helps the company sell more products, or products of higher value, has a value in itself. Service

---

3. http://www.truste.com/.

providers can acknowledge this value and share it with customers through the paid-permission mechanism.

The second benefit of paid-permission follows on from the first. By acknowledging the value of customer information, the mobile commerce service provider helps to build trust with the customer. User and service provider are equalised through an open commercial relationship. This mirrors the loyalty card model used frequently in bricks-and-mortar retail stores and successfully migrated to the Web through reward schemes such as Beenz.

The third benefit of the paid-permission model is its corrosive effect on some of the softer areas of online marketing. Customer information obtained from mobile users is detailed, accurate, and meaningful and can be readily priced. This situation contrasts starkly with the traditional unknown of marketing: the proportion of marketing spend wasted in any campaign. Players in the fixed e-commerce world have experimented with paying users to look at ads, adding a flimsy prop to the already shaky edifice of online advertising economics. Knowing a user's location, assembling the data needed to make an educated guess on his current goal states, and being connected to him at all times: a mobile commerce service provider in this position has a recurring stream of true one-to-one sales opportunities, the potential value of which makes even the smartest advertising look like a scattergun going off in the dark.

Our scenario for successful treatment of the privacy issue has one other interesting effect. The paid-permission model may privilege people in their consumer roles above their work roles. As employees we accept, either tacitly or by contract, certain bounds on our privacy. In the traditional setting, our employers and colleagues can see how we are dressed and how diligent we appear to be. Corporate networks can monitor work rates, screen e-mails, and restrict access to Web sites. The disclaimers at the foot of most corporate e-mails form a quaint species of millennial literature: incantations mouthed to deny the employer's liability for any statement made by the employee. There may be fewer suits in evidence in the business world, but conformity is alive and well. There is, of course, a difference between the expression of individuality and the maintenance of privacy, but the two issues are intimately linked.

With the spread of mobility amongst workers, the corporate impulse to monitor employees grows stronger. Work rates of home-based staff remain an item of concern for many companies, despite the usual findings that home-based workers achieve higher productivity. The real problem of home working is not output of work but separation from corporate culture and opportunities for advancement. Home-based staff need to visit formal workplaces regularly in order to maintain relationships. With truly mobile staff, equipped with everything they need to perform their functions without being tied to a building, employers can monitor their productivity, whereabouts, and hours of working with ease. The mobile channel becomes the only means of performing one's duties, and every action committed in the channel can be committed to the corporate memory.

Few companies are likely to monitor their workers' activities in fine detail as a matter of course. They are more likely to set up procedures that routinely look for exceptional patterns of behaviour. Such an exception might be an unusually high volume of image traffic circulating amongst a group of users with no formal working relationships or a repeated location report placing a key worker uncomfortably close to the premises of a competitor. The degree of paranoia or ease concerning internal privacy issues will become a key cultural issue as organisations turn mobile. Respect for the individual will rise to the top of our priorities in choosing the companies with which we work: we will transfer consumer values to our employee roles.

Health

The Cellular Telecommunications Industry Association (CTIA) now requires cell phone manufacturers to state the radiation output of their devices. Radiation is reported in terms of the quantity of radiation affecting the body while the device is in use, or the Specific Absorption Rate. The radiation-reporting policy sits uneasily alongside the wireless industry body's comprehensive public information resources on the status of research into the health effects (or noneffects) of wireless technology. The Web's distinctive FAQ (Frequently Asked Questions) format reveals as much about our hidden fears as our acknowledged concerns: "If it's so safe, why is the industry continuing to do all this research?"[4]

Health concerns continue to dog the wireless industry, despite the steady growth in both device ownership and connection time. There is clearly a disconnect between our actual behaviour and our attitudes. We are continuing to embrace the mobile lifestyle while occasionally fretting about its possible effects on our physical health. Our health concerns may therefore possibly be expressions of anxiety about changes in lifestyles or social values associated with mobility and connectivity. Just as environmental concerns seem to grow in correlation with car ownership and traffic density, so doubts about the safety of mobile devices increase with our growing dependence on them.

Consumers' health concerns operate on many levels. Most of us, despite our sophistication, instinctively fear novelty in any form. We tend to habituate ourselves to new technologies over time, increasing our exposure to a technology's benefits as our fears of its risks diminish. This is how we learn to ride a bike, drive a car, or surf the Web. Sudden immersion on the other hand – "in at the deep end" – is rarely a comfortable experience, though often effective in creating new skills.

We can conquer our innate fear of novelty when we can acknowledge a distinct benefit to be obtained from embracing a new technology. Thus, many consumers become users of cell phones because they want an emergency communications lifeline they can carry with them, particularly in the car. Once the device becomes part of the user's personal equipment, it becomes more friendly, approachable, and usable. Users who are issued mobile devices as essential tools for their jobs become even more rapidly habituated to device usage.

The dispersal of mobile devices around the body will help to ease consumer health fears and potentially clear the agenda for some more certain, but easily preventable, mobile device health issues. The first of these is the advisability of driving or operating machinery with only one hand. The increasing availability of hands-free kits for cell phones and PDAs is helping to address this problem, although more

---

4. http://www.wow-com.com/consumer/health/general/phones.cfm.

expensive car kits form a preferable solution for drivers. Some users resist hands-free kits because they prefer the mobile device to be visible while they are using it: not everyone wants to look like they are talking to themselves. For such users, wearable devices present a way of advertising their device usage without requiring them to clamp a unit to their head.

The second nonradiation health issue associated with mobile device usage is the risk of inattention. Mobile devices distract users and people nearby with incoming alert tones and vibrations. More seriously, users attempting to negotiate a complex function on a mobile device while walking through a busy street often blank out the external threats to which pedestrians are normally subconsciously alert. Simplicity in service design and brevity in messaging are key to ensuring mobile commerce services do not compromise users' ability to deal with environmental factors.

Inequalities of Access

The concept of information-rich and information-poor individuals, communities, and nations is steadily rising in the public agendas of policy-makers throughout the world. Arguments inevitably follow. Do people really need high-speed Internet access more than they need adequate food and health care? Are the richer nations really committed to granting e-commercial access to poorer nations, and if so is this commitment matched in traditional business channels? Do our children need a computer in every classroom (or on every desk, or in every pocket), or do we send them to school to learn how to think for themselves and interact with other people? Is the importance we attach to connectivity a true political issue or a contemporary piety?

Our usual assumption is that as the economy, government, education, and social spaces migrate online, those without access are disadvantaged with respect to employment, representation, personal development, and social participation. Attention currently appears to be focused on extending the benefits of networks to unconnected communities, particularly in the developing world. In fact, wireless technologies enable developing countries to establish networks much more rapidly than fixed-line technologies. Issues such as negotiation of land routes, surveying of terrain, securing routes in places with difficult access, and marshalling the teams needed to create fixed networks disappear with wireless technology. Spectrum can be allocated by the national government, and foreign technologies can be easily imported and implemented without disruption to other infrastructure elements. Wireless voice telephony is arguably the most important technology benefit the affluent North could bestow on the South: a technology usable by ordinary people to create personal opportunities and support the integrity of their communities. Access to information services can follow as a natural adjunct to basic voice connectivity.

An unspoken factor in many discussions about national inequalities of access is the assumption by our largely white, largely middle class, largely male, largely English-speaking technocracy that the coming knowledge economy is navigable only by superior beings like ourselves. People who don't share our extraordinary cuisine, denatured cities, and self-referential infotainment-scape can't possibly join in our hands-off, lights-out economy. They need to go through all the infant stages we (or actually our ancestors) endured on the road to enlightenment – but preferably making a lot less mess of the planet in the process than we did. Above all, we lack respect for the types of knowledge that operate in the developing world and tend to dismiss the abilities of people in developing nations to acquire and manipulate the types of knowledge that we venerate in our own culture.

History shows the folly of underestimating "foreign powers". The "long boom" of the 1990s in the United States and the slowdown of the Japanese economy seem to have erased memories of external competition. Yet the rhetoric surrounding the "sleeping giant" of China – imagining that society's reawakening as a distant prospect – is silenced by the hypergrowth achieved in China in the same period. Universities in India produce IT professionals who go on to create massively successful software development companies, undercutting American and European wages and proving more than equal to every new generation of technology. Wireless technology accelerates the growth of the global knowledge economy, creating a connectivity environment in which talent, imagination, and diversity will enrich mobile commerce.

Inequality of access is a greater issue at the personal level than at the national level. If the only way to access information about health care, social services, education, or benefits is through the Web, then many citizens are effectively disenfranchised. People need both connectivity and search skills in order to make the most of online resources. In many communities connectivity is available to disadvantaged citizens only though public libraries – themselves constant targets of budgetary cuts. The immaturity of the mobile channel makes it hard to establish whether mobile devices will fill the gap caused by lack of access to fixed computers and simplify the process of finding information. Cell phones have rapidly become classless, becoming common equipment for most people with disposable income. Falling cost of ownership and increasing physical mobility is helping the cell phone replace the fixed phone as the communications focus of many families, although the personal nature of cell phones gives them a different role from that of the household phone.

For the majority of people, the spread of mobile technology is an inevitable social force not unlike the dominance of pop music or fast food achieved in the post–World War II period. We participate in mobile commerce because it is part of our culture. Using mobile technology is easier, safer, and cheaper than driving cars – a once-strange activity that became habitual within a generation. Just as those who cannot afford a car are limited in their options with respect to car owners, so those who remain unconnected to the mobile channel will experience various types of exclusion. As entertainment migrates to the mobile channel, people without access will become detached from the evolving milieu. The connected will be in the swim, in the know; the unconnected will be living in a different – and perhaps less pressurised – world.

Privileged Places

Mobile commerce helps to blur the dividing line between work and private life. In so doing, mobile commerce also contributes to the erosion of workplace behaviours and loyalties, and the professionalisation of home life. In confusing these previously separate domains, mobile commerce generates options both for greater democratisation and greater privilege.

To consider democratisation first, we can readily appreciate how the loosening of physical work barriers may create a greater sense of personal freedom and self-determination among workers. If we release employees into the wilds of the market, armed with mobile devices, then we trust them to achieve the goals we agree with them in their own ways. We will balance the attempts we make to monitor their activities with the high degree of empowerment we have given them through the mobile device. As workers spend less time behind company walls and more time mixing with customers and partners, they begin to embody more of the organisation's knowledge in their individual rights. Each team member becomes an element of the corporate memory and the corporate potential, rather than a tool of the organisation. Mobile commerce also accelerates the importation of informal codes of behaviour into professional environments, making for more relaxed co-working situations.

The other way of looking at these effects is to consider how the blurring of boundaries creates opportunities for the already-privileged to improve their positions. For example, the importation of informal behaviours into the workplace does not benefit everyone equally. The stuffiness associated with some types of workplace may dissipate, only to be replaced with an atmosphere that excludes the unfashionable, the inarticulate, or the unrelaxed. More socially competent individuals will have an edge over others: the importance of "background" and a private education could be redoubled as social confidence commandeers the high ground in every business situation. Mastery of unwritten rules is always harder to acquire than mastery of public, objective knowledge.

Mobile technology has a significant effect on social mobility, muddying the clear waters that have hitherto defined private and public places. Like those other historic symbols of liberating technology, the car and the contraceptive pill, the mobile device represents affordable freedom and self-realisation. And like those symbols, the mobile device trails a new set of problems. As we embrace mobile connectivity, we relinquish our right to live in a world that runs at the speed of our choosing. We yield to the pressure to be "always on": online, onstage, on-message. We expand the share of our lives we devote to consuming, worrying about consuming, and paying for our consuming habits. We tear down the constructs that defined our old, inefficient world but that nevertheless gave us some orientation: there's no need to stand in line for anything anymore, and no need to go to a specific place to work.

Mobile commerce service providers will benefit by supporting users in these confusing times. By respecting individuality, recognising local differences and knowing when to leave users alone, smart service providers will position themselves as helpful, consistent, and discreet companions in a fast-changing world.

The Return of Geography

The business world is now familiar with the idea of the Internet removing geographical barriers, creating global markets, and hastening the effects of globalisation. Once a resource is on the Net, the resource is available throughout the world and the efforts of corporations or governments to block access are largely ineffectual. Dedicated Webmasters ensure the continued supply of news into closed states such as China by moving content as soon as it is blocked by the authorities. Individuals publish on the Web eyewitness accounts of events officially denied by their governments: an electronic message-in-a-bottle is instantly available to every beachcomber on every continent. Wireless technology has the potential to reverse this trend towards uncontrollable access.

The mobile channel differs markedly from the fixed Web in that content gateways are biased towards exclusion rather than inclusion. In the fixed environment, ISPs can block content by specifying a list of undesirable URLs at the proxy server. Since Web sites proliferate at a rapid rate, no authority can be completely certain of trapping every potential source of undesirable content. Wireless networks introduce an intermediary layer where the authorities may intervene. WAP systems, for example, use a WAP gateway to interface with the fixed Web. This creates another level of defence for the restrictive operator, who can choose to create an incrementable list of approved sites at the gateway. Governments may also control the supply of mobile devices into the state, insisting that available devices be preset with a limited list of sanctioned sites. In this case, the "walled garden" becomes a tool of political power rather than commercial restriction.

Wireless technology buttresses state power because spectrum is a national resource. Like airspace (or indeed air), the radio spectrum accessible within a given territory is controlled by the territory's government. Governments can generate revenue from the sale of spectrum for commercial use, but they can also exploit the finiteness of spectrum for political ends. Governments are clearly in a strong position to influence the number and type of mobile services accessible within their states. Although nations co-operate on technical standards issues, individual nations often seek to protect their home markets for home-grown companies.

With or without government blessing, incumbent network operators represent barriers to incoming competitors through the sheer weight of their sunk investment and aggregated bulk of their customer relationships. But the factors that make an operator strong at home also restrict the operator's movements abroad. Take the case of Japan's i-mode service. Given the phenomenal success of i-mode in Japan, i-mode might reasonably be identified as a candidate favoured mobile commerce environment for the rest of the world. However, i-mode runs on a packet-based wireless network, barring the system from entry to the nonpacket-based European scene. Outside of the Japanese market, the only i-mode phone manufacturer is Nokia, which is heavily invested in alternative technologies. i-mode content is written in Compact HTML (cHTML), a form of HTML unused elsewhere. Some claim cHTML is an easier development environment than WML, but in practice this factor would not be enough to create a groundswell towards i-mode outside its home territory. Finally, one reason for i-mode's great impact in Japan has been its introduction of text messaging – a function already provided by SMS in the GSM territories, and by paging services elsewhere. i-mode may become a true competitor to WAP around the world as both systems evolve to converge on XHTML (eXtensible Hypertext Markup Language) and TCP (Transmission Control Protocol) as their underlying technologies. Despite the harmonisation efforts of the 3G movement, there will be no true interoperability for 3G devices across the major regions of the world. Multisystem devices will doubtless be developed, but these will necessarily cost more than single-system devices. The introduction of 3G services in the United States will create a regional wireless standard across North America, bringing the region the interoperability benefits already enjoyed in GSM regions such as Europe, but America, Europe, and Japan will still be separate technology islands.

Perhaps of greater importance is the dominance of domestic sites over global ones, a situation rarely found on the fixed Web. Global brands such as Yahoo!, Amazon, and eBay may have local operational units in different geographical areas, but they are essentially global offers. European book and CD buyers can choose to source their purchases from Amazon.com as well as from Amazon.co.uk, playing delivery charges against price and currency advantages. But the British user accessing Amazon from her WAP phone will be routed to Amazon.co.uk. More significantly, the presence of location and time dimensions in our mobile commerce model strongly suggest advantages for local service providers. A U.S. user looking for restaurant information for San Francisco will expect to use a U.S.-branded and -supplied service, whereas a German user in Berlin will want German advice. An American traveller in Berlin may prefer to receive information about the city from a familiar source, and local service providers will contract with foreign brands to supply such content. But will mobile commerce service providers in Northern California provide local information in German via German sites? Partnerships will emerge to service the local needs of global travellers via the mobile channel, but these are likely to trail local services for local users by some margin.

Domestic brands will regain some advantage from global brands by acquiring portal positioning with mainstream mobile commerce device offers. Cell phones aimed at national markets will come pre-baked with selected mobile commerce services, chosen from high-profile local brands. Synergy between bricks-and-mortar companies, local advertising, and intercustomer recommendations will further bolster the strength of local brands. A company can create a global brand relatively cheaply on the fixed Web, partly because the Web is a more or less closed referral system. Traditional advertising and media coverage certainly help to channel users' activities on the Web, but the majority of page views are generated by link activation. With mobile commerce, the resources of the mobile channel are more obviously integrated with other messages in the user's immediate environment: billboards, store promotions, and especially the advice of other users. This kind of influence is harder to buy than domain name recognition and an abundance of links: it requires the kind of multichannel marketing support more commonly associated with the promotion of music or movies. Local service providers have an advantage here, if only through superior knowledge of the local market.

Investment in Obsolescence

Obsolescence is the flipside of innovation. Technologies build on the achievements of their predecessors, but in so doing they often make their predecessors redundant. In many cases, superseded technologies are given scant time to grow old before they are retired. Computer equipment is typically cascaded throughout an organisation as new pieces of kit are purchased, with outlying parts of the business resigned to getting along with their existing platforms and applications rather than enjoying the benefits of the latest processors and software. When kit can no longer be dispersed through the organisation, it may join a recycling scheme and find its way to a nonprofit organisation, to a less affluent country, or to a scrap yard.

Network equipment, on the other hand, is less easily dispersed as it ages. A wireless network represents a considerable investment in hardware and real estate. Such a network is also hard to break into pieces for sale. Network economics encourage large networks, maximising coverage area to maximise customer count. Networks also need to be reliable and robust so as to give the best possible service at all times, meaning that individual components must be built to exacting standards. A new kind of network technology that makes an existing component type obsolescent is a threat to incumbent operators rather than an opportunity.

The stress of evolutionary technology among wireless network operators reflects the potential disruptive power of novel solution types in the network context. A player who does not have an existing network is advantaged over incumbent players when new technologies become available. Yet incumbents enjoy two powerful nontechnological advantages. First, an existing network operator owns a licence to operate in its area. Access to spectrum is an essential item and it can represent a substantial proportion of a network operator's valuation, regardless of the company's customer population or service reputation. Second, incumbent networks own antenna sites. We tend to notice masts in rural areas more often than urban ones, and where many rural sites are concerned there may be alternative sites with similar physical characteristics that could be used by a competitor. Sites in urban areas are in greater demand: more cells are needed to provide service in highly populated areas, real estate prices are already higher than most rural areas, and building height and composition impact the performance characteristics of antennas. Ownership of operating licences and real estate assets join with depth of technology investment to make network operators somewhat conservative with respect to novel technologies. Loss of an existing licence, or the availability of a new type of licence as in the introduction of 3G services, can act as more potent forces for change than the development of a new coding scheme or the addition of location-reporting functions.

Obsolescence is a major factor for consumers. The user is concerned not so much with the network operator's investment in network technology, but in her own investment in a mobile device. Cell phones are already heavily subsidised to make them attractive to mainstream consumers, but top-of-the-range models earn more realistic price tags. The smallest and lightest cell phones of their generation are generally the most expensive items in the range, but also the models most likely to followed by cheaper models in the following season. Cell phones have become fashion items, clothed in chrome or snap-on jackets, diversifying into youth-oriented and professional-oriented shapes, and splitting into masculine and feminine positioning. As cell phones mutate into multipurpose mobile devices, their fashion properties begin to clash with their role as irreplaceable personal equipment. Once a user has stored all his personal information on a device, moving it to a new one is painful. Even though information may be transferred via a docking device to an intermediary PC, or directly to a new device via local wireless connection or the cellular network, the transition step is still an awkward one for the user. Users who take advantage of mobile portals to outsource the management of their personal information will find it easier to change mobile device without losing their addresses, bookmarks, and music library, but it is unclear how quickly consumers will come to trust such third-party services.

Users who wish to take direct responsibility for the configuration and content of their mobile devices are more suited to the PDA-style mobile device than to the cell phone–derived device. Such users already grapple with trade-offs between different device types, manufacturers, and operating systems. For example, any user interested in listening to stored music on a mobile device must choose a type of permanent storage – unless he is content to work with the memory limit of the device, replacing his content selections at intervals. Two leading types of storage are CompactFlash and Memory Stick. Where should the user place his bet? A mobile device is highly unlikely to offer both options. The legendary Betamax/VHS format battle is being replayed wherever an opportunity exists for physically accessorising or personalising the mobile device.

Potential obsolescence of mobile devices is a predictable force that we see operating in the general consumer electronic market. There are an additional two levels of less obvious potential obsolescence of concern to mobile commerce players: the obsolescence of code, and the obsolescence of sites.

In the area of code, companies may well see their investment in writing WML written off as WAP embraces other implementations of XML for content markup. WAP 2.0, due for approval in mid-2001, should see the replacement of WML by XHTML (eXtensible Hypertext Markup Language).[5] XHTML is a reformulation of HTML 4 as

---

5. Stephen Lawson, "WAP Forum moves toward Net standards", *InfoWorld*, 14 September 2000: http://www.infoworld.com/articles/hn/xml/00/09/14/000914hnwap.xml.

an implementation of XML. As well as adding extensibility to HTML, XHTML has greater portability across different client environments. 2000 vintage WML will inevitably join the various generations and browser-specific variants of HTML as legacy resources. However WML is at least a lightweight asset, more easily cast aside or recycled than more expensive backend application code, and greatly restricted in its functional effect on browsers when compared to HTML. Being largely textual artefacts, WML assets will not be too painful to part with as more sophisticated user interface options become available to mobile commerce service designers. Code written to push alerts to users or to generate content on demand from database resources may be more vulnerable to obsolescence as device types and interaction methods evolve. The introduction and growth of voice-controlled interfaces will cause many service providers to reengineer their offers.

Some players considering mobile commerce services may dispense with WAP altogether on the assumption that a full "wireless Web" will replace WAP and its limitation-driven ethos. Hanging fire while this debate plays out is one way of avoiding potentially unnecessary investments in technology, but also excludes players from the market in the vital early learning stages. Even if WAP melts away as a separately identifiable technology in favour of "pure" Internet standards, mobile commerce will still make different demands of service developers than fixed e-commerce does. As we have seen in this book, mobile commerce users tend not to surf or research in the same way stationary users do. They are more likely to zero in on the resources and services they need, and more likely to be acting in response to a real-time suggestion from the mobile channel or their physical environment rather than an internalised program of discovery. As well as being interactive, mobile commerce services are proactive. This makes the design of their structure, navigation strategies, and content different from those of fixed sites. The implication of the divergence between the user experience in the mobile and fixed channels creates our second level of hidden obsolescence: the legacy e-commerce site.

Existing e-commerce sites are challenged by mobile commerce services, including those of the same company. A company running a successful online store or information service must plan the introduction of the mobile channel with respect to its existing channels and in the knowledge that the mobile commerce service may contradict or cannibalise such existing assets. A company running a directory service, for example, may find its mobile commerce directory service is more popular than the fixed Web version. In such a case, what happens to the business model upon which the fixed Web site is built? If the justification for the site is its contribution to awareness of the company or its services, then managers may feel that funds are better spent supporting the more popular channel for the directory. If the rationale for the site is the income it generates in advertising revenue, then the success of the mobile commerce service will spell the commercial failure of the fixed Web site. In practice, players will adapt fixed Web sites in response to the growth in significance of their assets in the mobile channel, much as they have evolved the function of their print and video media activities in the light of the rising influence of the Web. Smart players will not wait to watch the success of mobile commerce create a crisis of confidence in the fixed e-commerce world: they will adapt the components of their commerce portfolios at the same time as they introduce mobile commerce services.

Cost per Customer

The issues we have looked at so far in this section are largely concerned with the recognition and negotiation of certain types of boundaries. The relationship between possibility and probability, the assurance of security, and the thematically related issues of trust and privacy, and consumer concerns regarding health in relation to wireless technology, all reflect the potential for service providers and users alike to misconstrue the fundamental day-to-day effects caused by our transition to a mobile commerce environment. Debates around access and the blurring of places and roles reflect the mobile channel's disruptive effect on established prejudices about membership of economic elites. The return of geography as an active factor in commerce after its brief retirement during the dominance of the fixed Web is a clear instance of political and physical boundaries making an influence on the development of mobile commerce. Obsolescence challenges the scope of technology investment in mobile commerce and impacts spending on contingent channels.

These issues are therefore driven by the changing nature of the commercial landscape in the transitionary era between fixed and mobile commerce, and our need to establish new maps of the terrain. None of these issues are binary; that is, none will be settled once and for all, for good or for bad. Privacy, for example, will always remain a continuum rather than a binary attribute: each of us trades certain items of private information with other people in order to function in society, even if we merely express our needs. In the mobile commerce context, users at least surrender the absolute right to freedom from interruption. We will negotiate levels of privacy just as we attempt to optimise spending across different commerce channels or attempt to equalise access to services across different groups in society.

There is, however, one stark, unambiguous, and unavoidable issue that may yet thwart the development of mobile commerce, or at best delay its dominance by some years. This is the issue of cost per customer: the price that mobile commerce pioneers are being asked to pay in order to acquire customers. Specifically, how can network operators – and potentially their partners in the mobile commerce industry – recoup the heavy costs of 3G licences?

Sales of 3G spectrum have provided surprise windfalls to national governments and primed governments to expect further revenue spikes from further sales. Here, as we have noted, national governments hold the trump card. Operators of fixed networks cannot provide truly ubiquitous access, yet neither do they have a practical ceiling on the extent of those networks they can deploy. Wireless spectrum, on the other hand, can reach to every part of a territory, yet is a finite resource that must be organised and allocated by governments.

The United Kingdom's 3G licence auction raised more than £22 billion (around $35 billion) for the government. The victorious companies paid differing amounts for their lots, with Vodafone AirTouch paying £2 billion more than BT Cellnet for its 3G licence. Vodafone's B licence covers a larger share of spectrum, giving the company a better ratio of equipment cost to network capacity.[6] Given the inherent scarcity of spectrum and the rapid obsolescence of electronic equipment, ownership of spectrum is a good long-term investment for an operator and may even be tradable with other companies for short-term gain. Vodafone's purchase of Mannesmann in 2000 was discussed largely in terms of German attitudes to foreign takeovers and its status as the biggest ever acquisition, yet the deal's long-term significance lies in its aggregation of wireless spectrum. However, Vodafone still needs to find almost £6 billion to play in the 3G game – and this cost will have to be passed on to consumers in some fashion.

In Germany itself, the sale of twelve blocks of 3G spectrum in August 2000 netted nearly $46 billion from six bidders, compared to original government estimates of around $10 billion. Holland's earlier auction raised a mere $2.5 billion. France chose to award its 3G licences on a fixed price basis, raising around $4.5 billion. The fastest nations to allocate 3G spectrum passed up on the bonanza: 3G licences were allocated on merit in Spain and Finland.

The high cost of 3G licences will necessarily have an effect on the mobile commerce value chain. Network operators have made profit-sharing offers to build-out partners in return for their accepting deferred payments.[7] Even before work starts on 3G systems, network operators are saddled with the costs of improving their existing infrastructure. Investment in 2.5G networks is already high, with network operator Orange spending £37 million on an Ericson GPRS network during 2000.[8]

Network operators are betting on consumer appetite for the media and commerce service possibilities of 3G to recoup their investment in the necessary spectrum and platform assets. These players need to add yet more costs into their plans to cover the marketing activities needed to convert the possibilities of advanced mobile commerce ser-

---

6. Philip Hunter, "The final frontier", *Computer Weekly*, 22 June 2000.
7. Ibid.
8. Antony Savvas, "Orange spends £37m on Ericsson GPRS network", *Computer Weekly*, 6 April 2000.

vices into high probabilities. The sheer scale of the task ahead points to further mergers and acquisitions in the telco industry. The run-in period for true mainstream embrace of the mobile commerce lifestyle may be longer than network operators and media commentators hopefully predict. Players need to bulk up ahead of a potential wait while millions upon millions of users learn to make the mobile channel their preferred means of interaction.

Meanwhile spectrum sales represent a potentially addictive source of revenues for governments, leading political parties to assume future windfalls in their manifesto pledges. Yet spectrum is a finite resource, with drastically shorter reserves than other natural resources such as oil or minerals. Spectrum is also not a proven long-term earner for all owners in all circumstances, as are oil and minerals. If 3G offers fail in the market – perhaps because of the success of 2.5G offers from the same sources – then interest in dedicated spectrum will decline rapidly. Governments also run the risk of damaging their local mobile commerce industry by indirectly taxing it in this way, creating disparities with other nations. The Finnish decision to give away 3G spectrum was not based on an under-valuation of the asset's worth, but on a different attitude as to where that value should be applied. Finland chose to donate the asset to its strong indigenous wireless industry while the United Kingdom and Germany chose to fold the value of their spectrum into their general budgetary processes.

The mobile network operators' experience with 3G auctions in the United Kingdom and Germany led to greater industry caution in subsequent auctions. Italy's auction of five licences in October 2000 attracted only six bidders. When one of the bidding consortia withdrew early in the game the Italian government had no choice but to allocate the licences to the remaining players for a total of around $12 billion – half the government's forecast. The Swiss auction of December 2000 generated income close to the government's minimum price.

The speed with which customers embrace the mobile lifestyle and their private valuations of mobile commerce's benefits will determine the ability of network operators to bear the undoubtedly high cost of customer acquisition in the post-2G context. We need to remember that although consumers continue to rush to the mobile channel in large numbers, mobile devices can also represent but a single category of goods in a continually growing consumer electronics market. Mobile devices compete for consumer attention and dollars with technologies aimed at personal entertainment, such as DVD players and games consoles. Mobile commerce service designers need to find ways of attaching compelling interactive services to other consumer electronics devices in order to encourage buyers towards wireless versions of such products.

The challenges for mobile commerce service providers are by no means finalised. Can, for example, companies invent video applications that appeal to users in mobile situations? Will Hollywood reinvent movies as personal rather than collective experiences, or will music videos become the primary vehicle of a new many-to-many style of entertainment? Can the news industry adjust its clock speed to a population constantly connected and constantly moving between goal-states? Can retailers reinvent themselves as trusted companions rather than familiar destinations? Can the "them" of traditional commerce learn to mingle with the "us" of the mobilised human tribe? Can we live up to the promise of mobile technology while taming mobile technology for a worthy role in our business and private lives? We will need imagination, ingenuity, and investment to work through these and many more questions as mobile commerce continues to put the world in new motion.

Mobile Commerce Services Directory

This appendix lists a number of mobile commerce services running or announced at the time of writing. Each entry contains a brief description and a URL where further information can be found on the Web.

This is not an exhaustive guide to mobile commerce services, but a selection of leading service providers and useful demonstrations. Some of the resources listed in the directory are themselves directories, and these give wider coverage of the growing population of available services.

The directory is regularly updated on this book's Web site at http://www.verista.com/mobile/

Service Directories and Search Engines

Awooga   http://www.awooga.com/

Directory of rated WAP sites, also email and bookmark services

Gixom   http://www.gixom.com/

Catalogue of WAP sites

Mopilot   http://www.mopilot.com/

Searchable directory of wap sites; company also offers WinWAP, a WAP microbrowser for Windows; Web site also shows statistics of the mobile browser types being used to access the site

Orktopas   http://www.orktopas.com

Search engine for WAP sites

VoiceXMLCentral   http://www.voicexmlcentral.com

VoiceXML search engine and community

wapaw.com   http://www.wapaw.com/

WAP site directory

Mobile Portals and Community Services

CNN   http://www.cnn.com/mobile/demo/

Web-based demonstration of CNN Mobile with a mobile phone

Genie   http://www.genie.co.uk/

Mobile portal for U.K. digital cell phones. Web site includes free text messaging to any U.K. phone.

inkontact   http://www.inkontact.com/

Social and professional contact management service

iobox   http://www.iobox.com/

European mobile portal

Room33   http://www.room33.com/

Multichannel portal operating in a number of countries

Sessami   http://www.sessami.com/

Lifestyle portal for urban singles and groups

Wapprofit   http://www.wapprofit.com/

Mobile portal and content provider; Web site includes examples of portals developed for WAP and i-mode delivery

Your WAP   http://www.yourwap.com/

Personal information management portal for WAP users

Content and Messaging Services

AvantGo   http://www.avantgo.com/

Delivers content channels optimised for PDAs

myAlert   http://www.myalert.com/

Alerts pushed to cell phones

omnisky   http://www.omnisky.com/

Wireless services for PDAs

UltiVerse   http://www.ultiverse.com/

Multichannel messaging and information-management services

Unimobile   http://www.unimobile.com/

Text messaging for all types of mobile device

Entertainment Services

Ludiwap   http://www.ludiwap.co.uk/

Games for wireless devices

MatchOn   http://www.matchon.com/

Real-time soccer coverage, results, and statistics

WAPGag:)   http://www.wapgag.co.uk/

Jokes to your phone

Financial Services

http://www.724.com/demos/bofa.htm

Bank of America Wireless financial services demonstration using Palm V PDA and NeoPoint cell phone

Fingo   http://www.fingo.com/

Mobile financial portal, including brokerage services; Web site includes demos for WAP, Palm, PocketPC, EPOC devices

Reservation Services

book2eat.com   http://www.book2eat.com/

WAP restaurant-booking service launched initially in London

BookingZone   http://www.bookingzone.com/

Wireless reservations service for consumers and business users; includes restaurants and repair companies

Shopping Services

12snap   http://www.12snap.com/

Auctions and shopping in the U.K., Germany, and Italy

E-Compare   http://www.ecompare.com/

Wireless and online search engine for pricing, availability, and shipping costs on a wide range of products

Iqorder   http://www.iqorder.com/

Multi-channel shopping service

SCAN   http://www.scan.com/uk/

Best-price retailer, uses SMS solution in Europe and voice-based solution in the U.S.

Travel Services

biztravel.com   http://www.biztravel.com/

Flight schedules, fares, availability, and status to various types of mobile device

CitiKey   http://www.citikey.com/

Guides to major cities in Europe, with North America and Asia planned

GetThere DirectMobile   http://www.getthere.com/products_services/products/mobile_manager.html

Wireless travel reservation and information service; complements an existing Web-based service

Maptuit   http://www.maptuit.com/

Travel directions and maps delivered to mobile devices

OAG   http://www.oag.com/

Flight information for mobile devices, including Palm and PocketPC PDAs and WAP phones

TomTom   http://www.tomtom.com/

Wireless personalised travel information service

Webraska   http://www.Webraska.com/

Wireless travel information service using maps and directions

Mobile Payment Systems

PayPal   http://www.x.com/

Person-to-person payments system

ProPay   http://www.propay.com/

Cash "beaming" solution for PDA users

Mobile Device Emulators

i-mode Emulator http://www.sanpo.t.u-tokyo.ac.jp/~ryo/imode.html

A Web-based emulator showing i-mode sites on a virtual cell phone. Your browser will need the Japanese character set installed for best performance.

Wapalizer   http://www.gelon.net/

A Web-based emulator allowing users to access live WAP sites on a virtual cell phone. Different types of cell phones may be selected.

Glossary

2G Second generation: technology category for existing digital cellular networks.

2.5G Two-and-a-half generation: umbrella term for technologies designed to add 3G capabilities to existing cellular networks.

3G Third generation: new digital cellular network technology designed to enable very fast data transmission speeds and delivery of multimedia content.

activation The act of making a mobile device live on a network.

air interface Technology used to create wireless networks; examples include CDMA and GSM.

alert A message triggered by the occurrence of an event and sent to an individual, with message receipt usually accompanied by an audible tone.

AMPS Advanced Mobile Phone Service: analog cellular network system used in the U.S.

application A package of software features designed for a known or ideal user group.

ARIB Association for Radio Industry and Business: telecommunications standards body for Japan.

ASP Application Service Provider: a type of company that provides the functionality of a software application, such as a human resources application, on a remote-usage basis to corporate customers.

avatar An animated character representing a human actor in a computer system.

B2B Business-to-business: the category of e-commerce applications that are oriented to users acting in employee roles or to collaborating systems operated by business partners.

B2C Business-to-consumer: the category of e-commerce applications that are oriented to individuals acting in a personal or family capacity.

Bluetooth A low-power radio communications system for PANs.

CDMA Code Division Multiple Access: a type of digital cellular network where calls are split into packets and the packets are tagged with identifying codes.

cdma2000 An implementation of wideband CDMA; a 3G network type.

CDPD Cellular Digital Packet Data: a technology for adding data-transmission capabilities to AMPS networks.

cellular network A wireless communications network formed by a collection of contiguous cells, where each cell contains a transmitter/receiver servicing nearby users.

cell phone A wireless telephone device designed for use with a cellular network; usually called mobile [phone] in Europe.

CEPS Common Electronic Purse Specifications: a standard for smartcards.

channel A conduit for wireless connections; a branded carrier of entertainment or information; a permanent route to a group of customers.

cHTML Compact HTML: a restricted form of HTML used to encode content for the i-mode system.

churn The propensity of a service provider's customers to terminate their contracts.

connectivity Participation in a network.

convergence The growth in functional and market connections between the fixed Internet and mobile communications systems; also used to refer to the coming together of different types of communications, information, and entertainment features into single-product packages.

cryptography The science of rendering communications meaningless to all but their senders and receivers.

DoCoMo   A Japanese company offering i-mode wireless service.

EDGE   Enhanced Data Rate for GSM Evolution: an enhancement to bring the data-transmission rate of TDMA network up to the speed of basic 3G networks.

EPOC   Mobile device operating system offered by the Symbian company.

ETSI   European Telecommunications Standards Institute: telecommunications standards body for Europe.

event stream   A refined and standardised supply of news stories.

FDMA   Frequency Division Multiple Access: analogue wireless network technology.

GPRS   General Packet Radio Services: an enhancement designed to introduce packet-switching behaviour to GSM networks.

GPS   Global Positioning System: a system of 24 satellites and a set of ground receivers used to determine the position of an object on the earth.

GSM   Global System for Mobile Communications: a type of TDMA cellular network dominant in Europe.

HDML   Handheld Device Mark-up Language: predecessor language to WML.

HomeRF   A technical standard for wireless LANs used in the domestic environment.

HSCSD   High Speed Circuit Switched Data: a means of combining two 14.4 kbps GSM channels to deliver a 28.8 kbps service.

HTML   HyperText Markup Language: a scheme for embedding instructions about how text should be rendered within the text itself; the language used to create Web pages.

iconic tones   Audio elements signalling events or options; aural brand marks.

i-mode   A type of wireless Web information system operating in the Japanese market.

IMT-2000   International Mobile Telecommunications 2000: an ITU initiative aimed at harmonising the various regional efforts under way to create 3G networks.

IrDA   Infrared Data Association: a standard for infrared communications.

ITU   International Telecommunication Union: the standards body of the telecoms industry.

LAN   Local Area Network: a type of computer network designed for use within a building or area of a building.

Linux   An open-source version of the Unix operating system.

LMDS   Local Multipoint Distribution System: a broadband wireless alternative to the copper-wire "last mile" connecting phone subscribers to the local exchange.

mobile commerce   Electronic commerce using mobile devices such as cell phones as client devices.

mortal   A multichannel portal.

MultOS   An operating system for smartcards.

network effect   The increase in utility of a network created by the addition of network users.

one-to-one marketing   The practice of addressing commercial offers to individuals as individuals rather than as members of groups.

P2P   Person-to-person (or peer-to-peer): the category of electronic services conducted between individuals without mediation performed by any business.

Palm OS   The operating system of the Palm series of PDAs.

PAN   Personal Area Network: a type of wireless network designed for deployment in an individual's personal space.

PCS   Personal Communications Services: a digital cellular network type using the 1.9 GHz band in North America.

PDA   Personal Digital Assistant: a hand-held device used to store data and run personal applications.

PDC   Personal Digital Cellular: a cellular network type used in Japan.

personalisation   The tailoring of services for a specific individual's needs or preferences, performed either by the individual or by a service provider on his behalf.

PKI   Public Key Infrastructure: a security architecture that combines specialist authorities, digital certificate management systems and directory facilities to create secure networks on top of unsecured networks such as the Internet.

PocketPC   Device using the third version of Microsoft's WindowsCE operating system; also the name of that operating system.

portal   A site that guides users to resources and services which it recommends or which it partners with; a branded gateway to resources and services.

PPV   PrePaid Voucher: a mechanism for buying usage time on a cellular network without taking out a billing contract.

PSTN   Public Switched Telephone Network: the traditional fixed analog telephone infrastructure.

push   A type of technology for sending content to users.

SIM   Subscriber Identification Module: the smartcard that identifies GSM cell phones to the network.

smartcard   A plastic card with an embedded chip, typically used to store customer account data in electronic purses and in automated payment applications such as payphones and turnstiles.

SMS   Short Message Service: a means of conveying messages up to 160 characters long to and from GSM cell phones.

stickiness   The length of time visitors remain with a site; sometimes used to refer to users' propensity to return to a site.

SWAP   Shared Wireless Access Protocol: HomeRF's data and voice communications protocol; not to be confused with WAP.

synchronisation   The act of replicating information between a mobile device and a fixed device.

TACS   Total Access Communications System: a type of analog cellular network.

TDMA   Time Division Multiple Access: a type of digital cellular network in which calls are sliced into time periods and interleaved with others on the same channel.

TIA   Telecommunications Industry Association: telecommunications standards body for the U.S.

transaction   In the commercial sense, the agreement of contractual terms or the exchange of goods or services for value; in the technological sense, the completion of complementary data updates in two or more entities.

UMTS   Universal Mobile Telecommunications Service: an implementation of wideband CDMA; the 3G network type designated for Europe.

viral marketing   A means of growing a customer base by recruiting existing customers as active or passive recommenders of the offer.

walled garden   A collection of mobile commerce services offered by a network operator, device manufacturer, or portal to the user as the default or only set of mobile commerce options available to her.

WAP   Wireless Application Protocol: an architecture designed to provide Web-style content to limited-functionality mobile devices over low-bandwidth networks, but independent of the underlying wireless network technology.

wASP   Wireless Application Service Provider: see **ASP**.

WCDMA   An implementation of wideband CDMA; a 3G network type.

WIM   WAP Identity Module: a tamper-proof component designed to store private data (including key pairs, certificates, and PIN numbers) within a mobile device; in practice, a WIM is implemented using a smartcard.

WindowsCE   Microsoft operating system family for hand-held and portable devices.

WML   Wireless Markup Language: the component of the WAP architecture that embodies deliverable content.

XHTML   eXtensible Hypertext Markup Language: a reformulation of HTML 4 as an XML standard; stabilises the functionality of HTML, adds extensibility to HTML, and improves portability of HTML code.

XML   eXtensible Markup Language: a means of defining documents with associated structure and semantics.

Online Resources

This section contains a number of online resources that readers may find useful for tracking the development of the wireless industry in general and the mobile commerce movement in particular.

Each entry contains a brief description and a URL where further information can be found on the Web.

News, Background, and Discussion

allNetDevices   http://www.allnetdevices.com/

Comprehensive news on the wireless industry, updated daily

AnywhereYouGo   http://www.anywhereyougo.com/

News, features and tutorials on the wireless industry

ePaynews   http://www.epaynews.com/

News and background on payment solutions for e-commerce and mobile commerce

Fierce Wireless   http://www.fiercewireless.com/

Weekly report on mobile commerce

M-Commerce Times   http://www.mcommercetimes.com/

Weekly mobile commerce magazine biased towards features

Mobic   http://www.mobic.com/

Daily news on the wireless industry

MobileCommerce.org   http://www.mobilecommerce.org/

News from the wireless economy by Tod Maffin

Mobile Commerce World   http://www.mobilecommerceworld.com/

Regular updates on relevant mobile commerce topics

Thinkmobile   http://www.thinkmobile.com/

Wireless news, features and surveys

Unstrung   http://www.unstrung.com/

Features and reviews relating to the wireless internet

WAPsight   http://www.wapsight.com/

General wireless industry news

WAPWednesday   http://www.wapwednesday.com/

Organisation of mobile commerce forums based in major European cities and open to all professionals with an interest in WAP and mobile commerce; site often includes presentation materials from previous meetings

Wireless World   http://www.wired.com/news/wireless/

News from the wireless arena filed by Wired reporters

Standards Organisations

GSM Association   http://www.gsmworld.com/

Body responsible for the development and promotion of the GSM cellular network standard

Location Inter-operability Forum   http://www.locationforum.org/

Industry forum created to define, develop, and promote a common location services solution

Mobile Electronic Signature Consortium   http://www.esign-consortium.org/

Industry association formed to develop a secure cross-platform infrastructure for deploying mobile digital signatures

VoiceXML Forum   http://www.voicexml.org/

Industry organization chartered with establishing and promoting VoiceXML

WAP Forum   http://www.wapforum.org/

Home of the WAP architecture and source of WAP specifications

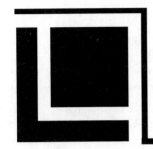

Index